AF663542

Ambedkar's Thoughts
on
Dalits, Politics
and
Women Empowerment

Ambedkar's Thoughts on Dalits, Politics and Women Empowerment

Edited by
Binay Barman

Kaveri Books
New Delhi-110 002

© Editor

Editorial Board & Co-Editors

Dr. M. Alankara Masillamani
Associate Professor, Palli Charcha Kendra, Visva-Bharati, Sriniketan.

Dr. K. Mavali Rajan
Assistant Professor, Department of A.I.H.C & A., Visva-Bharati.

Dr. Matilal Sen
Assistant Professor, Department of Mathematics, Saldiha College, Saldiha, Bankura.

Mala Laha
Assistant Professor, Department of Sanskrit, Saldiha College, Bankura.

ISBN: 978-81-7479-205-1
First Published in 2017

All rights reserved including the right to translate or to reproduce this book or part thereof in any form and through any means except for brief quotations in articles or critical reviews.

The responsibility for the facts stated or opinions expressed is entirely of the author and not of the editor or editorial board or co-editors.

Published by
Kaveri Books
4832/24, Ansari Road
New Delhi-110002 (India)
Tel: 011-23288140, 47072321
E-mail : info@kaveribooks.com
kaveribooks@gmail.com
Website: www.kaveribooks.com

Typeset at: Delta Book World, New Delhi - 110 002

PRINTED IN INDIA

Dedicated to

My Father Late Hara Chandra Barman
and
My Mother Phanibala Barman

Preface

This book is a compilation of twenty-six research oriented articles and each claims its own uniqueness. The salient feature of this volume is to depict the life and time of Dr. B.R. Ambedkar. For collecting articles and editing the volume, we cannot forget the effort and co-operation of Dr. M. Alankara Masillamani, Associate Professor, Palli Charcha Kendra, Visva-Bharati, Sriniketan, Dr. K. Mavali Rajan, Assistant Professor, Department of Ancient Indian History, Culture & Archaeology, Visva-Bharati. A very special word of thanks is due to Mala Laha, Assistant Professor, Department of Sanskrit, Saldiha College, for her effort in advancing our mission.

I feel privileged to present compilations outcome of U.G.C. sponsored national level Seminar on "125 Years Celebration of Dr. B.R. Ambedkar: Impact of His Ideas and Thoughts on Indian Politics" which was held at Saldiha College on 3rd and 4th September, 2016 in collaboration with the Department of Economics, Abhedananda Mahavidyalaya, Sainthia, Birbhum, West-Bengal. As, the editor, I have tried my best with the help of editorial board to maintain the publication of academic standard in publishing the volume as far as possible.

I am thankful to Dr. M. Alankara Masillamani, Associate Professor, Palli Charcha Kendra, Visva-Bharati, Sriniketan, Dr. K. Mavali Rajan, Assistant Professor, Department of Ancient Indian

History Culture and Archaeology, Visva-Bharati for their cooperation and guidance from time to time. I wish to express my gratitude to Dr. Shaikh Srajuddin, Principal, Saldiha College, Saldiha, Bankura for his constant encouragement, criticism, prudent support and tireless efforts in bringing out the book in this present form. I am also grateful to Mala Laha, Assistant Professor, Department of Sanskrit, Saldiha College, Saldiha and Bankura.

Dr. Shaikh Sirajuddin, Principal, Saldiha College, Saldiha, Bankura, West Bengal contributed the most instrumental factor behind the present work. Finally, I want to convey my regards to the publishers.

Binay Barman
Assistant Professor of History,
Saldiha College, Saldiha,
Bankura, West-Bengal, India.

Contents

Introduction

Dr. B.R. Ambedkar is the Father of Indian Constitution, who was one of the greatest personalities of world in 20th century. His life was a great chronicle of suffering, sacrifice and struggle. He was also a great freedom fighter, political leader, philosopher, economist, social reformer and more importantly the first Indian who fought for the advancement and upliftment of downtrodden in India. Ultimately he was a multi-faceted and multi-dimensional personality whose contribution to modern India was significant and substantial. B.R. Ambedkar, a determined fighter and outstanding scholar, who made his constant efforts to lead the society on the path of liberty, equality and fraternity. Being a pioneer of social justice, he always endeavored for the emancipation and empowerment of the weaker section. His principal objective was to build up an equal society with social justice. He created consciousness among poor and illiterate masses and inspired them to fight against the unjust social practices like caste discrimination, social inequality, child marriages and *devedasi* system. In other words, for the Indian Women's movement, Ambedkar provides a powerful source of inspiration to formulate a feminist political agenda, which simultaneously addresses the issue of class, caste and gender.

Despite the various shocking, painful experiences, humiliating inhuman treatment that he was meted out during his young age, he emerged as a bright, brilliant, brave and dedicated student. His hard work, commitment and dedication made him a talented student. His talent and intelligence was noticed by a few rational minded people of those times, who motivated him to pursue higher studies in abroad and made adequate arrangements for his funding and other things. His intelligence and higher qualifications equipped him with a power of rational arguments and empowered him to participate in intellectual discourses, with the learned people of both the western and Indian society.

Dr. Ambedkar by equipping himself with knowledge skill, aptitude and ability set as an example to the people of suppressed classes to follow. He started many journals and newspapers to propagate his revolutionary ideas among the depressed community. The journals and the newspapers that he started and societies he framed were devoted to the cause of eradication of untouchability from Indian society. He immensely contributed for the emancipation of the conditions of suppressed community, women and other under-privileged segments of the Indian society by ensuring legal rights for their protection. He launched varied forms of crusades for the betterment of oppressed and suppressed communities of Indian society.

Having been born in a marginalized family made him a victim of exclusionary practices to which the other people of his caste were treated. In his young age, during his school days he faced many problems. The disgrace, discrimination and severe social handicap that all Dr. Ambedkar experienced right from his early life stabilized and instilled in him the determination to liberate the depressed classes from the inhuman social practice. The painful and bitter experiences that he underwent, which pissing his education both during his school and high school days made him realize the curse of caste system.

B.R. Ambedkar, was a keen student of economics, the first Indian to pursue a doctorate in economics abroad. He argued that industrialization and agricultural growth could enhance Indian economy. He stressed the need for investment in agriculture as the primary industry of India. Ambedkar advocated national economic and social development, may be attained through education, public hygiene, community health and residential facilities as basic amenities. His D.Sc. thesis "The Problems of Rupees: its Origin and Solution (1923)" examines the causes for the Rupee's fall in value.

In his thesis he proved the importance of price stability over exchange stability. He analyzed the silver and gold exchange rates and their effect on the economy, and found the reasons for the failure of British India's public treasury. He calculated the loss of development caused by British rule. He contributed to the emergence of Land Revenue Tax and excise duty policies in the event of stabilizing the economy. He played an important role in land reforms and the state economic development. He emphasized a free economy with a stable Rupee which India has adopted recently. He advocated birth control to develop the Indian economy, and this has been adopted by Indian government as national policy for family planning. He emphasized equal rights for women for achieving economic development. He laid the foundation of industrial relations after Indian independence.

He played a pioneering role in the upliftment of women. Through his various writings he made an attempt to show how the gender relation and difference are constructed by Hindu Brahminical order. He questioned the laws of Manu and condemned it and attacked rule of *Manusmritis*. He gave much importance to the liberation of women and he valued them and wrote many articles on the contributions of women in social and political excellence. According to him woman is a companion of man gifted with equal rights of freedom and liberty with him. Woman is considered as the better half of humanity, not as the weaker section. He endeavored to mitigate the gender based discrimination. According to Ambedkar the contribution of women to the political, economic, education and social emancipation of the country was of overriding importance. He had immense faith in the capability of women to carry on a nonviolent crusade. Under his guidance and leadership, women shouldered critical responsibilities in India's struggle for freedom.

The main aim of the present volume is to analyze and evaluate the socio-political and philosophical ideas of Dr. B.R. Ambedkar. His philosophical contribution has revolutionized the areas of humanism, socialism and rationalism. He propounded a philosophy of humanism taking in account of both theory and practice. The social philosophy of Ambedkar can be understood by his monumental writings and speeches on various occasions. For him philosophy is not purely a theoretical matter but has practical potentialities. The concept of human dignity plays a pivotal role in Dr. B.R. Ambedkar's philosophical ideas. Human dignity means one is entitled to have respect by virtue of human nature. It has its roots in the problems of life and theories that have propounded return as a contribution for the reconstruction of the society. His social critique has developed into philosophy of thought and action leading to human emancipation. His thoughts on the week and deprived of the society are guiding principles for anyone working for their upliftment. The contribution of Ambedkar towards the upliftment and dignity of the Dalit and suppression had given to the Dalits, is simply unbelievable and unforgivable. Ambedkar's political philosophy combined a rational individualism with a social critique which sought to undermine the constraints which held back personal development, particularly caste discrimination and economic disparities. Dr. Ambedkar condemns the unjust behaviour-patterns in the social matters and the human relationship based on them.

The present work covers wide range of aspects on the ideas of Dr. B.R. Ambedkar and his struggle for social justice. It contains twenty-six articles covering the facet of Ambedkar's thoughts and its relevance to modern world; his social and philosophical thoughts; his ideas on economic development; role of Ambedkar in framing of Indian constitution; Ambedkar's thoughts on women rights and fundamental human rights; Ambedkar's Neo Buddhism; his contributions for the upliftment of downtrodden; his thoughts on the contemporary Indian politics; his vision on empowerment of women and suppressed communities; impact of his ideas in Indian political thoughts and social change and so on. I hope that the present volume fulfill the needs of the readers and will bring considerable light on the concepts and ideas of Dr. B.R. Ambedkar and his multi-faceted personality in the modern world.

Dr. M. Alankara Masillamani
Associate Professor, Rural Development,
Palli Charcha Kendra, Sriniketan, Visva-Bharati.

Dr. K. Mavali Rajan
Assistant Professor, Dept.of A.I.H.C.& A, Visva-Bharati

1

Early Life of Bhimrao Ramji Ambedkar: A Struggle for Survival

– Dr. Madhab Chandra Adhikary

Bhimrao Ramji Ambedkar (1891-1956), popularly known as Babasaheb, was an Indian jurist, economist, politician and social reformer who pioneered the Dalit movement and campaigned against social discrimination. He was the first law minister of Independent India and the architect of the Indian Constitution.

Ambedkar was born on 14 April 1891 in the town and military Cantonment of Mhow, near Indore in the Central Province, presently Madhya Pradesh. Ambedkar's family had a long History of military service, on both his mother and father's side. His grandfather Maloji Sokpal and father Ramji Sokpal were in British Indian Army. Ambedkar's family was belonged to the Mahar community. Of all the untouchable communities in the fold of Hindu society, the Mahar are the most robust, adaptable, intelligent, fighting, brave, virile and leading community. The Mahar are very sensitive to their position and they are conscious of their slavery. They were the first to come in contract with the Europeans in India. Consequently, they formed a part of the Bombay Army of East India Company just as the Dusads of Bihar and the Pariahs of Madras named the armies of the Company in those Provinces. Ambedkar's ancestral village is Ambavade, five miles away from Mandangad, a small town in the Ratnagiri District of modern-day Maharashtra. He was the 14th and last child of Ramji Maloji Sakpal and Bhimabai Murbadkar Sakpal.

Ambedkar's family belonged to the devotional Kabir school of thought. The followers of Kabir did not believe castes system and found consolation in the human attributes like compassion, benevolence and resignation to God. That was why some of the Untouchable families turned to the Kabir cult. The customs of followers of Kabir was that if anybody who worshipped God belonged to God irrespective of Caste and birth. They were very sincere to their Master and sang with their master as follows-

"Jat Pant puchhe na koi,
Har ko bhaje so harka hoi!"[1]

II

Bhima's mother, Bhimabai, came from the Murbadkars, an untouchable Hindu family. This family was rich from the village of Murbad in the Thane district of Bombay State. Her father and her six uncles were all Subedar Majors in the Army. They also belonged to the Kabir cult and discussed hotly and keenly the philosophy of Kabir and theology at troupes.

Bhima was only two years old when his father retired from military service. Ramji Sakpal came down to Dapoli in Konkan from Central India. Bhima was admitted to school at Dapoli when he was five years old. Bhima and his elder brother started their primary education there. His father could not stay long at Dapoli. Therefore, he moved to Bombay in 1897 and secured a job in the military quarters at Satara. As a result Bhima's family also moved to Satara. Shortly after their move to Satara, Baima's mother gave up her spirit. At that time, Bhima was only six years old. She was succeeded by three sons and two daughters out of fourteenth children. Balaram was the eldest, Anandrao was the second, then followed two daughters Manjula and Tulsi and the youngest was Bhima. The daughters were married and they looked after their brothers turn by turn. Ramji's sister, Mirabai, a physically handicapped but an experienced and having knowledge of the practical world who takes care of the family. Bhima, being the Benjamin in the house, claimed the special care and attention of his aunt. It is also natural that motherless youngest child Bhima became her favourite.

Ramji Sakpal lived a very industrious and intensely religious life. Stout, impressive, generous and valuable, he was a devotee. He offered prayers and devotions to God morning and evening. He inspired the children to join in his devotions .The sweet devotional lyrics and spiritual hymns of devotion flowed from his mouth. He was also the follower of Kabir. He made his children learn by heart all the *Bhajans, Abhangas* and *Dohas* of Kabir, woke up early in the morning to study. A chain of sweet songs of God would go on in a choir.[2] This was the compulsory routine of the Bhima's family till his fathers death.

Bhima's father read and recited to his children the great epics, the Ramayana and the Mahabharat, the two unfailing sources of inspiration. Ramji Sakpal also sang the spiritual songs from the Marathi peots like Moropant, Mukteshwar and Tukaram. The children derived immense benefits from this spiritual song. Thus religion had a deep impact on Bhima's mind. Bhima's father was not merely after the spiritual development of his children, he cared also for the worldly betterment of his children. He was a master of the Marathi language could teach having his pupils' and sons with appropriate word. He also having English could teach his sons the translation of books with confidence. Apart from this, at Mhow the family resided in military quarters. So a stern military discipline would have to be maintained in every family.

From his childhood Bhima was victimized by the evil of caste system. At Satara, he had experienced hardship because he was dalit. No barber would cut his hair, his elder sister shaved his head. Dhananjay Keer has mentioned here the measurable condition of Bhima's family in this way, "It was indeed a touching scene when Bhima came to know that his hair defiled the purity of razor of the barber who regarded even the buffalo-shaving as better and holier affairs than tonsuring a dalit who was his coreligionist and his countryman."[3] At Satara, Bhima completed his primary education and began his high school career along with his elder brother. During his school days Bhima realized painfully what stigma of untouchability meant.

When Ramji Sakpal was working on the scheme for famine stricken in Goregaon in Satara District, the family lived in Satara. Once, Bhima along with his elder brother and two nephews went to Goregaon on train. They got in at Padali Railway station and travelled up to Masur. As their father had not received their letter in time he did not turn up at the station. After waiting for long time, they could with difficulty persuade the station master, who was a caste Hindu, to secure them a bullock cart, and started for Goregaon. Hardly had the cart gone a few yards when the cart man came to know the boys identity as accursed Untouchables! In a fit of rage he threw them out on the road; for he felt they had polluted his wooden cart and impured the purity of his cart animals. But the boys soothed the cart man's anger by paying double the fare and Bhim's elder brother drove the cart and the regular driver following the cart on foot. Nobody had any sympathy for the children. For a whole day and a half they had to go without water because dalits were not allowed to drink water from the village wells. Every time people either pointed to the filthy water or asked them to go away. The exhausted children reached home in a critical situation. That day he knew that he belonged to a dalit family that was untouchable, degraded to drink and eat filthy things.[4] A few days later this impression became confirmed. Feeling very thirsty, one day, Bhima was drinking water stealthily at a public water course. Later on, he was discovered and was beaten black and blue.[5]

Although Bhima experienced humiliating treatment meted out to him because of his accident of birth in dalit family, he had also the good fortune to receive completely unexpected kindness from certain enlightened persons of the so-called upper castes. Reference may be given in this respect. Having made a bet with a schoolmate of his, he walked several miles to school in a heavy rain. His class teacher, a Brahmin namely, Pendse, who saw him in this condition was touched at the sight of the scantily clad Bhima shivering after his long and arduous journey, and asked his son to take Bhima to his house, give his dry clothes and warm food to eat.

There was another Brahmin teacher in the school with the surname Ambedkar, who somehow had a soft corner for Bhima and treated him like his own child. He shared a part of his own lunch with him every day. The original surname of Bhima's father was Sakpal. It was a family name Bhima drew his surname Ambavadekar from his native village Ambavade, as Maharashtrian surnames are often derived from the names of the ancestral village. It was the kindness of this teacher which made Bhima ultimately adopt Ambedkar as his surname. In fact, it was this teacher, Ambedkar, who himself changed Bhima's surname from Sakpal to Ambedkar in the school records. This is the surname by which Dr. Babasaheb Ambedkar was to go down in History.

Despite these oases of warmth, there was all around a scorching desert. Bhim and his brother were usually made to squat in a corner of the class on a piece of gunny cloth which they carried to school. The teachers would not touch their note books nor did some of them even ask them to recite poems or put questions to them for fear of being polluted! When these two boys felt thirsty in the school they turned their mouths upward and then somebody would kindly pour drinking water into their mouths as if through a funnel !

When Bhima was about ten years old, his father decided to marry again. Bhima naturally did not like the idea of having a step-mother and took the decision to be independent of his father for his daily needs. To achieve this, he even taking up a petty job in one of the cotton mills in Bombay. He even considered stealing some money from his aunt to enable him to reach Bombay. One day he was so fed up with life that like Siddharth Gautam, he left home.[6] But he thought of his aims in life and soon came back home. He could not bear to see the tearful eyes of his family. His good sense made him realize that he must somehow pursue his studies and make his mark in the world. From that day onwards, he became a diligent student and came to be loved even more by his teachers.

III

Another opportunity had come over Ambedkar family in 1897. When Bhima passed his fourth standard, Ramji moved his family to Mumbai. The family lived in a small room in a ***chawl (or a single room tenement)*** called the Dabak Chawal at Lower Parel. It was situated in the labour area with an environment of the underworld. Indeed a large number of families were hurdled together in these *chawls* and lived under almost sub-human conditions. His daughters had been already married and they also lived in Bombay. He got his sons admitted to the Maratha High School. Bhima's desire to concentrate on his studies became more intense after his family shifted to Bombay. This desire was generously supported by his father who even went to the extent of borrowing money from his two married daughters for purchasing books for Bhima. It was his ardent desire that his son should become a man of letters and light.

After some time, Bhima was admitted to the Elphinston High School which was one of the leading High Schools in Bombay. He now pursued his studies with single-minded determination, although he had to live in the single room apartment occupied by his entire family. There was no chance for the provision of a study and possibility of employing a tutor was beyond a dream. We came to know from different evidences that the small room was full of domestic article and utensils; smoky and crowded. Firewood was stored above head and also in corner, and in the other corner was the fireplace. The room served as a kitchen, a parlor, a lying in a room, a study – all in one! [7]

Ramji Sakpal solved the problem of his son study in his own way. He asked his son to sleep early. Bhima slept on a quilt. Near his head lay a grind-stone huddled into the wall and a she goat panted below his legs. His father sat up all night till two in the morning, and awakening his son for study, he retired. Bhima studied till early morning, now and then turning in his bed before a flickering kerosene oil-lamp which had no glass cover to serve as a chimney. After having a little sleep in the morning, he took his bath and went to school.

It is reasonable to say that he could have studied in the High School without enduring humiliations. But the Elphinstone High School was not free from the ever-present shadow of untouchability. We may give such example in this respect. Although Bhima was very much interested in learning Sanskrit, he was not allowed to do so as he was dalit. It was because of this reason that he was forced, much against his will, to choose Persian. But later on, Bhima's unconquerable will enable him to become a scholar of high caliber in Sanskrit, the very language, he was forbidden to learn in his school. The school was a miniature reflection of the vast insulting world outside. Once, Bhima was asked by the teacher to solve a geometrical theorem on the blackboard. But the students protested vehemently. It was only when they were allowed to remove the lunch packets that they had placed near the blackboard, Bhima could solve the theorem. All such offending and infuriating instances made Bhima rebellious. Despite all the hardships, ills and intolerable insults imposed upon him for being a dalit, and stimulated by his father to endeavour at rising to a high position in life and encouraged by broad minded men, Bhima prosecuted his studies. After school he went to Charniroad gardens and read all kinds of books. Another teacher, K.A. Keluskar, frequented the same garden to do his reading. One day he talked to Bhima and advised him to follow the proper method of studious reading. Bhima followed the valuable advice of Keluskar and finally he passed the Matriculation Examination in 1907 from Elphinstone High School. He scored the highest marks in the Persian Language. He was the first dalit to do so. This success inspired his people and evoked much celebration among the dalit.

Bhima's achievement in school education was no doubt an uncommon achievement for dalit. Even it was a milestone in the history of the dalits of India. So the event is celebrated by his community. In a special meeting Bhima was felicitated under the chairmanship of S.K. Bole, a well known Maharastrian social reformer along with K.A. Keluskar, a social reformer and an assistant teacher of Wilson High School, Bombay. K.A. Keluskar presented him a book entitled *Life of Gautam Buddha* in Marathi language written by himself. Needless to say that the book presented by Keluskar to Bhima had a great impact on the mind of latter and set up his mind for his ultimate conversion to Buddhism.[8]

IV

After a short period of his passing Matriculation Examination, Bhima was compelled to marry hardly at the age of 16 with a girl namely Rami of 9 years old daughter of Bhiku Valangekar as per the custom of those days. Dhananjoy Keer has given a description of the place where Babasaheb marriage was taken place. "It was the open shed of the Byculla Market in Bombay. After the day's market was over, at night the bridegroom and his men lodged in one auspicious corner of the open shed, and the other corner was occupied by the bride and her relatives. Small gutters of dry water flowed underneath their feet. The little stone-platforms in the market served them as benches, and the whole market place served as a marriage hall!"[9] The marriage took place with due ceremony and jollity, and the people vacant the place in the morning before the arrival of the fishermen. After her marriage, Rami was renamed as Ramabai. Bhima's early marriage could not extinguish Bhima's desire for knowledge, which was encouraged by his ageing father. After his matriculation, Bhima joined the Elphinstone College, Bombay. Misfortune, however, continue to dog his footsteps. After he passed the Inter Arts Examination he has no position to continue his education as his father ran out of funds. K.A. Keluskar, his old well-wisher, having come to know of Bhima's dificulties, personally approached the Maharaja of Baroda His Highness Sir Shreemant Sayajirao Gayakwad, a noble hearted man and broad-minded ruler. The Maharaja had made an announcement earlier offering his help to any worthy untouchable who wanted to pursue his higher studies. Keluskar made an arrangement for interview between Bhima and the Maharaja. At the request of Keluskar, the Maharaja asked Bhima and asked some searching questions and having satisfied with his replies, assured him financial help to his further education. Sir Sayajirao Maharaj awarded him a scholarship of Rs. 25 per month which was a big amount of money in those days.[10] Thus Keluskar has proved to be the real teacher. At Elphinstone College, Bhima was a favourite student of Professor Muller and Professor Irani. Prof Mullar loved Bhima very much and lent him books and gave his own shirt. But, it is seems, no professor in India like Oswald, George Anderson, principal Coverntorn could capture his mind. Moreover, the insulting environment and pitiable sights of the downtrodden must have added to his restlessness. The college hotelkeeper who was a caste Hindu would not give him tea and water. Taking in to consideration the poverty and apathy towards education amongst dalit, the ardor and the concern with which Ramji Sakpal encouraged Bhima to finish his degree course, is laudable. He passed the final degree in November, 1912, securing 282 marks out of 750.[11] Everybody became happy in this success of Bhima. Babasaheb often expressed his gratitude to his father who spent money and made such effort for his education.

After becoming graduate, Bhimrao Ambedkar applied for a job and took service in Baroda, the state of his benefactor. His father forbade Bhima to take the service. He was appointed to the post of a lieutenant in the Barada State Army. Unfortunately his service was not lasted for long time. After joining fifteen days to the post of lieutenant in January, 1913 he received a telegram informing him that his father was critically ill in Bombay. He immediately left for Bombay to look after his father. On his way home he got down at Surat station to buy sweet-meats for his father and lost his train. On the next day when he reached Bombay, he found that his father was dying. The sinking but searching eyes of the dying man moved on to his beloved son upon whom he had revolved his thoughts, his hopes and his existence. He moved his feeble hand over his son's back and the next moment death-rattle was in his throat. His eyes closed and his legs and hands became motionless. He breathed his last. On that day, February 2, 1913, Bhimrao Ambedkar was practically inconsolable. Thus, passed away a dalit, Subhedar Ramji Maloji Sakpal, who was to the end of his life industrious, abstemious, devotional and aspiring. Having infused in his son strength of will to resist worldly temptations and a depth of spirituality, he left him behind to fight the battle of life and to break the world to his way. Later on Bhimrao Ambedkar went to Europe for his higher education and secured M.A. and Ph.D degree. Despite western education and its influence, he had deep roots in the Indian soil and spent the rest of his life in identifying the problems of his motherland and in finding out ways to solve. From the above discussion, it is clear to us that poverty would be no obstacle to the indomitable will of mind. Dr. Bhimrao Ambedkar was a glorious example in this regard. In spite of poverty and socioeconomic discrimination, Bhimrao took challenges and established himself. He became the architect of Indian constitution and secured many honour in India and abroad in his latter life. He was the greatest inspiration to the downtrodden people in India.

REFERENCES

1. Dhananjay Keer, Dr. Ambedkar: Life and Mission, Popular Prakashan, Mumbai, First Published, 1954, Tenth Reprint, 2002, p.9.
2. Hudlikar, Satyabodh, The Navayug's Ambedkar's Special Number, 13 April 1947. cited in Dhananjay Keer, Dr. Ambedkar: Life and Mission, Popular Prakashan, Mumbai, First Published, 1954, Tenth Reprint, 2002, p.13.
3. Op.cit., p.13.
4. Ambedkar's Speech, *The Janata,* 20 November, 1937 cited in Dhananjay Keer, Dr. Ambedkar: Life and Mission, Popular Prakashan, Mumbai, First Published, 1954, Tenth Reprint, 2002, p.13
5. Dhananjay Keer, op.Cit., p.13.
6. Vanaudha Ramchandra, *Ambedkar's Life Struggle,* Allahabad, 1947, p.11 (in Hindi), cited in *Dr. Babasaheb Ambedkar,* Basant Moon translated by Asha Damle, National Book Trust, India,1991, p.4.
7. Dhananjay Keer, *Op.Cit.*, p. 17.
8. M.L. Shahare, *Dr. Bhimrao Ambedkar: His Life and Work,* NCERT, New Delhi, 1987, p.9.
9. Dhananjay Keer, *Op.Cit.*, p. 17.
10. The College records have the receipt of Rs. 120 as the amount of six months' scholarship till December, 1911 cited in Basant Moon, op. cit., p. 5; M.L. Shahare, Dr. Bhimrao Ambedkar: His Life and Work, NCERT, New Delhi, 1987, p.9.
11. Dhananjay Keer, *Op.Cit.*, p.21; Elphinstone College Record File cited in M.L. Shahare, *Op. Cit.*, p.6.

2

Contribution of Dr. B R Ambedkar to Indian Society and Education

– Dr. Bikash Mukherjee
– Sudipta Goswami

INTRODUCTION

Mother India has given birth to a galaxy of great sons Dr. Bhimrao Ramji Ambedkar is one of them. He is popularly known as Babasaheb Ambedkar, was one of the architects of the Indian Constitution. He was a well-known politician and an eminent jurist. Ambedkar's efforts to eradicate the social ill faith like untouchablity and caste conservativeness were remarkable. The leader, throughout his life, fought for the rights of the dalits and other socially disadvantage classes. Ambedkar was appointed as the nation's first Law Minister in the Cabinet of Jawaharlal Nehru. He was posthumously awarded the Bharat Ratna, India's highest civilian honor in 1990.

AMBEDKAR'S LIFE

Bhimrao Ambedkar was born to Bhimabai Sakpal and Ramji on 14 April 1891 in Madhya Pradesh. He was the fourteenth child of his parents. Ambedkar's father was a Subedar in the Indian Army and posted at Mhow cantonment, Madhya Pradesh. After the retirement of his father in 1894, the family moved to Satara. After a few days his mother passed away. Four years later, his father remarried and shifted to Bombay in 1912. After shifting to Bombay he cleared his matriculation in 1908.

Ambedkar was a victim of caste discrimination. Ambekar was from the Mahar community, an untouchable caste, whose profession was to clean under the command of the scriptural injunctions. Due to this, Ambedkar had to face severe discriminations from every corner of the society. The discrimination and humiliation haunted Ambedkar even at the Army school, run by British government. Fearing social outcry, the teachers would segregate the students of lower class from that of Brahmins and other upper classes. The untouchable students were often asked by the teacher to sit outside the class. After shifting to Satara, he was admitted to a local school but the change of school did not change the fate of young Bhimrao. Discrimination followed wherever he went. In 1908, Ambedkar got the opportunity to study at the Elphinstone College. Besides clearing all the exams successfully Ambedkar also obtained a scholarship of twenty five rupees a month from the then ruler of Baroda, Sahyaji Rao III. Political Science and Economics were the subjects in which he graduated from the Bombay University in 1912. Ambedkar decided to use the money for higher studies in the USA.

After coming back from the US, Ambedkar was appointed as the Defence secretary to the King of Baroda. Even, there also he had to face the humiliation for being an 'Untouchable'. With the help of the former Bombay Governor Lord Sydenham, Ambedkar obtained the job as a professor of political economy at the Sydenham College of Commerce and Economics in Bombay. In order to continue his further studies, in 1920 he went to England at his own expenses. There he was awarded honor of D.Sc by the London University. Ambedkar also spent few months at the University of Bonn, Germany, to study economics. On 8 June, 1927, he was awarded a Doctorate degree from the University of Columbia.

Dr. B R Ambedkar may be remembered for his contribution in the following areas:

(i) To know the impact of the pioneering work of Dr. B. R. Ambedkar in the field of human dignity, against caste discrimination in India.

(ii) To highlight his role as one of the founders of Modern India.

(iii) To analyze and assess his Legacy and Contribution to India.

(iv) To review his contribution to uplift Dalit community to the mainstream of the society.

(v) To highlight Ambedkar's role for empowerment of Indian women.

(vi) To show Ambedkars affection for the development of Dalits.

(vii) To find out his achievements in making several provisions in the form of Articles in the Constitution for the upliftment of the Dalits.

(viii) To recapitulate his contribution towards Dalit education.

DR. AMBEDKAR AS A SOCIAL REFORMER

Dr. Ambedkar believed in peaceful methods of social change. He was supported to constitutional lines in the evolutionary process of social transformation. He thought the factors like law and order which are indispensable for social life. He was opposed to the violent methods in social change as which obstacle the tranquility and create chaos. He had no faith in anarchy methods. A welfare state of all cannot be developed on the grounds of terror, force and brutal methods. According to him violent methods to a peaceful society is not only improper but also unscientific and immoral. He was a man of true Renaissance ie, a person who excelled in many different areas of inquiry. Though he was hated by orthodox Hindus and labeled as a destroyer of Hinduism.

Ambedkar played an important role in revitalizing Hinduism, reviving it by challenging everything that was unjust and unfair within it. In fact, he brought about a renaissance of Hinduism by provoking the Hindus to rethink some of the basic tenets of their religion. He had a great faith in social reformers who could create public opinion against gross inequalities in the society. He urged them to found organizations to deal with urgent cases of discrimination. The organizations should deal with the powerful section of society by giving a chance to the oppressed and depressed classes to work in different sectors. The Hindu society should give a space to depressed sections by employing them in their various sectors suited to the capacities of applicants. According to Dr. Ambedkar, social change and social justice are indeed critical to the egalitarianism that any democracy must aspire it.

As a social democrat Dr. Ambedkar stressed on a much broader notion of stable reconstruction of the country with inclusive growth and cultural integration without caste discrimination. As the architect of the Indian constitution, Dr. Ambedkar constructed the safeguards for establishing a more equitable society of millions of oppressed and depressed classes. In this process, Dr. Ambedkar emerges not only as a Valliant upholder of the Indian democratic republic, but also a unequal Indian Pantheon and rare intellectual mass leader who awakened the social conscience of Modern India. He was strongly believed that political institutions were responsible for reforming the existing social institutions by using legislative force to yield the results. Political institutions will survive only when they actively work for social reformation. Dr. Ambedkar was a freedom fighter of the truest kind, not merely dreaming of setting India by force from the British rule, but of transforming her into a country where freedom holds meaning for everyone. While Mahatma Gandhi led fellow Indians in a struggle against discrimination in South Africa, Dr. Ambedkar led a battle, too, against prejudice within his own country. While securing equality for his community, he has created a more equal world for us all.

TOWARDS THE EMPOWERMENT OF INDIAN WOMEN

On 11th April 1947 as the first Law Minister of India, Dr. Ambedkar for the first time really tried to defend the women of India specially the weaker sections in the form of Hindu Code Bill. The Bill has the provisions for a few basic rights to women. It attempted to establish monogamy as the only legal system and abolish polygamy systems prevalent among the Hindus. Its main aim was to encourage the right to property and adoption of women. It provided for restitution of conjugal rights and judicial separation. It sought to unite the Hindu Code with progressive and modern thought. This Bill invited strong protestation from the Hindu Orthodoxy in post independent India in 1948. Ambedkar tried his best to defend the Bill by pointing out the drawbacks of Indian Society and arguing that ideals in the Bill which are based on the constitutional principle of equality, liberty and fraternity. However, the Bill could not withstand the opposition of Hindu orthodoxy. Their major argument was that the bill will obsolete the entire flesh and blood of Hindu Society. Finally in 1951 Prime Minister Jawahar Lal Nehru dropped the Bill by saying that there was too much opposition. On this issue the then Law Minister resigned for the cause of the disadvantaged.

The operations of caste both at the systemic level and at the functioning of patriarchy, the growing caste or class divide in feminist political discourse makes Ambedkar's view on women's oppression, social democracy, caste and Hindu social order and philoshopy, significant to modern Indian feminist thinking. Although Ambedkar proved, himself to be a genius and was known as a great thinker, philosopher, revolutionary, jurist as par excellence with prolific writer, social activist and critic and strode like a colossus in the Indian sociopolitical scene unto his death, his thoughts never received adequate attention in the generality of Indian society just because he was born as a dalits. However, the contemporary social realities warrant close examination of the wide range of his topics, the width of his vision, the depth of his analysis, and the rationality of his outlook and there essential humanity of his suggestions for practical action. Hence, for Indian women's movement Ambedkar provides a powerful source of inspiration to formulate a feminist political agenda which simultaneously addresses the issues of class, caste and gender in the contemporary sociopolitical set up, which still keeps conservative and reactionary values in many respects, particularly on gender relations. The writings and Speeches of Ambedkar show what values India should develop and how they would modernize its social and political institutions. Ambedkar saw women as the victims of the oppressive, caste-based social system.

Dr. B R Ambedkar framed many laws for women labours in India:

1. Mines Maternity Benefit Act,
2. Women Labour welfare fund,
3. Women and Child, Labour Protection Act,

4. Maternity Benefit for women Labour,
5. Restoration of Ban on Employment of Women on Underground Work in Coal Mines,

AMBEDKAR'S ROLE FOR 'MATERNITY BENEFIT ACT'

The first Maternity Benefits Act was passed in India in 1929 by the Bombay Legislature. In this regard Ambedkar said, 'I believe that it is in the interests of the nation that the mother ought to get a certain period of rest during the Pre-natal period and also subsequently. I am prepared to admit this fact because the conservation of the people's welfare is primarily the concern of the Government. And in every country, therefore, the maternity benefit has been introduced, you will find that the Government has been subjected to a certain amount of charge with regard to maternity benefit. Therefore, the benefits contemplated by this bill ought to be given by this Legislature to the poor women who toil in our factories in this Presidency'. Subsequently the Madras Maternity Benefit Act was passed by the Madras Legislature Council in 1934 and subsequently in other provinces of India.

MINES MATERNITY BENEFIT BILL

As a Labour Minister in the Viceroy executive council between 1942 and 1946, Dr. Babasaheb Ambedkar was helpful in bringing the Mines Maternity Benefit Bill for women in all over India. Under this act, a woman working in the mine is entitled to maternity leave for a period of eight weeks. This period of 8 weeks is divided into two parts of four weeks each, one part preceding delivery and another part succeeding delivery. Later all the acts of Maternity Benefit of various states were repealed and a common Maternity Benefit Act-1961 was adopted by the Central Government for all states in India.

AMBEDKAR AS AN EMANCIPATOR OF THE DALITS

Ambedkar dedicated his life for the development of Dalits. He was opposed to the theory of caste based superiority and social disparity. He made a path for legal rights to enact the laws in connection with progress of dalits which could positively change their lives. Ambedkar said, "You can change your lot, but do not flock to temples hoping for justice to come to you in heaven. There is justice to be found on earth if you can fight for it. Ambedkar always led by example. He showed his followers, through the way he lived his own life, that education and hard work alone held the key to their liberation. The dalits had been a demoralized, helpless group of people, but Ambedkar taught them to stop waiting for help to come from the outside and to rely upon themselves instead. The idea was a revolutionary one for people who had always been told that their lot in life was preordained and that they had no control over it. This idea gave them a new courage and a sense of self respect that they had never known before. The Ambedkar statue was an icon for depressed and oppressed classes civil rights. His posture, constitution in his hand and showing a new path for millions of downtrodden people to words of modern society were symbols in the new age.

Ambedkar views were consistently been inspiring the depressed, suppressed and the downtrodden classes to challenge the dominant strands of political articulations in the country. He has always takes after in lives of millions of strong Dalit communities throughout the country.

STATES MEASURES FOR DALIT UPLIFTMENT BY AMBEDKAR

After independence Ambedkar became the First Law Minister of India. He was appointed as Chairman of the Constitution Drafting Committee by the Assembly to write India's newborn constitution. The text prepared by Ambedkar provided constitutional guarantees and civil liberties for individual citizens including freedom of religion, the abolition of untouchability and outlawing all forms of discrimination. He had a real visionary towards the fundamental rights of Indian citizens and upliftment of Dalits. He made several provisions in the form of Articles in the Constitution for the upliftment of the Dalits. Articles are given below:

- Article 13(2) which describe – "The State shall not make any law which takes away or abridges the rights conferred by this part and any law made in this contravention of this cause shall, to the extent of the contravention, be void".

- Article 14 of the Constitution declares that "the State shall not deny to any person equality before the laws or equal protection of laws".
- Article 15 of the Indian Constitution gives "fundamental rights to all Indian Citizens against any form of discrimination either by State or by any citizen on the basis of religion, race, caste, sex, place of birth or any of them".
- Article 15(4) of the Constitution of India declares that "Nothing can prevent the State from making any special provision for the advancement of any socially and educationally backward classes of citizens or for the Scheduled Castes (SCs) and the Scheduled Tribes (STs)".
- Article 16(4A) declares that "Nothing can prevent the State from making any provision for reservation in matters of provision with consequent seniority to any class or classes of posts in the services under the State in favour of SCs and STs which in the opinion of the State are not adequately represented in the service under the State".
- Article 16(4B) states that "Nothing in the Article shall prevent the state from considering any unfilled vacancies of year which are reserved for being filled in that year in accordance with any provision for reservation made under clause (4) or clause as a separate class of vacancies shall not be considered together with the vacancies of the year in which they are being filled up for determining the ceiling of 50% reservation on total number of vacancies of the year".
- Article 17 of the Indian Constitution declares that "Untouchability is abolished and its practice in any form is forbidden. The enforcement of any disability arising out of untouchability shall be an offence punishable in accordance with law". Based on this Article the Civil Right Protection Act 1965 and the Prevention of Atrocities (SCs and STs Act 1989) was enacted by the Parliament for the protection of Dalit rights.
- Article 330 of the Indian Constitution declares reservation of seats for SCs and STs in the House of the People for Scheduled Castes, Scheduled Tribes except some STs in the autonomous districts of Assam and Scheduled Tribes in the autonomous districts of Assam.

- Article 332 in the constitution of India states about the reservation of seats of SCs and STs in Legislative Assemblies of the States.
- 73rd amendment of constitution in the Article 243 declares that "Panchayat bodies must have proportionate representation of SCs and STs and women. Such reservation should also apply in the case of Chairperson and Deputy Chairpersons of their bodies". Besides these several programmes of the Indian State in the form of grants, scholarships, loans, stipends etc. are being provided for Dalits. This is all due to provisions of constitution drafted by Dr. Ambedkar. He was really a God Father for the Dalits in true sense.

CONTRIBUTION OF AMBEDKAR TOWARDS DALIT EDUCATION

Education is the backbone of human society. One can safely assume that a person is not in the proper sense until he is educated. It diverts the human mind to think and take the right decision. In other words, man becomes a rational animal when he is educated. By the grace of education only the knowledge and information received and spread throughout the world. Ambedkar wanted the people to cultivate the values of freedom and equality among themselves; it is possible only through education. Ambedkar had also given lot of emphasis on getting education. According to him "The backward classes have come to realize that after all education is the greatest material benefit for which they can fight. We may forego material benefits of civilization but we cannot forego our rights and opportunities to reap the benefits of the highest education fully. That is the importance of education. From this point of view he advised the backward classes to realize that without education their existence is not safe."

The influence of John Dewey, one of the greatest educationists of the 20th century, on Ambedkar appears to be deep and permanent. Therefore, Ambedkar approached the problem of educational upliftment of the masses as he believed that education was necessary to shake off their mental Sluggishness and satisfaction with their existing plight. He said that "We may forego material benefits, but we cannot forego our rights and opportunities to reap the benefits of highest education to the fullest extent."

Dr. Ambedkar to his Dalit people, 'Educate to organize and to Struggle' for their own betterment using whatever educational facilities they have. Ambedkar has been described as a philosopher, a patriot, scholar or a writer, a social revolutionary, a humanistic thinker, or the socialist and he had also contributed a great deal to the cause of education. He mainly emphasized that the education as a vital force for individual development and social change. Education plays an important role. It is an effective instrument of mass movement to safeguard life and liberty Ambedkar think that, education was an instrument for the change of the lives of untouchables. He declared that the elevation of the depressed classes was recognized to be the cause of all the enlightened people in the country. He thought that education would enlighten downtrodden people and bridge the gap between the rich and the poor to which the untouchables belong. Education could encourage the oppressed ones to fight and remove injustice and exploitation and pave ways for the liberal thinking.

He recognized that, lack of education was the main cause for the backwardness of poor. A singular role that Ambedkar played in the upliftment of the untouchables in the early 20th century and the importance that he gave to modern education for their betterment deserves special emphasis. In public lectures and meetings, Ambedkar encouraged untouchable youth to acquire education in order to raise their social status and image. His educational contribution starts on a wider scale of educating classes as well as masses. For Ambedkar, education was the main key to open the doors of light, vision and wisdom. He said, "Education is something which ought to be brought within the reach of every one. The object of primary education is to see that every child enters the portals of a primary school leaves it only at a stage when it becomes literate continuous to be literate throughout the rest of his life." Ambedkar's ideas for the dalits was to raise their educational standards so that they may know their own condition, have aspirations and rise to the level of highest Hindu and be in the position to use political power as a means. This is best reflected in Ambedkar's famous slogan of Educate, Agitate and Organize.

FINDINGS

Even though his early campaigns for access to public drinking water and Hindu temples met only with partial success, Ambedkar's activism caused a great social transformation from a Brahminical social system to a human centered one. In spirit, it was similar to the European Renaissance which reimagined human potential and extricated it from the ecclesiastical order. It is undeniable that Ambedkar's framework for reconceptualizing Indian society has yielded certain results that no other frame could achieve.

His drafting of the Indian constitution as a politically and legally liberating document for the Indian society was a remarkable project for envisioning a just social order. His projects touched different dimensions of human life and transformed them politically, socially, economically, and spiritually. Ambedkar's view on democracy reflects his basic emphasis on human equality: "A Democracy is a mode of associated living. The roots of Democracy are to be searched in social relationships, in terms of the associated life among the people, who form the society."

He has provided clear road maps for implementing social justice. By making the constitution a revolutionary document, he gave the Sudras socio-political and economic rights that were denied by the social system formulated in accordance with the codes of Manu.

Ambedkar emphasized the need for education in his community. Education and agitation against an unjust social order were the key ideas which he introduced. His revolutionary ideas inspired future dalit leaders and social activists to continue a persistent battle against social injustice.

Ambedkar's thought or'Ambedkarism' could simply be described as an "ideological expression on the basis of which historical analysis of the Indian society for making servile classes of India as a ruling class, in a classless society by liberating them through and the subjugated into the visions of a casteless society."

In Ambedkar's vision, opposition to of all kinds of discrimination based on race, creed and social status is inevitable. He advocated that some kind of governance is essential for peace and prosperity among people, particularly when people fail to abide by law and order. Such acts are the mission of a good government. And, in fact, without such quality, a true democratic society cannot be established. Indian leaders, who held differing opinions, too, co-operated with his vision of justice.

Saviour of labours, brought 8 hours of duty for them in India. Dr. Ambedkar changed the working time from 12 hours to 8 hours in 1942 which became a light for workers in India.

Dr. Ambedkar is "Champion of women's Rights in India". He strived hard for liberation and empowerment of Indian women and framed many laws for labours and also for women's in India like-Women labour welfare fund, Dearness allowances, ESI, Provident fund act, Women and child labour protection act, Maternity benefit for women labour bill, Divorce act, Right to Property, Leave benefit to piece workers, Revision of scale of pay for Employees, Restoration of ban on women working underground in mines etc.

CONCLUSION

Dr. Ambedkar was truly a multi-faceted personality. A veritable emancipator of Dalits, a great National leader and patriot, a great author, a great educationalist, a great political philosopher, a great religious guide and above all a real humanist without any parallel among his contemporary. Education according to Ambedkar was a blend of pragmatism of Dewey and 'dhamma' of Buddha. Education is not only a layer for their social mobility but also opens the doors for their modernization. Education is a instrument for Dalit upliftment. He regarded education as a means to reach the doors of light and perception to remove the regions of darkness and ignorance. The basic theme of his philosophy of education is: inculcating the values of liberty, equality, fraternity, justice and moral character among the boys and girls of all shades. Dr. B R Ambedkar strongly believed that the downtrodden and women also would have to come forward and to labour hard in all social, economical, educational and political fields to compete with the other members of the society.

REFERENCES

1. Chalam, K.S., *Modernization and Dalit Education: Ambedkar's vision,* Rawat Publications, New Delhi, 2014.
2. Jadhav, Narendra, *Ambedkar: Awakening India's social conscience,* Konark Publishers, New Delhi, 2014.
3. Narayan, J.S., Rao, Somasekhar, A., and Audiseshaiah, K., *B.R. Ambedkar, His relevance Today,* Gyan Publishing House, New Delhi, 1994.
4. Anand. S (Ed.), *Annihilation of Caste: The annotated critical edition* – B.R. Ambedkar – Introduced with the essay 'The Doctor and the Saint' by Arundhati Roy, Navayana Publishers, New Delhi, 2014.
5. Sahadevudu, D., G. Ramesh Babu, Y. Ramachandra Reddy & Venkateswarulu, (2015) The Role of Dr. B. R. Ambedkar in Modern India:A Study, *International Research Journal of Social Sciences,* Vol. 4(11), 20-23, November, 2015.
6. Jay Lakshmi, (2014), Relevance of Ambedkar's Contributions in the Upliftment of Modern Days Dalits and Women, *IOSR Journal of Humanities and Social Science (IOSR-JHSS),* Volume 19, Issue 2, Ver. Iv, February, 20142.
7. Nithiya, P. Ambedkar's Vision on the Empowerment of Dalit, Education, *International Journal of Multidisciplinary Educational Research,* Volume 1, Issue 2, June 2012.

Webliography:

http://ccnmtl.columbia.edu/projects/mmt/ambedkar/web/index.html

http://mahadalitmission.org/BMVM-Introduction.php#EWEU9aKwLa.

http://en.wikipedia.org/wiki/Dalit.

3

Dr. B.R. Ambedkar and Human Rights

– Dr. M. Alankara Masillamani

Human rights are inalienable rights of an individual which help essentially maintaining the dignity of mankind in our society. Universal Declaration of Human Rights (UDHRs) signed on 10th of December 1948 and a majority of nations including those of imperial powers and newly independent states agreed to practice certain principles of human life as inevitable guidelines in maintaining individual rights and social relations. Human Rights came into effect after the agreement of UDHRs as a negation of historical struggle for social reform effecting human rights. In Indian sub-continent the struggle for Human Rights led by Buddha as a reform which was carefully organized in a right path by Thomas Paine and Jyotiba Phule and strongly echoed by Dr. B.R. Ambedkar. Such struggle for human dignity and human rights are as old as the exploitation of human beings in ancient times when some of its people termed it as "lesser fortunate". That was clearly reflected in the mindset, and justified everything in the name of religion and customs and hence this exploited community by a few was termed as "unfortunate".

The origination of Human Rights traced in ancient doctrine of Natural Rights based Natural law advocated by social contract thinkers such as Hobbes, Locke and Rousseau. Human Rights for them were meant to maintain the right to life, liberty and the pursuit of happiness. Dr. B.R. Ambedkar being a son of modernizations, globalization and internationalism, what exactly he meant Human Rights for the feeling of "humanness". He was of the view that if Indian/Hindu society had to improve, it must be formed on the bases of liberty, equality and fraternity. For B.R. Ambedkar, human dignity reform and humanity reform were much bigger than any other reforms on Earth.

Ambedkar felt that all human beings were equal and all had the right to be treated equally. Unlike many others of his time who respected the prevailing notion of inequality imposed by birth must be accepted as it had religious sanction. But Ambedkar was against it notion and strongly held that all human beings were equal and all must be treated equally on the basis of certain rights as a man or a woman. Some of his ideas were the reflection of his concern for human rights and the activities he undertook throughout his life were only for attaining human rights of all. Dr. Ambedkar might be better understood in the light of his interest as a champion of human rights.

Two of Ambedkar's most fundamental ideas are those of the state and the religion on which most of his political thoughts and actions are based. These ideas or thoughts are analyzed from the point of view of his concern for human rights. His opinion about these ideas manifest his vision of an institution which protects the rights of all citizens and of a system which guarantees the freedom of all sections of people to select and practice a religion of their choice that gives them their appropriate status. Thus, his commitments to the cause of human rights inferred from these notions followed/ supported by his other ideas.

DR. AMBEDKAR'S THOUGHT OF STATE

Ambedkar does not consider state as a creation of God and holds the view that state is a human institution. An organization which he meant to serves the interests of individuals. In his opinion the aims of the state are:

(i) to maintain the right of every subject to life, liberty and pursuit of happiness to free speech for free exercise of religion;

(ii) to remove social, political and economic inequality by providing better opportunities to the submerged classes, and

(iii) to make it possible for every subject to enjoy freedom from want without any fear.

Ambedkar propagated the freedom of men/women and differentiated between a good state and a bad state on the basis of state's capacity and willingness to protect the freedom of citizens. He maintained to say a good state that guarantees protection against persecution of one community by another causing internal disturbances, violence and disorder in any part of its territory. He simply opposed discriminatory approach to any group and exploitation of one by another.

Dr. Ambedkar does not find a supernatural source of law. For him, law is made by human beings to deal with human affairs. The ultimate aim of law is to serve the interests of human beings. He considers law as an instrument of providing happiness to man. To him laws are made by man for man. Law has not created man, but man has created law for serving his own purpose. Thus, he believes law is not above man and its objective is not to harass him. As it has a human purpose it must be applicable to all equally i.e., social and universal in its effect.

To maintain an ideal social condition there must be rule of law. If a society is governed by law and not by the whims of man so that individual is able to enjoy his freedom. His unflinching faith in individual liberty and dignity led him to emphasize rule of law.

However, Dr. Ambedkar underlines the rule of law and points out the importance of law in providing a better condition to people to avail their rightful position against the caprices of the vested interests. He does not accept that law alone can safeguard the rights of individuals who are at the lower strata of social ladder. But he invokes the conscience of society. Rights are not protected by law but the social and moral consciences of society recognize rights which law chooses to enact will be safe and secured. But, if the fundamental rights are opposed by the community, no law, no parliament, no judiciary can guarantee them in the real sense of the word.

Dr. Ambdekar had experienced many humiliating situations in his life as a result of the misbehaviors of the upper class people and the state was unable to protect him from such conditions as the state was controlled by the very persons who were the perpetrators of those humiliations. He stated that if the state's power remained in the hands of higher class then there could be no justice for all, especially for those who are outside the decision making process. Other words, the controllers of decision making authority would likely to victimize those innocent people who have no such power.

Dr. Ambedkar's idea of state indicates some amount of autonomy from the hegemony of any class. He prefers a set of principles to be followed in the governance of the state. To him, the state is expected to act according to the principles of the constitution and therefore, he made attempts to incorporate certain principles into the constitution which he considered favourable to his fellowmen. Many of the provisions found in the constitution for the downtrodden people of India and aims at implementing affirmative actins for them.

Dr. Ambedkar also understand that the state might be an instrument in the hands of the ruling classes to serve their interests unless the subjugated people themselves became the rulers, the state might not work for them. Ambedkar wanted to make the lower caste people politically powerful. He argued and encountered the reservation of seats for the scheduled caste people of India long before India attained independence despite opposition from many other Indian leaders in the process. The First Round Table Conference 1930 marked the beginning. But Gandhi refused to consider separate electorate for the depressed classes and opposed any form of political representation or reservation of seats. I do not mind the oppressed converting to Islam or Christianity that I tolerate but I do not tolerate, if there are two divisions in Hinduism in each and every village. Gandhi said those who speak of political representation for the lower classes do not know India and the Indian society which is today constructed. I shall resist this thing with my life, Gandhi held. Though there were contrary opinions with regard to reservation in the constituent assembly Nehru made it clear that Reservation of seats for scheduled castes and scheduled tribes was a historic turn in our destiny. K.T. Shah told in the "Constituent Assembly", this discrimination on particular classes of our society is our unfortunate legacy of the past requiring special treatment for establishing real equality of all citizens.

Dr. Ambedkar was conscious of the need for political empowerment as he felt that without political power there could be no social and economic power. He considered (that the) lower caste people and regulate the social system as the latter has the power. He therefore encouraged and motivated his followers to capture political power so that the hold of the upper caste people over different social structures would end and there would be equality for all in different fields. According to Ambedkar political power only as a means and not an end and it is to attain some better conditions for his own people.

Dr. Ambedkar had firm faith in democracy. He visualized the establishment of a society free from any kind of exploitation through democracy. His conception of democracy appears to be purely people oriented which allowed involvement of all in decision making process. It envisaged complete abolition of inequality. He set in motion a social revolution to lay the foundation of an egalitarian social system by transformation of the traditional Indians society into a classless society in which there could be perfect social justice and no place for untouchability. For this purpose he wanted to empower the downtrodden people of India. He strongly held the view that devoid of power and knowledge for the non-brahmins and the depressed classes could not make any progress.

DR. AMBEDKAR'S CONCEPT OF RELIGION

Ambedkar was against the Brahmin's tradition which perpetuated the domination of the upper castes over the backward class people. He felt that the upper caste people had spread their brand of religion so that they could continue their hold over the various structures of the social system and monopolize all the benefits. There was an upper class bias in Hindu religion, he commented. As a result, Hindu religion defended only the interests of upper castes and completely disregarded those of the backward classes. The low born people of the Hindu society were subject to different type of cruelty and humiliation and these degrading acts had the support of various religious sanctions.

He rejected the doctrine of the infallibility of the Vedas (the Holy Scriptures of Hinduism) and the *Varna-Vayavastha* which divided the society into four *Varnas* or orders such as *Brahmins, Ksatriyas, Vaisyas and Shudras* occupied positions in descending order. He held the *Varna* system responsible for social inequality in India. He felt that so long as Hindu religion reined Indian society there was no remedy for the exploitation of lower caste people. He had a firm belief that Hinduism would never end the domination of Brahmins as the Hindu religion was controlled by Brahmins and the persisting inequality would continue in Indian society indefinitely. Therefore, Ambedkar motivated his followers to prefer for another religion which would provide them an equal status with others. He advised them to select only that religion in which they would get equal status, equal opportunity and equal treatment.

Since the untouchables were the followers of Hindu religion they were enjoying basic rights as human rights. To have human rights the low caste people had to choose and follow a religion which would guarantee equality and enjoyment of ordinary rights as human beings. When Ambedkar fail to gain equal status and ordinary rights as a human being within the Hindu society he searched for another religion which he believed would give equal status, equal rights and fair treatment to an untouchable like him. His statement in this regard was quite revealing at Yeda Conference in 1935.

He revealed that the religion must recognize the fundamental principles of liberty, equality, and fraternity. Otherwise, religion itself would be instrumental in dividing the society into different sections on the basis of inequality. To his mind, Hinduism had been just doing that. The Hindu society had been divided into different classes with the patronage of religion and the principles of inequality had been entrenched with religious sanction. This is the main cause of Hindu religion for making untouchables experiencing all the sufferings at the hands of the higher castes.

Further, Hinduism stressed on the need for conformity to the commands of the higher caste people and its tenets were beyond its scrutiny. All had to respect its principles without any protest even if those were inimical to their interests. It imposed many prohibitions on ordinary followers, favourable to legendaries/leaders/interpreters and disadvantageous to others. Hinduism was nothing but a multitude of commands and prohibitions. It excluded Shudras, people of low birth from all religious practices and relegated them to a position of ignominy. The Shudras belong to a stratum in the social system, Hinduism explains and outside the ashram theory, which divided life into four stages viz. *brahmacharya*, *grahasthya*, *vaṇaprastha* and *sanyasa* only to the 'twice born' castes who had the privilege of entitling to these four stages of life. Thus, inequality was in-built into different schemes of Hinduism as a result of which there were social and religious inequality very much prevailing in Hindu society.

Another thing that Ambedkar had in mind was economic security. Without economic self-sufficiency with empty stomach lower class people would not think of liberty and their liberty might be mortgaged with the people who provided them food. He felt three things in Hinduism worked against economic security. First, Hinduism denied freedom of occupation in the code of Manu and accordingly individual's occupation preordained before his/her birth. Secondly, Manu directed Shudras to serve the higher classes. Thirdly, Hinduism did not allow Shudras to accumulate wealth. To seek equality and economic security, he realized lower class people must have potentialities and access to knowledge. But, this was also monopolized by the higher caste people. He did not find necessary requirements of liberty in Indian society as here are not congenial situations for the enjoyment of liberty. Therefore, he wanted to reform the Indian society.

Dr. Ambedkar's search for a rational religion ended in Buddhism. He regarded Buddhism as a much more rational religion compared to Hinduism. Because Buddhism does not have different strata on the basis of untouchability and it adopts the principles of equality. Buddhism propagated equality among all its disciples, it does not discriminate one follower from another as it consider all as equal human beings. It was the only suitable religion to be practiced by all, Ambedkar viewed. He praised Buddhism as he believed it to be a religion based on moral principles. He also, pointed out that the founders of other religions consider themselves as emissaries of God but Buddha considered himself as a guide and not above moral principles. Thus, he gave a new meaning to the concept of religion.

Dr. Ambedkar raised his voice against exploitation of the backward class people. He concerned about caste system which subjugated more than one fifth of the population to levels worsen than animals, and institutionalized inequality with the help of different religious principles. He attacked Hindu religion from the standpoint of its victims-the untouchables. He was merciless in his denunciations of the pettiness perversities and the hypocrisies of Brahminism which, to him was a wicked and mischievous agent of the social exploitation of the backward and untouchable sections of the Hindu society.

Dr. Ambedkar has been the most renowned and the most militant champion of the untouchables. He paid his attention not only for the emancipation of untouchables but also towards eliminating annihilation of the entire caste system. He dreamed of an ideal society in which all would have justice. He envisioned his ideas in the famous three principles: liberty, equality and fraternity. These principles were the bases for establishing an ideal society of his conception, i.e. a society free from any kind of exploitation.

Dr. Ambedkar led Satyagrahas to assert human rights. He advocated three traits: educate, organize and agitate. Indeed the first principle will provide rational thought, the second principle will give mental or physical strength and the third principle will lead to fight for human rights, be it a man or woman. He advocated the land shall be let-out to villagers without distinction of caste or creed and in such a manner there will be no land, no tenant and no landless labourer.

In view of the social and political injustice, he questioned. How it could be possible for any future government which believes in doing justice socially, economically and politically without a socialist economy. He opined that labour must have both equality and liberty guaranteed by a constitution from the point of labour. In other words, the economic structure of a society would serve the interest of labour best from the establishment of "state socialism" through parliamentary democracy.

Dr. Ambedkar emphasized secularism being the only way to solve the minority's problems on a more rational basis as a part of democracy. He did not accept the form of democracy, where there are only privileges for some and disabilities for the majority of others. A democratic form of government presupposes a democratic form of society, he added.

Dr. Ambedkar was an extensive model philosopher. He did not confine to any single school in his philosophical approach. We can find multi schools in his idea, thought, vision, practice and implementation. His philosophy is not narrow based; it is a broad-based. The ultimate goal of his philosophy is justice for humankind.

Dr. Ambedkar was on a vivid rationalist His rationalism was on a basis of reason and raised so many questions i.e. what, where, how, when and why against the existence of God Rama and Krishna and social evils- *Varna* and caste. He exhorted the people to know about human life rather than the existence of God and *Atma*. He denied the dogma and accepted human reality, and he had high confidence on human reason which helps man come out from darkness to enlighten.

Dr. Ambedkar categorically explains human beings needs material results in social structure rather than spiritual results. Nature provides liberty, equality for all human beings irrespective of caste, colour, creed and sex. But Hindu society has made authority and tyranny over individual life. So, he vehemently condemned over the authority of Hindu society which consists of social evils like inequality, injustice, discrimination and inhuman. That's why he defended human rights which are part of the natural rights in nature. These rights are essential for all human beings without discrimination of caste and sex. He denied the authority of man over woman, man over man. He gives the highest place to fraternity which is being the only safeguard against the denial of liberty, equality and fraternity.

Dr. Ambedkar was a pragmatist. To pragmatism action (utility) is more important than thought or idea. He called upon the masses to do action and hard work rather than sitting idly and following others' opinions and beliefs. Human action must help to fulfill the material welfare or need of the people. Human hard work would enrich the quality of life was his strong belief. It helps change one's conditions from time to time. He never confined to the ideas of imaginary things without human welfare. He expressed human experience will guide him towards (social, political, economic) utility.

Dr. Ambedkar worked for social humanism which stands for the fact or truth and it must serve the human interest and not the interest of any supernatural being. The results and benefits of such humanism will reach the door of each and every human being living in human society. All things can be true only when they work for all people ultimately. Ambedkar's knowledge, intellectual highness, thoughts and actions he sacrificed for the people who are living in gloomy social conditions. Throughout his life he had been fighting for human rights and fundamental rights which are essential for all human beings who live in the nature. His social humanism is relevant even today for not only the people of Indian sub-continent but also each and every individual who live in the world society. He created human rights for all and tried to bring all men/women on a par socially. His contribution was not related to personal benefit but it was essentially social/human beings who were suffering from slavery, injustice, tyranny and exploitations. He recognized the social stigma of women in Hindu society and stressed the need for women human rights by introducing Hindu Code Bill in Indian Parliament in 1956. Though the bill was rejected at that moment and Dr. Ambedkar had to resign from the Central Ministry later on it was passed in the Parliament and became a legislation or Act. Dr. B.R. Ambedkar is a father of social justice, a man of courage and devotion, a role model to all pains and pleasures, a modern human rights fighter, practitioner and winner. He is a lighting lamp to the society. His foot prints are permanent on Indian soil. He is a lover of nature. He was born for knowledge only. His views will be continued remaining permanent forever. We everyone of Indian society should accept and recognize all citizens are equal before nature and conform to the ever strongest philosophy of Dr. B.R. Ambedkar.

REFERENCES

1. Sadashiv, S. Mugali : "A Perspective Study of Human Rights in India", *International Journal of Research Granthaalaya,* Vol. 2, Issue. 1, October 2014.
2. Nancy Flowers: "Human Rights Here and Now – Celebrating the Universal Declaration of Human Rights", University of Minnesota Human Rights Resource Centre, 2016, pp. 1-4.
3. Henry, Thiagavaj : "Ambedkar and Human Rights Education" (A talk at a JNU Seminar), Human Rights Education Movement of India, July 29, 1998 pp. 1-6.
4. Joseph, Benjamin : "Dr. B.R. Ambedkar 'An Indefatigable Defender of Human Rights", *FOCUS*, Vol. 56, June 2009, pp. 1-5.
5. Editor:"National Campaign on Dalit Human Rights", info@ncdhr.org.in, 8 August, 2016, pp. 1-3.
6. Maneesh Chhibber : "Is anyone listening to Ambedkar?" The Indian Express, December 21, 2016 p.9.
7. S.N. Mishra: *Socio-economic and Political Vision of Dr. B.R. Ambedkar*, Concept Publishing Company, New Delhi, 2010 pp. Ambedkar A Champion of Human Rights. A.N. Panda, pp. 222-232 the process write up.
8. Christopher, Jaffrelot : *Dr. Ambedkar and Untouchability Analyzing and Fighting Caste*, Permanent Black, Delhi, 2008, pp. 1-203.
9. Justice V.R. Kirshna Iyer : *Human Rights and Inhuman Wrongs*, B.R. Publising Corporation, Delhi, 1990 pp. 1-111.
10. S.L. Dhani: *Dr. B.R. Ambedkar Man of Millennium for Social Justice*, Kalpaz Publications, Delhi 2007. pp. 1-314.
11. J.P. Yadav: *Human Rights and Social Security*, Anmol Publications, New Delhi, 2004, pp. 1-266.
12. Volerian Roadrigues: *The Essential Writings of B.R. Ambedkar*, Oxford University Press, New Delhi, 2002 pp. 1-553.
13. Umakand N. Netragaonkar: *Social-Legal Philosophy of Bharat Ratna B.R. Ambedkar*, Decent Books, New Delhi, 2009, pp. 1-203.

14. Vidya Bhushan Rawat : "Ambedkar As a Human Rights Defender", Countercurrents. Org. 5 December, 2007.
15. B. Syam Mohan David Raju: "Life and Philosophy of Dr. B.R. Ambedkar's for Mankind", *Indian Journal of Research – PARIPEX*, Vol. 3, issue. 5, June 2013 pp. 67-69.
16. A. Venkata Rao: "Bharata Ratra Dr. B.R. Ambedkar", A Champion of Human Rights.

4

Religion and Modernity: A Study of Dr. Ambedkar's Neo Buddhism

– Dr. K. Mavali Rajan

The theme of my presentation is very vast. It is not possible to cover all the facets of Dr. Ambedkar's visions on the Buddhism and his efforts on the social change. Even though I have tried here to highlight my observations on the proposed theme. To understand the relation between Ambedkar's view on religion and modernity, it is essential to understand the realities of Brahmanism and practice of untouchability in Indian context. The practice of untouchability is a strange phenomenon, which has been a part and parcel of Hindu Brahmanical order, based on the concept of ritual purity and pollution. According to historical tradition the term 'untouchability' denotes the socio-religious practice by which Hindus (Brahmanism) keeps a large number of the lower castes from touching or coming near their persons, houses, temples, tanks, and sometimes even public roads. The term ordinarily stand for a particular condition of a man or a woman rendering him unfit for being touched by the other persons.[1] About the origin of untouchability Dr. Ambedkar offered several inter woven theories. One of the theories says that the untouchables were originally '*broken man*', people who had been isolated from the community, or in the other ways. These '*broken men*' were then allowed to live along with other communities but on the outside of the main village.[2] Ambedkar called the 'broken men' as 'unfortunate' who were always treated as outcastes by upper community and branded as the untouchables and unapproachable community in realm of society.

In his entire life Dr. Ambedkar vehemently struggled against the evil practice of untouchability. He undertook imperative task to liberate and emancipate the downtrodden from the oppression of Hindu social order and converted mass of people from the orthodox Hinduism to liberal Buddhism. His main conversion strategy was to provide a way to liberate himself and his people from the depression of untouchability and thereby to bring out a radical social change among the suppressed community. According to him it was not for liberation of just one individual but of the people those who in quest of self- respect and equality. Consequently his complete struggle for liberation not only for the oppressed and suppressed communities but for all Indians, to break down their shackles and bonds by looking for truth in the Buddhist way of life and creating a new society of harmony and happiness around them. Through his priceless speeches and writings Dr. Ambedkar created consciousness among the followers on the Buddhist doctrines and established that the social equality can only be accessible through the path shown by the Buddha and his *Dhamma.*

I

Before entering to the concern discussion it is essential to understand the early attempt made by the leaders of the subaltern groups in uplifting the marginalized communities. Since the 19th and early years of the 20th century the leaders from the subaltern groups had been strongly complaining about the oppression meted out to these communities by the dominant rural groups. The leaders of the suppressed people opined that illiteracy and ignorance of the poor had enabled the oppressive sections of the society to hold them in a position of subordination. They often requested the colonial government to introduce special concessions for the socio economic improvement of the poor sections.[3]

Gail Omvedt in her work "*The Dalit and Democratic Revolution: Dr Ambedkar and Dalit Movements in Colonial India*" argues that "the leaders of the depressed class challenged the 'Hindu-Natiónalism' which was emerging as a consequence of the elite organizing from 19th century onwards to define Indian society. They asserted that the Hinduism had not been the religion and culture of the majority but rather was an imposed religion; and that escaping exploitation today encouraging the low castes to reject this imposition to define themselves an 'non-Hindu' and take a new religious identity".[4] In the emerging circumstances Jotiba Phule tried to formulate a new, theistic religion; Periyar promoted atheism; Dr. Ambedkar turned to Buddhism; others in the Tamilnadu non-Brahmin movement tried to claim Saivism as an independent religion; Narayana Guru formulated "one religion, one caste, one god" while his more radical follower Ayyankali proclaimed "no religion, no caste and no-god to mankind". Whatever the specialties, the rejection of Hinduism remained a feature differentiating the anti-caste radicals from the reformers.[5]

Prior to Dr. Ambedkar, Jotiba Phule (1827-1890), a social revolutionary in the early decade of the 19th century played vital role in emancipation of oppressed in India. He is considered as the father of the depressed castes and non-Brahmin movements in South India, he was the first Indian leader to start a movement for the removal of the social and economic inequality of the lower castes suffered for ages. Jotiba Phule tried to secure social equality and social justice for the depressed castes of Maharashtra such as the Mahar, Mang, Dhed and Chamar who occupied the lowest social status in the Hindu social hierarchy. Gail Omvedt notes that "Phule is today taken as a founding figure in Maharashtra not simply by the anti-caste but also by the farmers, women and rural-based environmental movements. He questioned the Aryan race theory which was prominent during the time and greatly influenced some of the Dalit leaders of the 1920s who framed their movements according to race or ethnicity".[6]

Jotiba Phule, the main founder of the anti-caste movement in India, attacked the Brahmin domination and orthodox Hinduism. Against the traditional Hindu marriage ceremonies he introduced new marriage ritual, following many peasant traditions but without the use of Brahmin priests, and stressing equality between men and women, and in the end of his struggle he took the radical step of proclaiming a new, theistic religion, the "*Sarvajanik Satya Dharma*" (common religion of truth) with a strong, moralistic emphasis.[7] In many ways, *dharma* and caste are at the centre of Phule's thought. His opposition to Brahmanism did not relate only to the *Varna* system, also related to almost everything within the Hindu system. In his view Hinduism as we know it originates in the *Shrutis* (the *Vedas*) and the *Smritis.* He was convinced that these books were a part of the Brahmanical attempt at creating texts which would nationalize and perpetuate their dominance. The Brahmanical tradition claimed the *Chaturvarna* system to be god-given and eternal, and therefore unassailable. As such Brahmin superiority had divine origins. He rejected the supremacy of the Brahmins and useless Vedic rituals.[8] For Phule and Ambedkar the Brahmanism was historical, constructed over time, and since it was an ideology of oppression and dominance, it had to be opposed and ultimately smashed. Further he states that there was nothing sacred or divine about it, because it presented itself as divinely ordained; so it was necessary to oppose this system in complete form in Indian society. The bulk of Phule's writings on religion therefore, consist of a severe polemic against Brahmanism, and discrimination on the basis of castes.[9]

He struggled hard for the restoration of the dignity of individual and human rights as he considered all Indians are equal. It was Jotiba Phule who first opened a school for the depressed castes children in his own house in 1848. In 1873 he also founded an organization called '*Satya Shodhak Samaj*', a society for seeking truth, which was the first well known depressed class organization taking over the amelioration of the condition of the untouchables.[10] The main vision of Jotiba Phule, was to open schools and organize organizations to save mainly "lower castes from the hypocritical Brahmins and from their opportunities scriptures".[11]

In the contemporary period Pandit Ayothidas, a well known south Indian social reformer among the subaltern intellectuals, worked for the upliftment of the poor section of the society. He was very familiar with early Tamil classical works and seemed to have been learned in the philosophical thought of Hinduism, Buddhism, Jainism, Islam and Christianity. He was a Tamil *Siddha* physician, considered to be the pioneer of the Tamil Dravidian and non-Brahmin movements. Ayothidas, a depressed class by birth and Buddhist by faith, was an outstanding personality in the emancipation of the depressed class. He was a rationalist writer, strongly criticized the age old establishment of the caste system and the contents of the Vedic, Puranic and Brahmanical literatures. According to him caste system was an invention of self-seekers, who wanted to suppress the poor and depressed section of the society. He argues that Hinduism stands against liberty, equality and fraternity, so he wanted that the caste system to be destroyed. He criticized and hated the claim of the Brahmin's superiority.[12] Because of his rationalistic ideas and reform activities he was called as the '*morning star of rationalist movement*' in Tamil Nadu. His rationalistic view predated the political expression, non-Brahmin mission in the Madras Presidency and it paved the way for the non-Brahmin movement. Thus, Ayothidas became the pioneer of the non-Brahmin movement and rationalist movement in Tamil Nadu.[13]

In course of his movement Pandit Ayothidas established a society called '*Sakya Buddhist Sangam*' in Rayappetah of Madras.[14] The very name indicates a claim of heritage, for they believed that the Valluva Sakya, a sub-caste of the Paraiyas were descendents of Siddhartha's own *Sakya* clan.[15] The society organized regular lecture on Buddhism, atheism, and invited many speakers from the different capacity and the main speakers included Lakshminarasu, M. Singaravelu including Ayothidas himself.[16] The society attracted both subaltern group and non-Brahmin upper castes. His interpretation of Buddhism took up redefinition of what have been considered to be the basic teaching of Buddhism. The followers of the society were not ready to accept the notions of *karma* and rebirth, since these had been used in the Brahmanic frame work to define their untouchability. The interpretation of *karma* and rebirth made by the votaries of Sakya Buddhism, seem to have paved the way for Ambedkar's rejection of it.[17]

The Sakya Buddhism of Ayothidas spread mostly with the migration of the Paraiya community. We could find the branches of the society in Kolar gold mines region, where the Paraiyas were migrated as labourer and worked as miners. And the branches of the society also spread over to Burma and South Africa. It found its support largely among those Paraiyas, who had become urbanized, moving away from their traditional village occupations and finding themselves in a new life.[18] The famous Tamil rationalistic reformer E.V. Ramasamy Periyar was associated with the Sakya Buddhist movement during his early career. He was a frequent visitor to the Kolar gold fields during the period where his discontent with Congress was crystallized and he was about to launch the Self-Respect Movement (*Suyamariyathai Iyakkam*) in Tamil Nadu. Periyar wrote many articles in his journal about the ideology of the Sakya Buddhism.[19] Ayothidas spent much of his times to install so many branches of Sakya Buddhist Association, around 28 of Buddhist societies mostly in the northern districts of Tamil Nadu including in Kolar Gold mines, a few from outside India, in South Africa, among the migrant workers from north Tamil Nadu. He organized Buddhist ways of worshiping and meditating, taught his comrades Buddhist principles, structured Buddhist festivals and created a self-confident set of people who would represent themselves as Buddhists. He called upon the downtrodden people to get converted into Buddhism. He organized Buddhist cremation grounds in Chennai. He appealed to the British Government to give representation to the downtrodden people in local administration, education and government jobs.

Ayothidas's Buddhism is not a neo-Buddhism. He is very much traditional and his Sakya Buddhism is mostly constructed from the ancient Tamil and Pali texts. He had learned the Pali language and he was able to read and write Pali. His masterly Buddhist work, *Adhi Vedham,*[20] contains many Pali quotes, their Tamil translations and the Tamil quotes from Thirukkural and other Tamil works. The Buddhism, Ayothidas represents is very much away from the known versions of Buddhism in English or in Sanskrit. He even criticizes those who construct Buddhism from English translated sources. One can find the earliest post-Colonial critique of orientalist writings on Buddhism in Ayothidas's writings. In this sense, Sakya Buddhism is unique of its kind.

Ayothidas believed that the Buddhism is the biggest and highly original narrative of ancient Indian culture. He realized the emancipatory potential of the Buddhist tradition and drawing. On the earlier connection of the Buddhist tradition, Ayothidas tried to interpret the Tamil's history, religion and literature from the view point of Buddhism.[21] The Buddhism represents the casteless and classless social culture and ethos of ancient India which has determined the entire course of development of the religious culture of the country. The latter religions of India had either inherited or imprecise the religious thought of Buddhism in course of development. He intelligently gleans out the original memorandum of Buddhism even from the distorted texts of latter religions. At times, one feels that Ayothidas was trying to construct a grand narrative of Buddhism that would include not only Jainism but also the Saivite, Vaishnavite and Siddha thoughts of Indian tradition, particularly the Tamil tradition.[22]

II

In the beginning of the 20th century Dr. B.R. Ambedkar laid great stress on the elevation of the depressed castes through education. He saw education as human rights and as a fundamental civic right. Ambedkar awakened his people to their age-old disabilities and instigated them to fight for their emancipation. He urged the downtrodden to fight for self elevation. He launched his social movement in 1924 and founded a society called '*Bahishkrit Hitkarini Sabha*' as a central institute for removing difficulties of the poor masses and placing their grievances before the government. The founding principle of the *Sabha* was 'educate, unite, and agitate, (in Tamil *karpi*, *onrucher* and *purachichey*). Through the *Sabha* he worked for the promotion of education, culture and economic development of the depressed class. He convinced that without the right knowledge (education) no fruitful social change is attained. Also, well educated with unity of action (unite) the goal becomes distant. But with proper education and unity among the community, strengthens an agitation (agitate) to demand what is rightfully ours, a movement will be a definite success. Consequently to promote higher education among the depressed community Ambedkar founded the 'People's Education Society', which established institutions of higher education such as the Siddhartha College at Bombay in 1946 and the college of arts, science and commerce at Aurangabad in 1950.[23]

Dr. Ambedkar was known to the intellectual and academic world of America, England, and Germany since he took his post graduate and higher research studies in the well known universities of the said countries during the period between 1915 and 1924. He became well known in India and abroad as the leader of the subaltern, the excluded, and the oppressed-suppressed and poor neglected masses of the Indian Hindu society. He became widely known through his famous speeches at conferences and seminars at different parts of the world and also through his writings on the theme of national and international importance. Above all he was involved in the works of social reform, religious revolutions and political and economic developmental activities with the aim of liberating the suppressed section of people from the caste barriers, injustice and inequality of the Hindu system.[24]

Ambedkar, after returning to India sometimes in the early 1920s from earning a law degree in the United States, involved in politics and the plight of downtrodden. In 1936 Ambedkar founded the 'Independent Labour Party (ILP)' as a way to fight for the Dalit cause from inside the political sphere. It was a worker-peasant party with goals that aimed to eliminate caste discrimination, but also focused on problems with capitalism, wealth distribution and equal access to resources. Ambedkar remained involved in both sides of the movements; the political process and the grassroots organization.[25] He focused his intellectual energies on the task of socio economic liberation of the oppressed community.

III

Most of us only knew that Dr. Ambedkar was an architect of Indian constitution and he was also a great teacher, educationist, lawyer, economist, anthropologist, sociologist, author, orator, politician, trade union leader, statesman, preacher, philosopher, thinker, and above all he was a social revolutionary. In short he was a multifaceted personality, an intellectual revolutionary in India. In Indian land many social reformers emerged to struggle against injustice, inequality in favour of depressed communities, however a few leaders successfully communicated their own ideas to societies through their constant protest against the suppression. Particularly Dr. Ambedkar worked for the upliftment of suppressed communities, women, backward castes, minorities, and working class people and spends all his life for the human dignity and self-respect.

According to Ambedkar the Hindu social structure mainly based on the four Varnas, breeds inequality and has been the parent of the modern caste system and untouchability, which are merely forms of inequality. In Hinduism everything caste-oriented and hierarchy is based on their birth. Caste determines one's social status in society. Man is unavoidable if he is born in a lower caste. He says that the system is not just based on system of labour, but hierarchical division of labourers. He hated the hierarchical order and caste inequality of the Hindu society. He believed that the rights are equal and common to all human beings. He declared that "we are demanding equal rights which are the common possession of the entire humanity but due to inhibitions created by the *Shastras* we have been denied these human rights."[26] He further says that "rights are protected not by law but the social and moral conscience of society. If social conscience is such that it is prepared to recognize the rights, which law chooses to enact, rights will be safe and secure. But if the fundamental rights are opposed by community, no law, no parliament, and no judiciary can guarantee them in the real sense of the word".[27] He believed that the equality before law is the main base of social equality.

He rebelled against the orthodox Hindu society, attacked the Hindu social order, and declared in the strongest languages his opposition to caste-system and the social evils prevalent in the Indian society. He fought bravely against the protagonists of equality and exploitation and made heroic efforts to inspire the downtrodden classes to raise the banner of revolt against the Hindu social order. He realized the pain of the suppressed communities and tried to inculcate a new life to them. He exhorted them to revolt against their slavery and serfdom. Through his numerous speeches, talks and writings he made these classes conscious of their degraded position; its cause, and the way to relieve from it.

To create consciousness among the suppressed community he undertook many agitations for their liberation from the caste barriers and the Hindu social slavery. Under his leadership, the suppressed communities for the first time (in 1927) asserted their human rights by drinking water from the forbidden tank. The next important battle against the oppression fought by Dr. Ambedkar was to secure the right of entry in to the Hindu temples at Nasik. He advised his people 'to abjure Hinduism and embrace some other faith that would give them an equal status, a secure position and rightful treatment'.[28]

Ambedkar believed that conversion to other religion would give social justice to the suppressed community. He observed that Buddhism is the best way to be adopted to promote peaceful social life. On the eve of conversion Ambedkar expressed his choice of Buddhism as the least harmful route for the country since Buddhism is "a part and parcel of Bharatiya culture". In the conversion ceremony he announced that "I have taken care, my conversion will not harm the tradition of the culture and history of this land."[29] His main conversion method was to build a separate Buddhist moral community rather to attempt alteration of Brahminical ideology through the mobilizing of shared moral values among the suppressed communities.

Anne M. Blackburn holds the view that "religious sanction for Ambedkar, relies upon shared social experience and such experience is limited to individuals within the moral community of religious kin established by commensality and the adoption of a common ancestral tradition. Religion itself, as a social mechanism, also creates a moral community consisting in relations to equality and individuality among its members".[30] This understanding of religion and its role in the creation of a moral social order makes it clear that Ambedkar's conversion to Buddhism aimed to develop a community of Neo-Buddhist morality existed parallel with other religious communities in post independence India.[31]

When he decided to renounce the Hindu religion in 1935, he said at Yeola conference that "although I am born as a Hindu because I had no control over it. But I will not die as a Hindu because I do have control over it".[32] Ambedkar's view point was simple. In India, the greatest barrier to the advance of the downtrodden was Hinduism itself. He thought that Hinduism is the main source of birth of India's social evil. He bravely announced in a public meeting that "you must... destroy the sacredness and divinity with which caste has become invested. In the last analysis, this means you must destroy the authority of the *Shastras* and the *Vedas*... you must take the stand that Buddha took. You must take the stand which Guru Nanak took. You must not only discord the *Shastras*, you must deny their authority as did Buddha and Guru Nanak. You must have courage to tell the Hindus that what is wrong with them is their religion- that has produced in them this notion of the sacredness of caste".[33] He strongly criticized the caste system and urged for the social justice.

Dr. B.R. Ambedkar took decision for conversion to Buddhism because of the following factors;

(1) the rational consciousness of assessing things for better life of human beings,

(2) the freedom of choice in which man realizes his individual dignity,

(3) the revolt against suppression and enslavement of humanity, and

(4) the entire change of traditional pattern of society for providing physical facilities for all and finally the emancipation of ignored humanity and the revitalization of overlooked reality.[34]

He said at a conference in Bombay in May 1936 that "the Hindu religion does not appeal to my conscience. It does not appeal to my self-respect... I tell you very specifically, religion for man and not man for religion. To get human treatment, convert yourself. Convert for becoming strong. Convert for securing equality. Convert for getting liberty." He delivered his speech in Marathi at the Mahar conference on 30-31st May 1936 which was first published by the government of Maharashtra in the special number of Lok Rajya dated 16th April 1981.[35]

In the conference he announced for the renouncing of Hinduism. He delivered his famous speech on '*which way to emancipation*? (*mukti kon pathe* ?). That was;

> "If you want to gain self-respect,
> Change your religion;
> If you desire independence,
> Change your religion;
> If you want equality,
> Change your religion;

If you wish to create a society that ensures Co-operation and Brotherhood,

> Change your religion;
> And if you wish to make happy the world in which you live,
> *Change your religion.*"[36]

Thus he urged the depressed communities to change their religious identity. Through the ideas of conversion he wanted to bring about a radical social change, an ideological revolution in the Hindu mind. In an interview occasion he clearly stated that "Buddhism is based on equality and liberty. Brahmins did not approve of them. If Buddhism were to succeed, caste system would have been abolished, and Brahmanism would not have been stabilized". He also added that "a religion is needed to control human life; the philosophy of Marx will not satisfy the downtrodden".[37]

According to Ambedkar, "Caste is religion and religion is anything but an institution. It may be institutionalized by not as same as the institution in which it is embedded. Religion[38] is an influence or force immersed through the life of each individual molding his character determining his actions and reactions and his likes and dislikes. These likes and dislikes action and reaction are not institution, which can be lopped off".[39]

Dr. Ambedkar delivered many speeches and wrote on several occasions during the years 1950 to 1956 and wrote much on various aspects. In his speeches, he repeatedly expressed the need of religion for the existence of human society, equally maintaining necessity of morality and law. On every religion, Ambedkar said, if it is going to serve humanity, will have to declare how it proposes to relieve the sufferings of the oppressed psychologically and ethically. The modern world, as for him needs religion more than ever before... He believes that Buddhism is the religion of the intellectual, and spells out its way of life which is in principle rational, moral, humanist and social. Buddhism rejects the Hindu doctrine of *Chaturvarna*, in the same way as it rejects belief in god, the soul and the *Vedas*. Also as a religion of intellectual, Buddhism does not believe in idol worship and provides to every individual the liberty to examine everything in the light of his reasoning faculty. In brief, Buddhism is in consonance with man's scientific outlook.[40]

Ambedkar says that Buddhism is not a religion but '*Dhamma*'. Here '*Dhamma*' is a term which stands for the Buddha's thought. According to this system '*Dhamma*' is distinct from religion and from non-religion (non-*Dhamma*) also. Romila Thapar says that "the Buddhist *Dhamma* was universal ethic of family and community, privileging non-violence, tolerance and respect for individuals. These values applied equally to all since they assumed the equality of all and the inter-connection of all sentiment beings. The ethic was encapsulated in conduct towards various social categories such as parents, friends, teachers and those for whom the individual worked and those who worked for the individual.[41]

Ambedkar considered the following beliefs are not-*Dhamma*. They are:

- *Belief in the supernatural is not Dhamma;*
- *Belief in god is not essentially part of Dhamma;*
- *Dhamma based on union with Brahma is a false Dhamma;*
- *Belief in soul is not Dhamma;*
- *Belief in sacrifices is not Dhamma;*
- *Belief based on speculation is not Dhamma;*
- *Belief in the infallibility of books of Dhamma in not Dhamma.*[42]

From the above description it is clear that if religion is considered of non-human elements, then it is non-religion and if it refers to its human subject then it is a religion.

In his whole life he laid great stress on the three principles; liberty, equality and fraternity. On one occasion he delivered a public lecture in All India Radio on 3rd October 1954, where he proclaimed his social philosophy. He announced that "positively my social philosophy may be said to be enshrined in three words; liberty, equality and fraternity. Let no one; however, say I have borrowed my philosophy from the French Revolution. I have not. My philosophy has roots in religion, and not on political science. I have derived them from the teachings of my master the Buddha".[43] Ambedkar also stressed on the morality of the people in his *Dhamma* principles. In Buddhism, he says '*morality is dhamma*' and '*dhamma is morality*' and there is no god in *dhamma*.[44] Further he says that morality is at the root of the *Dhamma*. Religion is concerned with god, soul, prayers, worship, rituals, ceremonies, sacrifices, etc. Buddhism is not concerned with any of this religious practices.[45]

IV

One of the most abiding aspects of his life and career which history will remember is his conversion to Buddhism, leading the mass conversion in one time. Before deciding to convert to Buddhism he underwent an in-depth study of the Buddha *Dhamma*. He preferred Buddhism because he found the religion of Buddha rational, scientific and epitome of morality, liberty, equality and fraternity. He also found that Buddhism can raise the downtrodden to the highest level as it had done in the past. In his well-known work "*The Buddha and His Dhamma*" and other writings, he announced that "I prefer Buddhism; it gives three principles in combination which no other religion does. All other religions are bothering themselves with god and soul and life after death. Buddhism teaches wisdom (*prajna*), love (*karuna*) and equality (*samata*). This is what man wants for a good and happy life on earth".[46] Again Ambedkar says that 'Buddhism to my mind is essentially rationalist and humanist in its approach to life". In his writings he noticed evidences in several places in support of his own rationalist outlook. Some of the examples of his statement I have noted here; Buddhism is nothing if not rationalism, Buddha's path is the path of reason and this is the way of emancipation from superstitions. In Buddha's rationalism and humanism there is no place for coercion and exploitation. Even in the brotherhood of Buddhism, there is no vow of obedience to be made. Ambedkar's ultimate aims at liberating man from the all chains and fetters through Buddhism. That is liberation, freed man from belief in god, from the domination of the Vedas, from the discrimination of caste hierarchy.[47]

Buddhism came to Ambedkar through books. As he studied more and more about Buddhism, the love for Buddha and his Dhamma became stronger in him. He studied Buddhist texts, philosophy and teaching and also visited many places connected with the Buddhism. Gradually the love for Buddhism became stronger to him and it came to be reflected in various ways. He visited many Buddhist places and discussed his plans for revival of Buddhism in India. In 1954 after returning from Burma Ambedkar concentrated all his attention on the plan for the conversion ceremony.[48] Initially Dr. Ambedkar had announced that the conversion ceremony would be held in Mumbai but his close associate convinced him to shift over to Nagpur. Finally, he decided to arrange the ceremony in Nagpur. He invited senior *Bhikkus* from Kushinagar to join the conversion ceremony.

On the ceremony day Ambedkar woke up in early morning and had bath and reached the ceremonial ground along with his wife Maisaheb Ambedkar and his close associates. There was a crowd of five lakhs who received their emancipation in the new religion. At last he embraced Buddhism on 14th October 1956, the auspicious day of *Vijaya Dashami*, a few weeks before his death on 6 December 1956. The historic conversion ceremony at Nagpur marked the end of his pilgrimage journey. After the ceremony he addressed the vast gathering, he said in an emotional voice "I started the movement of renouncing the Hindu religion in 1935 and since then I have been continuing struggle. This conversion has given me enormous satisfaction and pleasure unimaginably. I feel as if I have been liberated from hell".[49] Again to quote Ambedkar "by discarding my ancient religion which stood for inequality and oppression today I am reborn, I have no faith in the philosophy of incarnation; and it is wrong and mischievous to say that Buddha was an incarnation of Vishnu. I am no more a devotee of any Hindu god or goddess. I will not perform any ritual. I will strictly follow the eight-fold path of Buddha. Buddhism is true religion and I will lead a life guided by the three principles of knowledge, right path and compassion".[50] This emotional words from Ambedkar voice attracted the vast gathering. As per his statement the Buddhism formed the best possible choice for Ambedkar because it was an egalitarian religion born in India, not the creation of outsiders.

The kind of Buddhism he adopted and propagated is known as Neo Buddhism (*Navayana*) in the history. He developed the term '*navayana*' (new vehicle) to his new religious order. This *navayana* was understood as a direct expression of the prior tradition and pristine purity of early Buddhism.[51] Ambedkar's Neo Buddhism included some noticeably recent influences of modernism. He charged contemporary monks to adopt Christian forms of social action and argued that successful propagation of Buddhist *Dhamma* required a "Buddhist Bible".[52] The Neo Buddhism does not give any importance to the spiritual part of original Buddhism. It does not accept that Buddha gave any sermon related to other world. It applies all the doctrines of Buddha in the modern social context.

The primary notion of Ambedkar's conversion was not so much of religious but of social and political nature. His main intension consisted in developing the worldly emancipation of the suppressed communities. Ambedkar's Neo Buddhism obviously appears to be 'a religion of liberation for the oppressed in society'. On the one hand through this definition Ambedkar's Neo-Buddhism became the strongest rival of Christian and Muslim social ideologies and the on the other hand, the sharpest opponent of the caste-Hindus. The caste-Hindus prevented very successfully with the help of the Indian National Congress the emancipation of all the downtrodden. Because of the numerical dominance of Hindus within the Indian orthodox community Ambedkar developed an abstract of anti-Hinduism blaming the Hinduism as such for the illusion of untouchability.[53]

M.G. Mishra in his article '*Dr. Ambedkar the Liberator*' emphasizes that Dr. Ambedkar's conversion to Buddhism along with his followers as a return to the original faith to which they belonged in the ancient times. In fact, it was not 'conversion' but liberation.[54] It was liberation from Hinduism and liberation of millions of people,[55] who suffered through ages from the curse of caste and inequality. His complete mission was to liberate and emancipate the downtrodden from the yoke of Hindu social order. As he considered that the Hindu religion incapable of giving either spiritual solace or social equality to the depressed and oppressed, he finally decided to renounce Hinduism and embrace Buddhism.[56]

Dr. Ambedkar's love for and devotion to the Lord Buddha has left in imprint on the national symbols also. It was due to his efforts as the architect of India's constitution that the Buddhist wheel of law (*dharma chakra*) was incorporated in the national flag, and Lions from an Asokan Pillar at Saranath were adopted as national emblem by the constituent assembly.

He was devoted for the cause of providing social justice to the downtrodden community. He himself faced many inhuman situations in life. Hence, he made a strong resolve that he would eradicate the failure of the society and fight for human rights of the suppressed community.

V

Ideologically, if we compare Gandhi with Ambedkar, both were different in their views on the Indian society. Ambedkar strongly protested the Hindu caste system. But Gandhi did not want to disturb the Hindu Varna system and wanted a reform within that framework. Gandhi believed that for the abolition of untouchabiliy, there was the need of change of mind set up on the part of Caste Hindus. He stressed apology on the part of the upper castes. But Ambedkar wanted to eliminate the Hindu Varna system completely from the society and wanted political power as well as legal protection for the downtrodden. Ambedkar said that mere changing the name from untouchables to *Harijan*, as proposed by Gandhi, was not going to improve their life. Just change of name like '*Harijan*' meant to give a new identity, did not help in the eradication of untouchability and inequality. The new name in fact sealed the 'broken men' more effectively in their own category. It did not give them self-respect. Ambedkar believed that changing social identity through converting in to Buddhism is only way to escape from the caste exploitation in Hindu society. He aimed at eradicating social distinctions, based on their birth and establishing a new social order, based on liberty, equality and fraternity. The purpose of his Neo-Buddhism he says is to reconstruct the world.

NOTES AND REFERENCES

1. For detailed account about origin and growth of untouchability refer K.R. Hanumanthan, *Untouchability: A Historical Study up to 1500 A.D. (with special reference to Tamil Nadu)*, Madurai, 1979.
2. K. Mavali Rajan, "Social Oppression: Prevalence and Practice of Untouchability in Early Tamil Society", *Golden Research Thoughts*, Vol.2, Issue 10, April 2013, p.72.
3. Raj Sekher Basu, *Nandanar's Children: The Paraiyas Tryst with Destiny, Tamilnadu 1850-1956*, New Delhi, 2011, p.xxii.
4. Gail Omvedt, *Dalits and the Democratic Revolution: Dr. Ambedkar and Dalit Movements in Colonial India,* New Delhi, 2010, p.12.
5. *Ibid.* In India many social reformers strongly protested against the philosophical ideas of Hinduism. Among them E.V. Ramasamy Periyar, a founder of atheist philosophy, criticized the orthodox Hindu ways of worship and blind beliefs on gods. He wrote many articles in journals and periodicals criticizing the role and character of gods in Hinduism, which perpetuates suppression of women and downtrodden communities. He published his atheist views in verse form for the first time in a meeting at Thiruvarur (in May 1967) in his own words, which has been published in the journal '*The Modern Rationalist*', (Vol. III, Chennai, February 1974, p.21). He proclaimed that;

   "*There is no god,*
   There is no god at all,
   One who conceptualizes god is a fool,
   One who propagates god is a scoundrel, and
   One who worship god is a barbarians".
6. *Ibid.*, p. 100.
7. *Ibid.*

8. G.P. Deshpande (ed.), *Selected Writings of Jotirao Phule*, Fifth Impression, Delhi, 2010, p.5; also see K.Mavali Rajan, "Nationalism from Below: The Suppressed Class Uprising in Tamil Nadu", *Golden Research Thoughts*, Vol.3, Issue 5, November 2013, p.3
9. *Ibid.*, p.6.
10. S. Manickam, *Facets of History: A Spectrum of Thought,* Madurai Kamaraj University, Madurai, 1998, pp.102-103.
11. Quoted in Charles H. Heimsath, *Indian Nationalism and Hindu Social Reform*, Princeton, 1984, p.103.
12. K. Mavali Rajan, "The Role of Pandit C. Ayothidas in Uprising Subaltern Consciousness in Madras Presidency", *Proceedings of ICHR sponsored Three day National seminar* on Subaltern Freedom Fighters in the Madras Presidency organized by Rajapalayam Raju's College, Rajapalayam, 2015, pp.25-32.
13. G. Thangavelu, *Tamilan Iyodhi Thass Pandithar*, Madras, 1999, pp.25-34.
14. G. Thangavelu, *Tamil Desiaya Unarvin Munnodi 'Tamilan' Iyothee Thassa Pandithar* (Tamil), Chennai, 1999, p.8.
15. Gail Omvedt, *Buddhism in India: Challenging Brahmanism and Caste*, Sage Publication, New Delhi, 2013, p.237.
16. V. Geetha, S.V. Rajadurai, "Dalits and non-Brahmin Consciousness in Colonial Tamilnadu", *Economic and Political Weekly*, XXVIII, No.39, September 25, 1993, p.2091.
17. Gail Omvedt, *Buddhism in India: Challenging Brahmanism and Caste,* p.239.
18. *Ibid.*
19. G. Aloysius, *Religion as Emancipatory Identity: A Buddhist Movement among the Tamils under Colonialism*, New Delhi, 2000, pp.191-193.
20. Ambedkar Priyan, *Pandithamani Iyothee Thassar* (Tamil), Chennai, 1997, pp.5-12.
21. G. Aloysius, *Nationalism without a Nation in India*, (seventh impression), Oxford University Press, New Delhi, 2006, pp. 58-59.
22. *Ibid.*
23. M.E. Prabhakar "Dalit Education and Youth", in (ed.) Bhagavan Das and James Massey (eds), *Dalit Solidarity*, Delhi, 1955, p.99.
24. C.D. Naik, *Ambedkar's Perspective on Buddhism and other Religions*, Kalpaz Publication, Delhi, 2004, p.285.

25. Lisa A. Daily, *Constructing a New Nationalism from Below: The Dalit Movement, Politics and Transnational Networking*, Graduate School Theses and Dissertations Paper- 1920, University of South Florida, 2009, p.44.
26. P. Mohan Larbeer, *Ambedkar on Religion: A Liberative Perspective*, ISPCK, 2003, p.69.
27. *Ibid*, p.73.
28. D.C. Ahir, "Buddhism and Social Change" in A.K. Narain and D.C. Ahir (eds,), *Dr. Ambedkar Buddhism and Social Change*, Buddhist World Press, Delhi, 2008, p.3.
29. Anne M. Blackburn, "Religion, Kingship and Buddhism: Ambedkar's Vision of a Moral Community", *The Journal of the International Association of Buddhist Studies*, Vol.16, No.1, 1993, p.10.
30. *Ibid.*, p.9.
31. *Ibid.*
32. Dhananjay Keer, *Dr.Ambedkar: Life and Mission*, Popular Prakashan, Bombay, reprint, 1987, p.138.
33. Dr. Babasaheb Ambedkar writings and Speeches, Vol. I published by Government of Maharashtra, Bombay, 1979, p.69; cited by Gail Omvedt, *Buddhism in India: Challenging Brahmanism and Caste*, p. 252.
34. A. Ranjitkumar, "Ambedkar's Notion of Social Justice-A Different Perspectives", *International Journal of Scientific and Engineering Research*, Vol.2, Issue 12, December 2011, p.2.
35. Cited by A.C. Ahir, *op.cit.*, p.3.
36. K.N. Kadam (ed.), *Dr. Babasaheb Amdedkar and the Significance of His Movement: A Chronology*, Popular Prakashan, Bombay, 1991, p.108; still now Hindu temple continues to be spaces for oppressing and resistance and remain a major source of caste clashes in southern district of Tamil Nadu. *Dalit* are at the receiving and in issues like enter to temples and rights to participate in festivals and they face stiff opposition and attack from caste-Hindus. It highlights that the *Dalit* communities do not have accessing civil rights and they are not allowed inside temples. The *Dalit* have little access to temples, kids, made to sit separately in schools. That is why Ambedkar strongly pronounced for the change of religious identity to obtain human treatment.

37. Vasant Moon, *Dr. Babasaheb Ambedkar*, Translated by Asha Damle, National Book Trust, New Delhi, First Edition 2002, reprint 2012, p.39.
38. Romila Thapar holds the views that "the public articulation of religion is related to social institution. Consequently one aspects of religion in India is the degree to which the institution of caste as the basic organization of Indian society, structure religions. Every religion reflects an acceptance of caste in differing degree. Some Hindu sects are obsessive about castes other are more flexible. Islam and Sikhism have denied it in theory but confirm to much of it in practice, particularly in rules of marriage and of inheritance of property. Some religious sects formulated and furthered caste organization and some opposed it in various ways: Romila Thapar, *The Past and Present: Forging Contemporary Identities through History*, Aleph Book Company, 2014, p.129.
39. P.P. Vijayan, *Reservation Policy and Judicial Activism*, Kalpaz Publication, New Delhi, 2006, p. 18.
40. K.N. Kadam, "Dr.Ambedkar and Buddhism as an Instrument of Social Change" in A.K. Narain and D.C. Ahir, (eds.)., *Dr.Ambedkar, Buddhism and Social Change*, Buddhist World Press, Delhi, 2010, p.41.
41. Romila Thapar, *The Past and Present: Forging Contemporary Identities through History*, Aleph Book Company, 2014, p.132; for further details about Buddha and His Dhamma see page nos.133 to 150 in D.D. Bandiste, *Dhamma Our Only Savior*, Buddhist World Press, Delhi, 2008.
42. Dr. B.R.Ambedkar, *The Buddha and His Dhamma*, Siddharth Publication Bombay, 1957, IIIrd edition 1984, pp.174-195; cited by C.D. Naik, *op.cit.*, p.315.
43. K.N. Kadam, "*Dr. Ambedkar and Buddhism as an Instrument of Social Change*", pp.43-46; Vasant Moon, *op.cit.*, p.205.
44. *Ibid.*
45. *Ibid.*
46. Dhananjay Keer, *op.cit.*, p.490.
47. K.N. Kadam, "*Dr. Ambedkar and Buddhism as an Instrument of Social Change*", p.43.
48. In 1956 Dr. Ambedkar, along with half a million other Dalits, converted to Buddhism. Dr. Ambedkar's interpretation of Buddhism

is a modern and humanistic one. Such is the intensity of the problem and the yearning for dignity that many Dalits are converting to Christianity, and thereby foregoing the meager advantage of educational and job reservations for Dalits, but denied to those who convert to Islam or Christianity.

49. D.C. Ahir, *Buddhism in Modern India*, Bhikkhu Niwas Prakashan, Nagpur, 1982, p.35.
50. P. Mohan Larbeer, *op.cit.*, p.82.
51. Anne M. Blackburn, *op.cit.*, p.11.
52. *Ibid.*
53. Edmund Weber, "Ambedkar and the Hindu Culture", *Journal of Religious Culture*, No.18b (1999), pp.6-7.
54. A.K. Narain and D.C. Ahir (eds.), *op.cit.*, p. XIII.
55. His conversion of Buddhism is an instrument of social change in India. It is clear that his conversion to Buddhism triggered a mass movement, the number of Buddhists reported by the Census of India increases over a thousand present in a decade, increased from 181, 000 in 1951 to 3, 250, 000 in 1961. For further details refer to Christopher S. Queen, "Ambedkar Modernity, and the Hermeneutics of Buddhist Liberation", in A.K.Narain and D.C. Ahir (eds.), *op.cit.*, p.100; D.C. Ahir, *op.cit.*, pp.10-25.
56. D.C. Ahir, 'Dr. Ambekar's Pilgrimage to Buddhism', in A.K. Narain and D.C. Ahir (eds.), *op.cit.*, p.1.

5
Leaders of Modern India: B.R. Ambedkar

– Dr. Jitesh Chandra Roy
– Dr. Matilal Sen

Bhimrao Ramji Ambedkar 14 April 1891 to 6 December 1956 A.D., popularly known as Babasaheb, was an Indian jurist, economist, politician and social reformer who inspired the Dalit Buddhist Movement and campaigned against social discrimi-nation on Untouchables (Dalits), while supporting the rights of women and labour. He was Independent India's first law minister and the principal architect of the Constitution of India.[1]

Ambedkar was a prolific scholar, earning doctorates in economics from both Columbia University and the London School of Economics, and gained a reputation for his scholarship in law, economics and political science. In his early career he was an eminent personality in all these subjects mentioned. His later life was marked by his political activities; he became involved in campaigning and negotiationing for India's independence, publishing journals advocating political rights and social freedom for Dalits and contributing significantly to the establishment of the state of India. In 1956 he converted to Buddhism, with mass conversions of Dalits.[2] In 1990, the Bharat Ratna, India's highest civilian award was posthumously conferred upon Ambedkar. Ambedkar's legacy includes numerous memorials and depictions in popular culture.

Ambedkar was born on 14 April 1891 in the town and military cantonment of Mhow in the Central Provinces (now in Madhya

Pradesh). He was the 14th and last child of Ramji Maloji Sakpal, an army officer who held the rank of Subedar and Bhimabai Murbadkar Sakpal.[3] His family was of Marathi background from the town of Ambavade (Mandangad taluka) in Ratnagiri district of modern-day Maharashtra. Ambedkar was born in a poor low Mahar (dalit) caste, who were treated as untouchables and subjected to socio-economic discrimination.[4] Ambedkar's ancestors had long worked in the army of the British East India Company and his father served in the British Indian Army at the Mhow cantonment. Although they attended school, Ambedkar and other dalit children were segregated and given little attention or help by teachers. They were not allowed to sit inside the class. When they needed water, someone from a higher caste had to pour that water from a height as they were not allowed to touch either the water or the vessel that contained it. This task was usually performed for the young Ambedkar by the school peon and if the peon was not available then he had to go without water; the situation he later in his writings described as "No peon, No water". He was required to sit on a gunny sack which he had to take home with him.

Ramji Sakpal retired in 1894 and the family moved to Satara two years later. Shortly after their move, Ambedkar's mother died. The children were cared of by their paternal aunt, and lived in difficult circumstances. Three sons– Balaram, Anandrao and Bhimrao– and two daughters– Manjula and Tulasa– of the Ambedkars would go on to survive them. Of his brothers and sisters, only Ambedkar passed his examinations and graduated to high school. His original surname Ambavadekar comes from his native village 'Ambavade' in Ratnagiri district. His teacher, Mahadev Ambedkar, who was fond of him, changed his surname from 'Ambavadekar' to his own surname 'Ambedkar' in school records.

EDUCATION

In 1897, Ambedkar's family moved to Bombay where Ambedkar became the only untouchable enrolled at Elphinstone High School. In 1906, when he was about 15 years old, his marriage to a nine-year-old girl, Ramabai was arranged.

In 1907, he passed his matriculation examination and in the following year he entered Elphinstone College, which was affiliated to the University of Bombay, becoming the first dalit to do so. This success evoked much celebration among dalit and after a public ceremony; he was presented with a biography of the Buddha by Dada Keluskar, the author and a family friend.

By 1912, he obtained his degree in economics and political science from Bombay University, and prepared to take up employment with the Baroda state government. His wife, by then 15 years old, had just moved his young family and started work, when he had to quickly return to Mumbai to see his ailing father, who died on 2 February 1913.

In 1913, Ambedkar moved to the United States at the age of 22. He had been awarded a Baroda State Scholarship of £11.50 (Sterling) per month for three years under a scheme established by Sayajirao Gaekwad III (Gaekwad of Baroda) that was designed to provide opportunities for postgraduate education at Columbia University in New York City. Soon after arriving there he settled in rooms at Livingston Hall with Naval Bhathena, a Parsi who was to be a lifelong friend. He passed his M.A. exam in June 1915, majoring in Economics, and other subjects of Sociology, History, Philosophy and Anthropology. He presented a thesis, Ancient Indian Commerce. Ambedkar was influenced by John Dewey and his work on democracy.

In 1916 he completed his second thesis, *National Dividend of India-A Historic and Analytical Study* for another M.A. and finally he received his Ph.D in Economics in 1927 for his third thesis, after he left for London. On 9 May, he read his paper 'Castes in India: Their Mechanism, Genesis and Development' before a seminar conducted by the anthropologist Alexander Goldenweiser.

In October 1916, he enrolled for the Bar at Law course at Gray's Inn and at the same time enrolled at the London School of Economics where he started working on a doctoral thesis. In June 1917, he returned to India because his scholarship from Baroda ended. His book collection was despatched on different ship from the one he was on and that ship was torpedoed and sunk by a German submarine. He got permission to return to London to submit his thesis within four years. He returned at the first opportunity and completed a master's degree in 1921. His thesis was on the "The problem of the rupee: Its origin and its solution". In 1923, he completed a D.Sc. in Economics, in the same year he was admitted into Bar at Law by Gray's Inn. His third and fourth Doctorates (LL.D, Columbia, 1952 and D.Litt., Osmania, 1953) were conferred honoriscausa.[5]

OPPOSITION TO ARYAN INVASION THEORY

Ambedkar viewed the Shudras as Aryan and adamantly rejected the Aryan invasion theory, describing it as "so absurd that it ought to have been dead long ago" in his 1946 book *Who Were the Shudras?*[6]

Ambedkar viewed Shudras as originally being "part of the Kshatriya Varna in the Indo-Aryan society", but became socially degraded after they inflicted many tyrannies on Brahmins.

According to Arvind Sharma, "Ambedkar noticed certain flaws in the Aryan invasion theory that were later acknowledged by western scholarship. For example, scholars now acknowledge anâs in Rig Veda 5.29.10 refers to speech rather than the shape of the nose."[7] Ambedkar anticipated this modern view by stating:

The term Anasa occurs in Rig Veda V.29.10. What does the word mean? There are two interpretations. One is by Prof. Max Muller. The other is by Sayanacharya. According to Prof. Max Muller, it means 'one without nose' or 'one with a flat nose' and has as such been relied upon as a piece of evidence in support of the view that the Aryans were a separate race from the Dasyus. Sayanacharya says that it means 'mouthless,' i.e., devoid of good speech. This difference of meaning is due to difference in the correct reading of the word Anasa. Sayanacharya reads it as an-asa while Prof. Max Muller reads it as a-nasa. As read by Prof. Max Muller, it means 'without nose.' Question is: which of the two readings is the correct one? There is no reason to hold that Sayana's reading is wrong. On the other hand there is everything to suggest that it is right. In the first place, it does not make non-sense of the word. Secondly, as there is no other place where the Dasyus are described as noseless, there is no reason why the word should be read in such a manner as to give it in altogether new sense. It is only fair to read it as a synonym of Mridhravak. There is therefore no evidence in support of the conclusion that the Dasyus belonged to a different race.[8]

Ambedkar disputed various hypotheses of the Aryan homeland being outside India, and concluded the Aryan homeland was India itself.[9] According to Ambedkar, the Rig Veda says Aryans, Dâsa and Dasyus were competing religious groups, not different peoples.

OPPOSITION TO UNTOUCHABILITY

As Ambedkar was educated by the Princely State of Baroda, he was bound to serve it. He was appointed Military Secretary to the Gaikwad but had to quit in a short time. He described the incident in his autobiography, waiting for a Visa.[10] He tried to find ways to make a living for his growing family. He worked as a private tutor, as an accountant, and established an investment consulting business, but it failed when his clients learned that he was an untouchable. In 1918, he became Professor of Political Economy in the Sydenham College of Commerce and Economics in Mumbai. Although he was successful with the students, other professors objected to his sharing a drinking-water jug with them.

Ambedkar had been invited to testify before the Southborough Committee, which was preparing the Government of India Act 1919. At this hearing, Ambedkar argued for creating separate electorates and reservations for untouchables and other religious communities. In 1920, he began the publication of the weekly *Mooknayak* (Leader of the Silent) in Mumbai with the help of Shahaji II (1874–1922), Maharaja of Kolhapur.

Ambedkar went on to work as a legal professional. In 1926, he successfully defended three non-Brahmin leaders who had accused the Brahmin community of ruining India and were then subsequently sued for libel. Dhananjay Keer notes that "The victory was resounding, both socially and individually, for the clients and the Doctor".[11]

PROTESTS

While practising law in the Bombay High Court, he tried to promote the education of dalits and their upliftment. His first organised attempt was his establishment of the central institution Bahishkrit Hitakarini Sabha, which intended to promote education and socio-economic conditions besides improving the welfare of "outcastes", referred to as depressed classes. For the defense of Dalit rights, he started many periodicals like *Mook Nayak, Bahishkrit Bharat* and *Equality Janta.*[12]

He was appointed to the Bombay Presidency Committee to work with the all-European Simon Commission in 1925. This commission had sparked great protests across India, and while its report was ignored by most Indians, Ambedkar himself wrote a separate set of recommendations for the future Constitution of India.

By 1927, Ambedkar had decided to launch active movements against untouchability. He began with public movements and marches to open up public drinking water resources. He started a struggle for the right to enter Hindu temples. He led a satyagraha in Mahad to fight for the right of the dalits to draw water from the main water tank of the town. In a conference in late 1927, Ambedkar publicly condemned the classic Hindu text, the Manusmriti (Laws of Manu), for ideologically justifying caste discrimination and "untouchability", and he ceremonially burned copies of the ancient text. On 25th December 1927, he led thousands of followers to burn copies of Manusmrti. Thus annually 25th December is celebrated as *Manusmiriti Dahan Din* (Manusmriti Burning Day) by Ambedkarites and Dalits.

In 1930, Ambedkar launched Kalaram Temple movement after three months of preparation. About 15,000 volunteers assembled at Kalaram Temple satygraha making one of the greatest processions of Nashik. The procession was headed by a military band, a batch of scouts, women and men walked in discipline, order and determination to see the god for the first time. When they reached the gate, the gates were closed by Brahmin authorities.

POONA PACT

In 1932, the British announced the formation of a separate electorate for "Depressed Classes" in the Communal Award. Gandhi fiercely opposed a separate electorate for untouchables, saying that such an arrangement would divide the Hindu community.[13] Gandhi protested by fasting while imprisoned in the Yerwada Central Jail of Poona. Following the fast, Congress politicians and activists such as Madan Mohan Malaviya and Palwankar Baloo organised joint meetings with Ambedkar and his supporters at Yerwada. On 25th September 1932, the agreement known as Poona Pact was signed between Ambedkar (on behalf of the depressed classes of Hindus) and Madan Mohan Malaviya (on behalf of the other Hindus). The agreement gave reservation of seats for the depressed classes in the Provisional legislatures, within the general electorate. Due to the pact, the depressed class received 148 seats in the legislature, instead of the 71 as allocated in the Communal Award earlier proposed by the British Prime Minister Ramsay MacDonald. The text uses the term "Depressed Classes" to denote Untouchables of Hindus who were later called Scheduled Castes and Scheduled Tribes under India Act 1935, and the later Indian Constitution of 1950.[14]

HIGHLIGHTS ON THE UNTOUCHABILITY OFFENCES ACT, 1955

The Rajya Sabha passed on September 2, 1976, the Bill to amend the Untouchability (Offences) Act, 1955 and changed its title to the "Protection of Civil Rights Act". This Bill had proposed stringent measures against those who still practise untouchability. It sought to make wilful negligence on the part of investigating officers of complaints relating to untouchability tantamount to abatement.

The Bill was then passed by the Lok Sabha. It provides that persons disqualified under the Act would be barred from contesting elections to the central or state legislature. The provision has also been made to have a deterrent effect on the commission of untouchability offences. It has proposed surveys and fieldwork for determining the areas where untouchability is practiced. It envisages setting up of committees for implementing the Act and grant of adequate facilities to persons subjected to disabilities arising out of untouchability so that they will be in a position to avail their rights.

The Act has also brought under its purview the privately owned places of worship along with lands and subsidiary shrines and such places used for public worship by the content of the owners. The Act makes the direct or indirect preaching of untouchability or its justification on historical, philosophical or religious grounds an offence

The 17th Paragraph of the Indian Constitution states that untouchability is a punishable offence. For the eradication of untouchability the Untouchability Offences Act was passed by Indian Government in 1955 in which any person forcing the disabilities of untouchability can be sentenced to six months imprisonment or a fine of Rs. 500/- or both for his first offence. For every subsequent offence the sentence will include both a term in jail as well as fine. If considered necessary, the punishment can also be increased.

This Act provides penalties for the offences like preventing a person from entering into public temples or places of worship, preventing the drawing of water from sacred lakes, tanks, wells etc. Enforcing all kinds of social disabilities such as preventing people from the use of a '*dharmasala*', any shop, public restaurant, public hospital, hotel, educational institutions or any other place of public entertainment denying the use of any road, river, well, water top, river bank, cremation ground, etc.

Enforcement of occupational, professional or trade disabilities in the matter or enjoyment of any benefit under a charitable trust preventing Harijans from pursuing any general occupation. Refusing to sell goods or render services to a Harijan, for molesting, injuring or annoying a person or organizing a boycott or taking part in the excommunication of a person on the basis of untouchability.

ALL INDIA SCHEDULED CASTES FEDERATION

All India scheduled castes federation, was a first all India political party exclusively for Scheduled Castes. SCF was founded by Dr. Ambedkar in a national convention of the Scheduled castes held at Nagpur during 17-20 July 1942. It was presided by Rao Bahadur N. Shivraj, a renowned Dalit leader from Madras. An executive body of All India SCF was elected in the convention. Rao Bahadur N. Shivraj was elected as President and P.N. Rajbhoj

(Bombay) was elected as general secretary. The convention passed the following resolutions;

(1) Cripps proposals were condemned as they failed to consider the interests of the dalits.

(2) The separate identity of the dalits be recognised.

3) Special provision should be made in the budgets of respective provinces for the higher education of dalits.

(4) The dalits should get adequate representation in the central and provincial ministries.

(5) Certain seats should be reserved in the government services.

(6) The untouchables should get representation in the legislatures and local self-governments in proportion to their population.

(7) Their representatives should be elected by separate electorate.

(8) There should be provision in the constitution for the separate settlements of the Scheduled castes.

(9) They should be given arable uncultivated land for their livelihood.

In March 1946, general elections were held for the provincial assemblies. The SCF as other political parties actively participated in the elections. It contested altogether for 51 seats (Madras-24, Bombay-5, Bengal-6, UP-5, CP and Berar-11). Of all the contestants' one from Bengal (S.N. Mandal) and other from the CP and Berar (R.P. Jadhav) were elected to the respective assemblies.

In order to find a solution to the Indian problem, the cabinet mission came to India on 24th March 1946. The representatives of various political organisations, including Dr. B.R. Ambedkar on behalf of SCF met the cabinet mission. The cabinet mission declared its plan on 16th May 1946, which contained no references to the demands of the Scheduled castes. It was proposed that a constituent assembly consisting of 210 members elected by the general electorate, 78 by the Muslim electorate and 4 by the Sikh electorate would be formed to frame the new constitution. It was proposed that there would be an interim government composed of the Congress and the Muslim League. Both the major parties, however, accepted the Cabinet mission plan.

In view of the apathetic attitude of the cabinet mission, the SCF started satyagraha on 15th July 1946 at Poona under the leadership of P.N. Rajbhoj. The satyagrahas were launched at other places as well like Bombay, Nagpur, Kanpur, Lucknow etc.

J.N. Mandal (Bengal SCF chief) was included in the Interim ministry under the leadership of Pandit Nehru. In 1946, Dr. B.R. Ambedkar was elected to the constituent assembly, firstly from Bengal and after partition from Bombay legislative assembly. He became chairman of the drafting committee of the constituent assembly and law minister of India.

In the first general elections held in 1952, the SCF contested for 34 Lok Sabha seats (4 from Bombay, 3 from CP and Berar, 9 from Madras, 2 from Punjab, 8 from UP, 4 from Hyderabad, 1 from Rajasthan, 1 from Delhi, 1 from Himachal Pradesh and 1 from Vindhya Pradesh. Out of them only 2 candidates were elected. They were P.N. Rajbhoj from Solapur (Maharashtra) and other was M.R. Krishna from Karimnagar. However Dr. Ambedkar, who contested from Bombay (north), could not get elected. Again he contested from Bhandara Lok sabha by-election.

The SCF contested for 215 seats in the legislative assemblies of various states. Of all the 215 seats, the party won 12 seats (5 from Hyderabad, 2 from Madras, 1 from Bombay, 2 from Mysore, 1 from Pepsu and one from Himachal Pradesh. Dr. Ambedkar got elected from Bombay legislative assembly to the Rajya Sabha and J.H. Subbiah, the SCF leader from Hyderabad got elected to the Rajya Sabha in 1952.

POLITICAL CAREER

In 1935, Ambedkar was appointed principal of the Government Law College, Bombay, a position he held for two years. He also served as the chairman of Governing body of Ramjas College,University of Delhi, after the death of its Founder Rai Kedarnath. Settling in Bombay (today called Mumbai), Ambedkar oversaw the construction of a house, and stocked his personal library with more than 50,000 books. His wife Ramabai died after a long illness. It had been her long-standing wish to go on a pilgrimage to Pandharpur, but Ambedkar had refused to let her go, telling her that he would create a new Pandharpur for her instead of Hinduism's Pandharpur which treated them as untouchables. At the Yeola Conversion Conference on 13 October in Nasik, Ambedkar announced his intention to convert to a different religion and exhorted his followers to leave Hinduism. He would repeat his message at many public meetings across India.

In 1936, Ambedkar founded the Independent Labour Party, which contested the 1937 Bombay election to the Central Legislative Assembly for the 13 reserved and 4 general seats, and secured 11 and 3 seats respectively.[15]

Ambedkar published his book Annihilation of Caste on 15 May 1936. It strongly criticised Hindu orthodox religious leaders and the caste system in general, and included "a rebuke of Gandhi" on the subject. Later, in a 1955 BBC interview, he accused Gandhi of writing in opposition of the caste system in English language papers while writing in support of it in Gujarati language papers.

Ambedkar served on the Defence Advisory Committee and the Viceroy's Executive Council as minister for labour.

In his work *Who Were the Shudras?*, Ambedkar tried to explain the formation of dalits. He saw Shudras and Ati Shudras who form the lowest caste in the ritual hierarchy of the caste system, as separate from Untouchables. Ambedkar oversaw the transformation of his political party into the Scheduled Castes Federation, although it performed poorly in the 1946 elections for Constituent Assembly of India. Later he was elected to the constituent assembly of Bengal where Muslim League was in power.[16]

Ambedkar contested in the Bombay North first Indian General Election of 1952, but lost to his former assistant and Congress Party candidate Narayan Kajrolkar. Ambedkar became a member of Rajya Sabha, probably an appointed member. He tried to enter Lok Sabha again in the by-election of 1954 from Bhandara, but he placed third (the Congress Party won). By the time of the second general election in 1957, Ambedkar had died.

Ambedkar also criticised Islamic practice in South Asia. While justifying the Partition of India, he condemned child marriage and the mistreatment of women in Muslim society.

DRAFTING INDIA'S CONSTITUTION

Upon India's independence on 15 August 1947, the new Congress-led government invited Ambedkar to serve as the nation's first Law Minister, which he accepted. On 29 August, he was appointed Chairman of the Constitution Drafting Committee, and was appointed by the Assembly to write India's new Constitution.[17]

Granville Austin described the Indian Constitution drafted by Ambedkar as 'first and foremost a social document'. 'The majority of India's constitutional provisions are either directly arrived at furthering the aim of social revolution or attempt to foster this revolution by establishing conditions necessary for its achievement.

The text prepared by Ambedkar provided constitutional guarantees and protections for a wide range of civil liberties for individual citizens, including freedom of religion, the abolition of untouchability, and the outlawing of all forms of discrimination. Ambedkar argued for extensive economic and social rights for women, and won the Assembly's support for introducing a system of reservations of jobs in the civil services, schools and colleges for members of scheduled castes and scheduled tribes and Other Backward Classes, a system akin to affirmative action. India's lawmakers hoped to eradicate the socioeconomic inequalities and lack of opportunities for India's depressed classes through these measures. The Constitution was adopted on 26 November 1949 by the Constituent Assembly.

During the debates in the Constituent Assembly, Ambedkar demonstrated his will to reform Indian society by recommending the adoption of a Uniform Civil Code. Ambedkar resigned from the cabinet in 1951, when parliament stalled his draft of the Hindu Code Bill, which sought to enshrine gender equality in the laws of inheritance and marriage. Ambedkar independently contested an election in 1952 to the lower house of parliament, the Lok Sabha, but was defeated in the Bombay (North Central) constituency by a little-known Narayan Sadoba Kajrolkar, who polled 138,137 votes compared to Ambedkar's 123,576.[18] He was appointed to the upper house, of parliament, the Rajya Sabha in March 1952 and would remain as member till death.

OPPOSITION TO ARTICLE 370

Ambedkar opposed Article 370 of the Constitution of India, which granted a special status to the State of Jammu and Kashmir, and which was included against his wishes. Balraj Madhok reportedly said, Ambedkar had clearly told Sk. Abdullah: "You wish India should protect your borders, she should build roads in your area, she should supply you food grains, and Kashmir should get equal status as India. But Government of India should have only limited powers and Indian people should have no rights in Kashmir. To give consent to this proposal, would be a treacherous thing against the interests of India and I, as the Law Minister of India, will never do it." Then Sk. Abdullah approached Nehru, who directed him to Gopal Swami Ayyangar, who in turn approached Sardar Patel, saying Nehru had promised Sk. Abdullah the special status. Patel got the Article passed while Nehru was on a foreign tour. On the day the article came up for discussion, Ambedkar did not reply to questions on it but did participate on other articles. All arguments were done by Krishna Swami Ayyangar.[19]

ECONOMIC PLANNING

Ambedkar was the first Indian to pursue a doctorate in economics abroad. He argued that industrialization and agricultural growth could enhance the Indian economy. He stressed investment in agriculture as the primary industry of India.[20] According to Sharad Pawar, Ambedkar's vision helped the government to achieve its food security goal.[21] Ambedkar advocated national economic and social development, stressing education, public hygiene, community health, residential facilities as the basic amenities. His D.Sc thesis "*The problem of the Rupee: Its origin and solution*" (1923) examines the causes for the Rupee's fall in value. He proved the importance of price stability over exchange stability. He analysed the silver and gold exchange rates and their effect on the economy, and found the reasons for the failure of British India's public treasury. He calculated the loss of development caused by British rule.[22]

In 1951, Ambedkar constituted the Finance Commission of India. He opposed income tax for low-income groups. He contributed in Land Revenue Tax and excise duty policies to stabilise the economy. He played an important role in land reform and the state economic development According to him; the caste system divided labourers and impeded economic progress. He emphasised a free economy with a stable Rupee which India has adopted recently. He advocated birth control to develop the Indian economy, and this has been adopted by Indian government as national policy for family planning. He emphasised equal rights for women for economic development. He laid the foundation of industrial relations after Indian independence.

RESERVE BANK OF INDIA

Ambedkar was trained as an economist, and was a professional economist until 1921, when he became a political leader. He wrote three scholarly books on economics: *Administration and Finance of the East India Company, The Evolution of Provincial Finance in British India, The Problem of the Rupee: Its Origin and Its Solution.*[23]

The Reserve Bank of India (RBI) was based on the ideas that Ambedkar presented to the Hilton Young Commission.

CONVERSION TO BUDDHISM

Dikshabhumi, a stupa at the site in Nagpur, where Ambedkar embraced Buddhism along with many of his followersAmbedkar considered converting to Sikhism, which encouraged opposition to oppression and so appealed to leaders of scheduled castes. But after meeting with Sikh leaders, he concluded that he might get "second-rate" Sikh status, as described by scholar Stephen P. Cohen.[24]

Instead, he studied Buddhism all his life. Around 1950, he devoted his attention to Buddhism and travelled to Ceylon (now Sri

Lanka) to attend a meeting of the World Fellowship of Buddhists. While dedicating a new Buddhist vihara near Pune, Ambedkar announced he was writing a book on Buddhism and that when it was finished, he would formally convert to Buddhism. He twice visited Burma in 1954; the second time to attend the third conference of the World Fellowship of Buddhists in Rangoon. In 1955, he founded the Bharatiya Bauddha Mahasabha, or the Buddhist Society of India. He completed his final work, The Buddha and His Dhamma, in 1956 which was published posthumously.[25]

After meetings with the Sri Lankan Buddhist monk Hammalawa Saddhatissa, Ambedkar organised a formal public ceremony for himself and his supporters in Nagpur on 14 October 1956. Accepting the Three Refuges and Five Precepts from a Buddhist monk in the traditional manner, Ambedkar completed his own conversion, along with his wife. He then proceeded to convert some 500,000 of his supporters who were gathered around him. He prescribed the 22 Vows for these converts, after the Three Jewels and Five Precepts. He then travelled to Kathmandu, Nepal to attend the Fourth World Buddhist Conference. His work on The Buddha or Karl Marx and "Revolution and counter-revolution in ancient India" remained incomplete.

DEATH

Annal Ambedkar Manimandapam, Chennai Bust of Ambedkar at Ambedkar Museum in Pune Since 1948, Ambedkar suffered from diabetes. He was bed-ridden from June to October in 1954 due to medication side-effects and poor eyesight. He had been increasingly embittered by political issues, which took a toll on his health. His health worsened during 1955. Three days after completing his final manuscript The Buddha and His Dhamma, Ambedkar died in his sleep on 6 December 1956 at his home in Delhi.

A Buddhist cremation was organised at Dadar Chowpatty beach on 7 December, attended by half a million grieving people. A conversion program was organised on 16 December 1956, so that cremation attendees were also converted to Buddhism at the same place.

Ambedkar was survived by his second wife, who died in 2003, and his son Yashwant (known as Bhaiyasaheb Ambedkar). Ambedkar's grandson, Ambedkar Prakash Yashwant, is the chief-adviser of the Buddhist Society of India, leads the Bharipa Bahujan Mahasangh and has served in both houses of the Indian Parliament.[26]

A number of unfinished typescripts and handwritten drafts were found among Ambedkar's notes and papers and gradually made available. Among these were Waiting for a Visa, which probably dates from 1935-36 and is an autobiographical work, and the Untouchables, or the Children of India's Ghetto, which refers to the census of 1951.

A memorial for Ambedkar was established in his Delhi House at 26 Alipur Road. His birth-date is celebrated as a public holiday known as Ambedkar Jayanti or Bhim Jayanti. He was posthumously awarded India's highest civilian honour, the Bharat Ratna, in 1990.

On the anniversary of his birth and death, and on Dhamma Chakra Pravartan Din (14 October) at Nagpur, at least half a million people gather to pay homage to him at his memorial in Mumbai. Thousands of bookshops are set up, and books are sold. His message to his followers was "educate, organise, agitate".

The Ambedkar Memorial at Lucknow is dedicated in his memory. The chaitya consists of monuments showing his biography.

Ambedkar and his Egalitarian Revolution– Struggle for Human Rights. Events starting from March 1927 to 17 November 1956 in the chronological order; Ambedkar and his Egalitarian Revolution– Socio-political and religious activities. Events starting from November 1929 to 8 May 1956, in the chronological order; Ambedkar and his Egalitarian Revolution– Speeches. (Events starting from 1 January to 20 November 1956, in the chronological order.

REFERENCES

1. Edwin Bryant, *The Quest for the Origins of Vedic Culture*, Oxford: Oxford University Press, 2001. pp. 50-51.
2. Christophe Jaffrelot, *Ambedkar and Untouchability: Fighting the Indian Caste System*, New York, Columbia University Press, 2005, p.2.

3. Dhananjay Keer, *Dr. Ambedkar: Life and Mission.* Mumbai: Popular Prakashan, 1954, pp.37-38.
4. Dhananjay Keer, *Dr. Ambedkar: Life and Mission.* Mumbai: Popular Prakashan, 1954, pp.37-38
5. Dhananjay Keer, *Dr. Ambedkar: Life and Mission,* Popular Prakashan, 1990, p.61.
6. Edwin, Bryant, *The Quest for the Origins of Vedic Culture,* Oxford, Oxford University Press, 2001, pp- 50.
7. Arvind Sharma, *Dr. B. R. Ambedkar on the Aryan Invasion and the Emergence of the Caste System in India*; J Am Acad Relig; 2005, pp-849.
8. Arvind Sharma, *Dr. B. R. Ambedkar on the Aryan Invasion and the Emergence of the Caste System in India*; J Am Acad Relig; 2005, pp-851.
9. Arvind Sharma, *Dr. B. R. Ambedkar on the Aryan Invasion and the Emergence of the Caste System in India*; J Am Acad Relig; 2005, pp-863.
10. Dr. B.R. Ambedkar "Waiting for a Visa". http://www.columbia.edu. Columbia University, Retrieved 15 April 2015. External link in website.
11. Dhananjay, Keer, *Dr. Ambedkar: Life and Mission.* Mumbai: Popular Prakashan. 1971, pp.37-38.
12. Ian Harris (ed.), *Buddhism and politics in twentieth-century Asia.* Continuum International Group, Retrieved 17 July 2013.
13. Shabnum Tejani: "From Untouchable to Hindu Gandi, Ambedkar and Depressed class question 1932", Indian secularism: a social and intellectual history, 1890-1950, Bloomington, Ind.: Indiana University Press, 2008, pp.205-210. Retrieved 17 July 2013.
14. Christophe Jaffrelot: *Dr Ambedkar and Untouchability: Analysing and Fighting Caste.* London, C. Hurst & Co Publishers, 2005, p.4.
15. Dhananjay Keer , '*Man of The Hour', Dr. Ambedkar: life and mission* (Third ed.), Mumbai, Popular Prakashan, 1954, pp.63-64.
16. Dr. Ambedkar, National Campaign on Dalit Human Rights ; Retrieved January, 2012.
17. Archived from the original on 11 May 2011; On 29 August 1947,: Parliament of India. National Informatics Centre, the Constituent Assembly set up an Drafting Committee under the Chairmanship of B. R. Ambedkar to prepare a Draft Constitution for India.

18. Granville Austin, (1999), *The Indian Constitution: Cornerstone of a Nation,* Oxford University Press; Constituent Assembly Debates Clause wise Discussion on the Draft Constitution 15th November 1948 to 8th January 1949. Retrieved 12 January 2012.
19. D.L. Sheth, Reservations Policy Revisited; *Economic and Political Weekly.* 22: 1957-1962. 1987, Retrieved 10 October 2013.
20. S.N. Mishra, (Edited) *Socio-economic and political vision of Dr. B.R. Ambedkar*; New Delhi: Concept Publishing Co., 2010, pp.173-174.
21. The Times of India. Retrieved 15 October 2013; Ambedkar had a vision for food self-sufficiency'.
22. Jayashri Purushottam Sarode, "Impact of Dr. B.R. Ambdekar's thoughts on Indian Economy"; *International Indexed & Refereed Research Journal.* IV (42). (March 2013). Retrieved 15 October 2013.
23. M.R. Ingle: "Relevance of Dr. Ambedkar's Economic Philosophy in the Current Scenario"; *International Research Journal.* I (12); Retrieved 19 October 2013.
24. Dhananjay Keer, *Dr. Ambedkar: life and mission,* Mumbai, Popular Prakashan. 2005, pp.403-404. Retrieved 13 June 2012.
25. Sangharakshita, *Milestone on the Road to conversion; Ambedkar and Buddhism,* New Delhi: Motilal Banarsidass Publishers, 2006, p.72. Retrieved 17 July 2013.
26. The Hindu: 30 May 2003. President; PM; condole saving Ambedkar's death".

6

Dr. B.R. Ambedkar: Impact of His Ideas and Thoughts on Indian Politics

– Dr. Md. Salahuddin Munshi

In ancient India, Buddhism tried to change the social order of India based on equality. It tried to evolve a society based on equality, liberty, tolerance, love and sympathy. For the first time in the history of India attempt's were made in Buddhism to provide educational opportunity against Brahminism. But the Buddhist tradition of education could not continue for a long time, due to continuous disaster of Brahminism and Islam.

During the middle ages various efforts were made by religious leaders like Adi Shankaracharya, Ramanuja Charaya, Ramanand, Kabir, Gurunanak, Saint Namdev, Chaitanya, Mahaprabhu, Eknath, Tukaram and Ravidas etc., for reforming the religious and social order.

Even Islam and Sufism tried to preach a message of equality and universal brotherhood but all in vain. The Indian system of education remained as it was since the time immemorial. The efforts of saints during this period remained as a reformation movement in the domain of religion and philosophy.

During 19th century with efforts of social reformers in the field of education like Raja Ram Mohan Roy, Jothiba Rao Phuley, Swami Dayanand Saraswati, Swami Vivekanada, Rama Swami Periyar Naiker, Panchanan Barma, Justice Mahadev Govind Ranade, awaerness generated among proper masses. Their message could reach and influenced the oppressed masses to solve their educational problems to same extent. The colonial system of education during the British Raj has been criticized by many on the ground that it does not suit the needs of the Indian educational philosophers like M.K. Gandhi, Rabindarnath Tagore, Aurobindo, Swami Dayanand Saraswati, Swami Vivekanand and so on.

A view to provide alternative educational thoughts for evolving a rational, just and national system of education by M. K. Gandhi also had proposed a scheme of basic education but none of the above efforts was found to be satisfactory and covenanting to all. However, during the time of freedom struggle for the independence of India, a very distinct and outstanding thinker freedom fighter, social revolutionary and constitutional expert and economic visionary emerged as a force on the Socio-Political Map of India.

A GREAT PERSONALITY DR. B.R. AMBEDKAR

Ambedkar – Baba Sahab was first enrolled in the first standard as Bheem Rao Ramji Ambavadkar but he changed his title from Ambavadkar to Ambedkar as an emblem of love and respect.

B.R. Ambedkar was born on 14th April, 1891 A.D. in a poor family of Mhao community in Indore district of Madhya Pradesh. He belonged to a religious family and his father was Ramji Sakpal, a Subedar major. Moloji Sakpal was his grand-father who belonged to a village viz Ambavade, in the Ratnagiri district of the Konkan region of Maharashtra. He was from a good Mahar family who retired from the rank of Hawaldar in Military services. His father Sakpal came in close contact with Kabir in 1896 A.D.

Ambedkar was married to Ramabai, daughter of Bhiku Walungakar. He was then admitted to Maratha High School, later on shifted to Eliphinston High School, one of the best schools during that time in Bombay. B.R. Ambedkar had a habit of reading and as a student he was interested in learning Sanskrit and an optional subject Persian. He passed the Matriculation (X Std.) on 14th April, 1907 from the Eliphinston College, and B.A. examination in 1912 with English and Persian as subjects.

The Maharaja of Baroda decided to send some students to Columbia University of U.S.A. for higher studies from states expenses. Fortunately, Ambedkar had been selected for the scholarship and joined the Columbia University as a Gaekward Scholar.

The Fundamental Rights in the Indian Constitution include:

1. **Right to Equality:** All persons are equal before the law. This means that all persons shall be equally protected by the laws of the country. It also states that no citizen can be discriminated on the basis of their religion, caste or sex. Every person has a right to access to all public places including play ground, hotels, shops etc. The state cannot discriminate against any one in the matters of employment. Practice of untouchability has also been abolished
2. **Right to Freedom:** This includes the right to freedom of speech and expression, the right to form associations, the right to move freely and to reside in any part of the country, and the right to practice any profession, occupation of business.
3. **Right against Exploitation:** The constitution prohibits human trafficking, forced labour, and children working under article 14 years of age.
4. **Right to Freedom of Religion:** Religious freedom has been provided to all citizens, every person has the right to practice profess and propagate the religion of his choice.
5. **Cultural and Educational Rights**: The Constitution states that all minorities, religious or linguistic, can set up their own educational institutions in order to preserve and develop their own culture.
6. **Right to Constitutional Aspects:** This allows citizens to move the court if they believe that any of their fundamental rights has been violated by the state.

Indian Constitution recognizes 22 languages as statutory. There are Assamese, Bengali, Gujrati, Hindi, Kannada, Kashmiri, Konkari, Malayam, Manipuri, Marathi, Nepali, Oriya, Punjabi, Sanskrit, Sindhi, Tamil, Telugu and Dogri, Santhali, Mythili, Bodo, some of these are official languages in the states. It is to be noted that in this context Hindi has been regarded as the recognized official language of the country.

SOCIAL STATUS

In traditional India the social status implies occupation of a person though India is a large multi-lingual, multi-religious, multi caste, and multinational culture but it is to be noted that there must be a unity in diversity.

Contribution of Dr. B.R. Ambedkar: The National policy on Education (1986) took this aspect of value into consideration and emphasized on equality, and social justice in education to promote the country's Socio-cultural identity and to contribute national cohesion, promote tolerance, scientific temper and the concerned enshrined in the Indian constitution. The social values to be inculcated are friendliness, co-operation, compassion, courage self discipline and love for social justice.

Truth: Righteous conduct peace, love and non-violence are the core universal values representing the five domains of human personality, intellectual physical, emotional, psychological and spiritual.

In view of curriculum the following values are to be developed and inculcated in the students.

1. Cultural heritage
2. Environment
3. Right to Equality
4. Cultural and Educational rights
5. Scientific Temper
6. Secularism
7. Gender Equality
8. Social Justice
9. Right to Religion
10. Right against Exploitation.

RECOMMENDATION OF EDUCATION EQUALITY

National Policy on Education (1986) NPE made the following recommendations. Education for women's Equality , provision of educational opportunities to women has been an important programme in the education sector since independence. Between 1951 and 1981 the percentage of literacy amongst women has been improved from 7.93 percent to 24.82 percent. The number of illiterate women has been increased during this period from 158.7 million to 241.7 million excluding Assam.

Women, comprising 57 percent of the non-enrolled children of school stage are girls. Today inspite of efforts made so far, the educational system has not been able to make sufficient contribution to women's equality.

MINORITIES EDUCATION

The N.P.E. was formed for the education of the minority. Some minority groups are educationally deprived or backward. Greater attention will be paid to the education of these groups in the interest of equality and social justice. This will naturally include the constitutional guarantees given to them to establish and administer their own educational institutions and protection to their languages and culture.

Simultaneously, objectivity will be reflected in the preparation of text-books and in all school activities and all possible measures will be taken to promote an integration based on appreciation of common national goals and ideals, in conformity with the co-curriculum.

A Constitutional Approach for Social Change:

The functional and organizational structure of pre-independence educational system was not designed to be the custodian of total knowledge. Dr. B.R. Ambedkar as a Chairman of the drafting committee of Indian constitution made a number of provision for the safeguarding and self dependence of weaker classes.

> Article 15 (A): Provision for advancement in any society and educational backward classes or SC/STs.
>
> Article 15 (3): Prevents the state from depriving of any special provision for women and children.
>
> Article 17: Implies the abolition of untouchability and making every one equal.

Article 23: The provision of this article has been helpful in fighting the following evils and making social justice possible:

(a) Trade in girls and women.

(b) The custom of bonded labour and beggar of forced labour.

(c) The custom of slavery.

Not only women, even children fall into main the category of weaker section of society, even children had been deprived of several justice in traditional Indian society.

Article 29 (ii): admission into educational institution maintained by the state.

Article 30: Right to minorities to establish and administer educational institutions.

Article 30(ii): making any kind providing for compulsory acquisition of any property of an educational institutions.

Article 30(ii): granting aid to educational institutions.

Article 39(a): The citizens, men and women equally have the right to an adequate means to livelihood.

Article 39 (c): The health and strength of workers, men and women and the tender aged children are not abused and that citizens are not freed by economic necessity to enter a vocation unsuited to their age or strength.

As a social revolutionary, dynamic leader, great philosopher B R Ambedkar, the founding father of India Constitution, had left no stone unturned to solve the different problems of society, inhabited by different races of puple.

Dr. B.R. Ambedkar passed away in the early morning of 6th December 1956, on 7th December 1956 the dead body of Dr. B.R. Ambedkar was taken to Bombay from New Delhi. In the year 1960, A grand 'Stupa' was erected at "*Chaitya Bhoom*", Dadar Chaupati where the pyre was built by his son Yeshwant Rao.

Dr. B.R. Ambedkar studied Sanskrit subject, his efforts led the doors open for study of Sanskrit. He strongly believed that without the education of women, no social progress could be acheived. He was conscious of the need of education in general specially for depressed classes in directive principles of the state policy of universal and compulsory education system under Elementary Education, Secondary Education and Concrete Philosophy.

Dr B R Ambedkar's Chronological important events are as follows:

Speeches of Dr. B.R. Ambedkar:

Dr. B.R. Ambedkar's historic speeches, discussions and debates, writings and selected documents depict his lifelong struggle. He started to express his talent when he was a student of Post-graduate Course under the Columbia University. He presented a dissertation of 'Administration and Finance of the East India Company.' (Submitted to the same University on May, 15th 1915.

His other valuable writings and speeches include the following:

1916 A.D. : "Caste in India: Their Mechanism, Genesis and Development", a paper read out the Anthropology Seminar sponsored by Dr. A.A. Gold-Enweizer at the Columbia University, New York, U.S.A. published in Indian Antiquary, Vol.XXVI, 1917.

1916 A.D. : "Responsibilities of Provincial Governments in India", a paper read in the Economics Association of the Columbia University, 1916 A.D.

1918 A.D. : Small Holdings in India and Their Remedies. A paper published in the Journal of India Economic Society. Vol. 1, No.3, 1918 A.D.

1919 January, 16 : Dr. B.R. Ambedkar's letter under a non deplume on "The Duties of Higher Classes:. The Times of India, Bombay, January 16, 1919.

1920 A.D. : Mooknayak (Leader of the Dumb). A Marathi fortnightly. Bombay.

1923 A.D. : Evolution of Provincial Finance in British India. London, P.S. King & Sons.

1923 A.D. : Problem of the Rupee: Its Origin and its Solution. London, P.S. King & Sons.

1925 A.D.: Evolution of Provincial Finance in British India. London, P.S. King & Sons,

1927 April – 3 : Bahishkrit Bharat. A Marathi Fortnightly Bombay.

1928 May -29 : Statement submitted on behalf of the Bahishkrit Hitkarini Sabha to the Indian Statutory Commission.

1929 March: Samata, a newspapaer. Bombay.

1930 A.D.: Presidential Address to the All India Depressed Classes Congress, Nagpur. Bharat Bhusan Printing Press, Bombay, 1930 A.D.

1930 December: Janata, a weekly.

1931 November: Appeal on behalf of the Depressed classes Institute, Bombay.

1935 A.D.: "Annihilation of Caste", An Address which could not be delivered at the Annual Conference of Jaat Paant Todak Mandal, Lahore.

1936 August, 15: Independent Labour Party: Its Formation and Its Aims. A Pamphlet reprinted from " Parliamentary Democrcy", An Address at Poona.

1938 A.D.: Speech at the G.I. P. Railway Depressed class workman's conference, Manmad.

1939 January 29: "Federation Versus Freedom". Kale Memorial Lecture delivered at Gokhale Memorial Hall, poona and Published by Gokhale Institute of Economics and political Science, Poona.

1939 A.D.: Federation Versus Freedom. Bombay, R.K. Tatnis.

1940 A.D.: Toughts on Pakistan, Bombay, Thacker & Co.

1942 October 29: Grievances of the Schedule Caste. Memorandum submitted to his Excellency, the Governor General.

1942 October 30: Speech as the Labour Member at a Press Conference.

1943 July: What ails the World Today. Article. The Indian reader's Digest.

1943 A.D.: Mr. Gandhi and the Emancipation of the Untouchables (First issued as the Untouchables and the Indian Constitution). Bombay, Thacker & Co.

1943 A.D.:Ranade, Gandhi and Jinnah, Jullundur, Bheem Patrika Publications. Address delivered on the 101st Birthday Celebrations of M.G. Ranade, in Gokhale Memorial Hall, Poona.

1944 Sept. 24: "Scheduled Caste ask for future safeguards, Separate Electorates and Reservation in Public Services, Federation Committee on Fundamental Rights". The Mail, September 24, 1944. A.D.

1944 Sept. 25: "Rationalismin India : Revolution and Counter Revolution". The Liberator, Madras, September 25, 1944. A.D.

1945 A.D.: What the Congress and Gandhi have done to the untouchables, Bombay, Thacker & Co.

1945 February: Pakistan on the partition of India (Revised edition of Thoughts on Pakistan, 1940 A.D.)

1945 May, 6: "Communal Deadlock and A way to solve It." Address to the India Scheduled Castes Federation.

1945 A.D.: Communal Deadlock and A way to solve it. Delhi, F & O.

1946 A.D.: Mr. Gandhi and the Emancipation of the Untouchables. Bombay, Thacker & Co.

1946 A.D.: Cabinet Mission and the Untouchables, 1946 A.D. A pamphlet…3.

1946 A.D.: What Congress and Gandhi have done to the untouchables. Ed. 2. Bombay, Thacker & Co., 1946 A.D.

1946 A.D.: Who were the Shudras? How they came to be the fourth Varna in the Indo-Aryan Society? Bombay Thacker & Co.

1946 April, 5: Memorandum on behalf of the All India Scheduled Caste Federation Submitted to the Cabinet Mission.

1947 A.D.: History of Indian Currency and Banking Vol. I, Bombay, Thacker & Co.

1947 A.D.: State and Minorities : What are their Rights and How to secure them in the constitution of free India, Bombay, Thakcer & Co.

1947 July-16: "Joint Versus Separate Electorates : Hindu Argument against Separate Electorate is Insubstantial and Unsupportable". Jai Bheem, Madras, July 16, 1947 A.D.

1947 December 18: Letter from Ambedkar to the Prime Minister Jawaharlal Nehru, to draw the attention of Nehru to the complaints that Scheduled Caste evacuees from Pakistan are prevented from coming over to India and requesting him to take some steps that he suggested or Any other useful ones.

1948 A.D.: Maharashtra as a Linguistic province. Bombay Thacker & Co.

1948 A.D.: Untouchables: Who where they and why they became untouchables. New Delhi, Amrit Book Co.

1951 A.D.: Speech before the Buddha Gathering., Marathi, Published in Dharmachakra, 1951 A.D.

1956 A.D. :

(a) Buddhism and Communism, Speech.

(b) A Critique of the proposals of the Cabinet Mission of Indian Constitutional Change so far as they affect the Scheduled Caste (Untouchables). A Pamphlet.

(c) Rise and Fall of Hindus Women and Who is Responsible. A Pamphlet.

(d) Report of the round table Conference, 1930-32 A.D.

(e) Report of the committee apoointed by the Harijan Sevak Sangh, May 1933 A.D. to make a survey on Social andReligious Disabilities of the Harijans, Cawnpore, The Sangh,1934 A.D.

(f) Report of the seminar of the Indian Conference of the Social work, Bombay, on Casteism and Removal of untouchability, September 26 to October, 1955 Bomaby.

(g) Report of the Simon Commission on Indian constitutional reforms.

(h) Indian Labour party: Constitution and Rules Directory of Bombay Legislature. Bombay. K. Srinivasan, 1939 A.D.

Ambedkar's life and work as 'an eminent scholar and thinker of international repute', 'one of the finest flowers of the twenty first century', 'Fighter for human rights and dignity', shall remain a source of inspirations to men and women all over the World.

REFERENCES

1. Dhananjay Keer, *Dr. Ambedkar: Life and Mission.* Mumbai: Popular Prakashan, 1954.

2. Dhananjay Keer, *Dr. Ambedkar: Life and Mission*, Popular Prakashan,1991.
3. Edwin Bryant, *The Quest for the Origins of Vedic Culture*, Oxford, Oxford University Press, 2001.
4. Arvind Sharma, Dr. B. R. Ambedkar on the Aryan Invasion and the Emergence of the Caste System in India; J Am Acad Relig; 2005.
5. Arvind Sharma, Dr. B. R. Ambedkar on the Aryan Invasion and the Emergence of the Caste System in India; J Am Acad Relig; 2005.
6. Arvind Sharma, Dr. B. R. Ambedkar on the Aryan Invasion and the Emergence of the Caste System in India; J Am Acad Relig; 2005.

7

DR. B.R. Ambedkar: A Man of Vision

– Sujit Kujur

INTRODUCTION

The life of Dr. B.R. Ambedkar was full of struggle, but his outstanding capability to fighting with the all unfavourable conditions was path making for each of us. Our each and every freedom/right is due to only his struggle, efforts and vision. He is a great visionary, thinker and activist of India who has influenced India's development. The problem which he struggled to solve still defies solution is linked with unity and prosperity of India (Audi, Ambedkar's struggle for untouchables: reflections, 1989). Dr. B.R. Ambedkar popularly known as Babasaheb, was an Indian jurist, economist, politician and social reformer who inspired the Dalit, Buddhist movement and campaigned against social discrimination on Untouchables (Dalits), while supporting the rights of women and labour. He was Independent India's first law minister and the architect of the Constitution of India.

His original surname Ambavadekar comes from his native village 'Ambavade' in Ratnagiri district. His teacher, Mahadev Ambedkar, who was fond of him, changed his surname from 'Ambavadekar' to his own surname 'Ambedkar' in school records (Wikipedia).

EXPERIENCING UNTOUCHABILITIES

Childhood and school: Ambedkar was born on 14 April 1891 in the town and military cantonment of Mhow in the Central

Provinces (now in Madhya Pradesh) a poor low Mahar (dalit) caste, who were treated as untouchables and subjected to socioeconomic discrimination. He was the 14th and the last child of Ramji Maloji Sakpal, an army officer who held the rank of Subedar, and Bhimabai Murbadkar Sakpal. His family was of Marathi back-ground from the town of Ambavade (Mandangad taluka) in Ratnagiri district of modern-day Maharashtra.

(a) Once he and his brother took a train for Goregaon because their father had not come to the station they took a bullock cart for Goregaon. When the cartman came to know that they were untouchables and asked them to get off the cart, took them back only after they had paid him double the fare. After that the caste Hindu walked behind the cart with Ambedkar's brother driving it. This was the first rude and shattering shock to the budding mind of him (Wikipedia).

(b) He attended school but not allowed to sit inside the class, and was required to sit on a gunny sack which he had to take from home with him (Wikipedia).

(c) For drinking water, someone from a higher caste had to pour that water from a height as they were not allowed to touch either the water or the vessel that contained it. This task was usually performed by the school peon, and if the peon was not available then he had to go without water (Keer, 2009).

(d) A few days the earlier impression got confirmed when he was drinking water stealthily at a public watercourse, got caught, and was beaten black and blue (Palshikar, 1997).

(e) The barber refused to cut his hair so his sisters cut his hair (Keer, 2009).

(f) In Elphinstone High School, Ambedkar and his brother were not allowed to take up the study of Sanskrit – a key to the study of the Vedas, instead were forced to take Persian against their will (Keer, 2009).

During profession: As Ambedkar was educated by the Princely State of Baroda, he was bound to serve it. He was appointed Military Secretary to the Gaikwad but had to quit in a short time.

(a) He tried to find ways to make a living for his growing family. He worked as a private tutor, as an accountant, and established an investment consulting business, but it failed when his clients learned that he was an untouchable (Audi, Ambedkar's struggle for untouchables: reflections, 1989).

(b) In 1918, he became Professor of Political Economy in the Sydenham College of Commerce and Economics in Mumbai. Although he was successful with the students, other professors objected to his sharing a drinking-water jug with them (Wikipedia).

Dr. B.R. Ambedkar had been experienced bitter humiliation of untouchability throughout his life. There was enormous pain inside him and those pains provoked him to fight for the injustice, social discrimination, untouchability, rights of women and labour, etc. In those times whole India was fighting for the freedom from the British Rule, but Ambedkar was fighting and struggling for the basic rights of individuals like social discrimination, Hindu cast system and the life bondage, etc.

HIS VISION ON DIFFERENT ISSUES

EDUCATION

He was a playful child who was not keen on studies but liked to indulge in all sorts of hobbies, fancies and gardening. Ambedkar's father married again and he did not like this and so decided to earn his own livelihood, becoming a winding boy in a Bombay mill but unable to arrange the money for fare to Bombay. He decided to give up his truant habits, study hard and get through his exams as fast as possible so that he could be independent of his father. This marked a turning point in his life because he became so diligent that his teachers urged his father to give him the best possible education (Keer, 2009).

(a) In 1907, he passed his matriculation examination and in the following year he entered Elphinstone College, which was affiliated to the University of Bombay, becoming the first dalit to do so. This success evoked much celebration among dalits and after a public ceremony (Audi, Ambedkar's struggle for untouchables: reflections, 1989).

(b) In 1912, he obtained his degree in economics and political science from Bombay University, and prepared to take up employment with the Baroda state government.

(c) In 1913, Ambedkar moved to the United States at the age of 22. He had been awarded a Baroda State Scholarship of £11.50 (Sterling) per month for three years under a scheme established by Sayajirao Gaekwad III (Gaekwad of Baroda) that was designed to provide opportunities for postgraduate education at Columbia University, New York City (Wikipedia).

(d) In 1915, he passed his M.A. in Economics, and other subjects of Sociology, History, Philosophy and Anthropology. He presented a thesis, Ancient Indian Commerce.

(e) In 1916 he completed his second thesis, National Dividend of India - A Historic and Analytical Study for another M.A., and finally he received his Ph.D. in Economics in 1927 for his third thesis, after he left for London. On 9 May, he read his paper Castes in India: Their Mechanism, Genesis and Development before a seminar conducted by the anthropologist Alexander Goldenweiser (Keer, 2009).

(f) In October 1916, he enrolled for Bar at Law course at Gray's Inn, and at the same time enrolled at the London School of Economics where he started working on a doctoral thesis. In June 1917, he returned to India as his scholarship from Baroda ended. He got permission to return to London to submit his thesis within four years and completed a master's degree in 1921. His thesis was on the "The problem of the rupee: its origin and its solution" (Keer, 2009).

(g) In 1923, he completed a D.Sc. in Economics, and the same year he was called to the Bar by Gray's Inn. His third and fourth Doctorates (LL.D, Columbia, 1952 and D. Litt., Osmania, 1953) were conferred honors causa. (Wikipeadia).

Dr. Ambedkar was a brilliant scholar of his time and was the first Indian to receive Ph.D. in Economics from London School of Economics, London. He received the top most education degree of his time. When he was purusing postgraduate from Colombia University, New York, freedom fighter Lala Lajpat Rai and his guide

Prof. Selling wish him to take part in the movement of Indian freedom, but he denied because to complete his study at the earliest as he was on the Baroda State Scholarship. After submitting his thesis his supervisor guide said to him that your struggle is much tougher than the India's Freedom.

Ambedkar was known very well that to fight with the cast system in India is very difficult and education and knowledge is the only way to fight against it. The aim of education is not only to acquire knowledge but to utilise it for the betterment of the society. By his outstanding scholarship a thinker, lawyer, educationist, activist and what not made him to understand the situation of problems and to find to solutions. The Constitution of India is the best gift of his ability for the peoples of India.

JUSTICE FOR DALITS

Ambedkar was victimized by the caste system of India and that hindered the development of India too. He devoted his entire life for the basic rights of the dalits. His outstanding fight against the caste system made him 'Mesiha of dalits'.

(a) While practicing law in the Bombay High Court, he tried to promote the education of dalits.

(b) His first organized attempt was his establishment of the central institution Bahishkrit Hitakarini Sabha, intended to promote education and socio-economic improvement, as well as the welfare of "outcastes", at the time referred to as depressed classes (Audi, Ambedkar's struggle for untouchables: reflections, 1989).

(c) For the defense of Dalit rights, he started many periodicals like *Mook Nayak,* weekly (Leader of the Silent) in Mumbai with the help of Shahaji II (1874–1922), Maharaja of Kolhapur in 1920, *Bahishkrit Bharat,* and *Equality Janta.* He was appointed to the Bombay Presidency Committee to work with the all-European Simon Commission in 1925 and wrote a separate set of recommendations for the future Constitution of India. This commission had sparked great protests across India, and while its report was ignored by most Indians (Wikipedia).

(d) By 1927, Ambedkar had decided to launch active movements against untouchability. He began with public movements and marches to open up public drinking water resources. He led a satyagraha in Mahad to fight for the right of the dalits to draw water from the main water tank of the town (Keer, 2009).

(e) In a conference in late 1927, Ambedkar publicly condemned the classic Hindu text, the Manusmriti (Laws of Manu), for ideologically justifying caste discrimination and "untouchability", and he ceremonially burned copies of the ancient text. On 25 December 1927, he led thousands of followers to burn copies of Manusmrti. Thus annually 25 December is celebrated as *Manusmriti Dahan Din* (Manusmriti Burning Day) by Ambedkarites and Dalits (Patel, 2000).

(f) In 1930, Ambedkar launched Kalaram Temple movement after three months of preparation. About 15,000 volunteers assembled at Kalaram Temple satygraha making one of the greatest processions of Nashik. The procession was headed by a military band, a batch of scouts, women and men walked in discipline, order and determination to see the God for the first time (Patel, 2000).

(g) Ambedkar had been invited to testify before the Southborough Committee, which was preparing the Government of India Act 1919. At this hearing, Ambedkar argued for creating separate electorates and reservations for untouchables and other religious communities (Wikipedia).

Ambedkar has a great vision for the upliftment of dalits and the depressed class of the society. He protested the caste system of Hindu religion (*Brhamin, Kshtariya, Vasya* and *Shudra*) and advocated the freedom of individuals. The depressed/ untouchables are very important part of the society and without their contributions to nation's economic growth and development cannot be imagined.

ECONOMICS

Ambedkar was an economist by his basic training and argued that industrialization and agricultural growth could enhance the Indian economy. He stressed investment in agriculture as the primary industry of India. Ambedkar advocated national economic and social development, stressing education, public hygiene, community health, residential facilities as the basic amenities. His D.Sc. thesis "*The problem of the Rupee: Its origin and solution*" (1923) examines the causes for the Rupee's fall in value. He proved the importance of price stability over exchange stability. He analyzed the silver and gold exchange rates and their effects on the economy, and found the reasons for the failure of British India's public treasury. He calculated the loss of development caused by British rule. In 1951, Ambedkar constituted the Finance Commission of India (which led to the establishment of the Reserve Bank of India). He opposed income tax for low-income groups. He contributed to Land Revenue Tax and excise duty policies to stabilize the economy. He played an important role in land reform and the state economic development. According to him, the caste system divided labourors and impeded economic progress. He emphasized a free economy with a stable Rupee which India has adopted recently. He advocated birth control to develop the Indian economy, and this has been adopted by Indian government as national policy for family planning. He emphasized equal rights for women for economic development. He laid the foundation of industrial relations after Indias independence (Wikipedia).

(a) Ambedkar offered an excellent exposition of the evolution of Indian currency in terms of its form as a medium of exchange and its equivalence in terms of precious metals, such as, gold and silver (Jadhav, 1991).

(b) Ambedkar provided statistical evidence to show that in Indian context, prices varied much less under the gold standard than under the gold-exchange standard (Jadhav, 1991).

(c) The caste system reduces mobility of labour as well as capital leading to inefficiencies in production, thus impeding economic growth. In a broader sense, change is the essence of the process of economic development, it calls for continuous changes in socio-economic patterns (Ambedkar, 1944).

(d) Ambedkar observed in his What Congress and Gandhi have done to the untouchables that "as an economic system, it (the caste system) permits exploitation without obligation. Untouchability is not only a system of unmitigated economic exploitation but is also a system of uncontrolled economic exploitation". In Ambedkars book '*The Untouchables*', he argued that the caste system was a "diabolical contrivance to suppress and enslave humanity. It's proper name would be infamy" (Jadhav, 1991).

(e) He believed that the thrust strategy for India's economic development should be on eradication of poverty, elimination of inequalities and ending exploitation of the masses (Jadhav, 1991).

(f) Ambedkar believed in a classless society but not in a stateless society. He maintained that the state would continue to exist as long as human society survived. Indeed in his book States and Minorities, he has entrusted 'an obligation on the state to plan the economic life of the people on line which would lead to highest point of productivity without closing every avenue to private enterprise, and also provide for equitable distribution of wealth' (Jadhav, 1991).

LABOUR

For the labours, Ambedkar was an activist who looked forward for the Human Rights. Human Rights are inalienable rights of an individual. He led a relentless social reform movement to educate dalits of the human rights to live a life of dignity and to organize among themselves to vindicate their rights, to self-confidence, self-help and to agitate for civil and political rights. He said about the depressed society, "Depressed by the government, suppressed by the Hindus and degraded by the Muslims, we were left in the most intolerable position of utter helplessness to which I am sure there is no parallel". Mahatmas have come and Mahatmas have gone, but, the untouchables have remained as untouchables. But it was him who redeemed these untouchables from their centuries old bondage through a non-violent movement and brought recognition to them as human beings and secured Human Rights to them (Rao A. V., 2006).

(a) According to Article 21 the right to life has been guaranteed to all including scheduled castes (Rao A. V., 2006).

(b) Article 25 guarantee right to religion. The scheduled castes are able to enter the temples and offer prayers and worship Gods and Goddesses (Rao A. V., 2006).

(c) Article 29 guaranteed right to education and so the scheduled castes are able to enter into the educational institutions and pursue their studies. Introduction of universal adult suffrage and the democratic form of Government provided political right to them and the right to vote (Rao A. V., 2006).

(d) Article 330 provided reservation of seats for the scheduled castes and scheduled tribes in the House of the people (Rao A. V., 2006).

(e) Article 332 provided reservation of seats for scheduled castes and scheduled tribes in the Legislative Assembly of the states (Rao A. V., 2006).

(f) Article 335 provided them reservation in appointments of Union and State Services (Rao A. V., 2006).

(g) According to 338 a special officer for scheduled castes and scheduled tribes is appointed by the president to look after the safeguards conceded to these sections (Rao A. V., 2006).

It was Dr. Ambedkar's single-handed effort and fight delivered the human rights of scheduled castes privileges and constitutional safeguards for their socio, economic, political, educational and cultural developments (Rao A. V., 2006).

He organized a conference at Mahad, for example, to exercise a human right and indispensable fundamental right to drink portable water from a common chowder tank dedicated to use by the public but was inaccessible to the dalits. Under his leadership, the dalits went peacefully to the tank and drank the water. He was a great champion of the dalit because he succeeded in turning the depressed classes movement into revolutionary movement (Rao A. V., 2006).

Ambedkar was understood that labour's are the backbone of the country's development but most of the injustice faced by them. The owner always thinks to take maximum efforts and strength of a labour by paying very low wages, emotional/physical harassments to women labour, involving children in the labour work, living standard of labour were without facility, and they are bond to live in dirty, unhygienic conditions, etc.

Ambedkar's vision in the form of the Constitution of India today we are having labour commission to look into the injustice of labours, decided wages, working times, holidays, sanity and hygiene, medical facility, etc. and all the basic rights of human being.

POLITICS

In 1936, Ambedkar founded the Independent Labour Party, which contested the 1937 Bombay election to the Central Legislative Assembly for the 13 reserved and 4 general seats, and secured 11 and 3 seats respectively. In his book '*Annihilation of Caste*' it strongly criticized Hindu orthodox religious leaders and the caste system in general, and included "a rebuke of Gandhi" on the subject. In another book *Who Were the Shudras?* he tried to explain the formation of untouchables and oversaw the transformation of his political party into the Scheduled Castes Federation, although it performed poorly in the 1946 elections for Constituent Assembly of India. Later he was elected the constituent assembly of Bengal where Muslim League was in power. He contested in the Bombay North first Indian General Election of 1952, but lost. He became a member of Rajya Sabha, probably an appointed member. He tried to enter Lok Sabha again in the by-election of 1954 from Bhandara, but he placed third (Wikipedia).

His political vision in a sense is an expression of vital human affairs and is a sincere attempt to bridge the gulf between theory and practice, materialism and spiritualism. His thought process arose out of his dejection with the inhuman treatment meted out to his community by the caste Hindus. The servile class consisting of the untouchables and the Shudras were forever condemned to a life of poverty, ignorance, ignominy, hatred and contempt. His main concern was the total emancipation of the servile class from the clutches of the privileged caste Hindus. Hence, "he was in total engagement throughout his life with the social phenomena, as a humanist who charitably looked for what made true humanity. These were later to figure in all his endeavours." Dr. Ambedkar had a 'mission' in his life and that was one of 'man-making.' (Rajasekhariah & Jayaraj, 1991).

INDIAN CONSTITUTION

Upon India's independence on 15 August 1947, the new Congress-led government invited Ambedkar to serve as the nation's first Law Minister, which he accepted. On 29 August, he was appointed Chairman of the Constitution Drafting Committee, and was appointed by the Assembly to write India's new Constitution (Wikipedia).

Granville Austin described the Indian Constitution drafted by Ambedkar as 'first and foremost a social document'. The majority of India's constitutional provisions are either directly arrived at furthering the aim of social revolution or attempt to foster this revolution by establishing conditions necessary for its achievement (Wikipedia).

The text prepared by Ambedkar provided constitutional guarantees and protections for a wide range of civil liberties for individual citizens, including freedom of religion, the abolition of untouchability, and the outlawing of all forms of discrimination (Athawale, 1977). He argued for extensive economic and social rights for women, and won the Assembly's support for introducing a system of reservations of jobs in the civil services, schools and colleges for members of scheduled castes and scheduled tribes and ther Backward Class, a system akin to affirmative action. India's lawmakers hoped to eradicate the socio-economic inequalities and lack of opportunities for India's depressed classes through these measures. The Constitution was adopted on 26 November 1949 by the Constituent Assembly (Wikipeadia).

During the debates in the Constituent Assembly, Ambedkar demonstrated his will to reform Indian society by recommending the adoption of a Uniform Civil Code. Ambedkar resigned from the cabinet in 1951, when parliament stalled his draft of the Hindu Code Bill, which sought to enshrine gender equality in the laws of inheritance and marriage (Patel, 2000). He was appointed to the upper house, of parliament, the Rajya Sabha in March 1952 and would remain as member till death (Wikipedia).

The vision behind the Constitution of India Ambedkar was very clear to make uniform equal rights, freedom to do anything, no cast system systems. Hindu Code Bill was the great proposal of Ambedkar to make change the traditional cast systems, and bring women forwards, Hindu marriage system, women part in the paternal properties, Uniform civil code etc. which can be are revolutionize the Indian economic status.

INDIA-PAKISTAN DIVISION

Ambedkar criticised Islamic practice in South Asia. While justifying the Partition of India, he condemned child marriage and the mistreatment of women in Muslim society (Wikipedia). He was never in favour of the partition of India, but Muslim league demanded for the separate country "Pakistan" for the Muslims. He wrote some books "*Thoughts of Pakistan*" and "*Pakistan or partition of India*" and his vision was against Pakistan partition because United India is benefited for both Hindu and Muslims communities, whatever will be matter between Hindus and Muslims can be resolved without partition.

RELIGION

In 1950, Ambedkar traveled to Sri Lanka to attend a convention of Buddhist scholars and monks. After his return he decided to write a book on Buddhism and soon, converted himself to Buddhism. In his speeches, Ambedkar lambasted the Hindu rituals and caste division. Ambedkar founded the Bharatiya Bauddha Mahasabha In 1955. His book "*The Buddha and His Dhamma*" was published posthumously (Ambedkar, 1973).

On October 14, 1956 Ambedkar organized a public ceremony to convert around five lakh of his supporters into Buddhism. He traveled to Kathmandu to attend the Fourth World Buddhist Conference. He completed his final manuscript, "*The Buddha or Karl Marx*" on December 2, 1956 (Ambedkar 1973).

His vision to covert from Hinduism to Bhuddhismave:

(a) Buddhism always impress because it is stand on three theories Pragya, Karuna & Samata.

(b) Religion should teach liberty, equality and fraternity and Bhuddhism do all theses.

(c) Based on non-voilence.

(d) For the favour of nation, Buddhism is the only way.

(e) Buddhism is out of cast systems and there is equality.

CONCLUSION

Since 1948, Ambedkar suffered from diabetes. He was bed-ridden from June to October in 1954 due to medication side-effects and poor eyesight. He had been increasingly embittered by political issues, which took a toll on his health. His health worsened during 1955. Three days after completing his final manuscript "*The Buddha and His Dhamma*", Ambedkar died in his sleep on 6 December 1956 at his home in Delhi (Wikipedia).

In 1990, the Bharat Ratna, India's highest civilian award, was posthumously conferred upon Ambedkar. His legacy includes numerous memorials and depictions in popular culture (Wikipedia).

Ambedkar was an ideal for many and still we thank for his outstanding visions and his work. His vision gave freedom, strength and equal status to each of us in our day to day life, women at work, house wife, we appeal for our right to different courts, every child should take the basic education, our working hours, labour wages, and the law for their justice. He awakened the depressed classes and gave strength on them to stand against the injustice and broke the traditional practices of the Hindu cast system. His restless life was making us free citizens of India and the constitution of India is caring each one of us. He was converted to Bhuddhism where all people are same and its teachings are based on logic. He was always impressed with the Bhuddhism. He published many books, articles, delivered speeches, but his many unpublished books published by the Government of Maharashtra like "*Philosophy of Hindusim*" volume 3 in 1987, "*Untouchables or the Children of India's Ghetto*" volume 5 in 1989, "*Pali Grammer*" volume 16 in 1998, "*Riddles in Hindusim*" in 1987 etc., it shows he was not only a social reformer, leader, advocate, educationist, but a great scholar. Still today we do follow his foot prints because his vision was very clear and essential for the development of India.

REFERENCES

1. Ambedka, B.R., *Buddha and his dhamma,* Bombay: online Jai Bhim, 1973.
2. Ambedkar, B.R., *Annihilation of Caste: With a reply to Mahatma Gandhi.* (V. Natarajan, Ed.), New Delhi, 1944.
3. Ambedkar, B.R., *Pakistan or partition of India.* Bombay: Thacker & Co. Ltd, 1946.
4. Athawale, D, Ambedkar and the Indian Constitution. *Economic and Political Weekly , 32* (15), 734, 1977.
5. Audi, M. J., Ambedkar's struggle for untouchables: reflections, *The Indian Journal of Political Science, 50* (3), 307-320, 1989.
6. Keer, D, *Dr. Ambedkar: life and mission.* Mumbai: Harsha Bhatkal, 2009.

8

National Integration and Development: A Relevant Thoughts of Dr. B.R. Ambedkar

– P. Karuppasamy Pandian

Some people born as great, some have greatness thrust upon them and some achieve greatness. Bharat Ratna Babasaheb Dr. Bhimrao Ramji Ambedkar belongs to the last category. He was a great nationalist, political thinker, reformer and revolutionary and prolific writer with prodigious ideas. He stood for all scientific and social activities which enhanced the cause of human progress and happiness. His contribution in the making of the Constitution of India was phenomenal. He constantly fought for the betterment of the oppressed classes. In this struggle, he showed rare crusading spirit, carving out in the process an important place for himself among the prominent architects of modern India.

Dr. Ambedkar was a brave national leader united all the suppressed community under one banner. He was not only a great national leader and an eminent jurist but also a distinguished scholar of International repute. He was a multi-faceted personality, an intellectual revolutionary and the statesman of the twentieth century, contributing immensely to enrich various facets of Indian national life. He had left an indelible mark on Indian polity, society and economy. His vision on nation building was closely related to his ideal of a good society which is based on liberty, equality and fraternity. Ambedkar's vision of national building was geared with social transformation and human progress. His contribution pervades the entire gamut of social life with equality and social justice. He is remembered and admired as nationalist, well known economist, brilliant lawyer, constitutionalist, author of various books, social activist, law maker, liberator, leader of oppressed classes and women, the chief architect of the Indian Constitution.

He was very much devoted to the reconstruction of modern India and contributed towards restricting the Indian social structure. He also contributed in the fields of agriculture, irrigation, industrialization and modernization, which reflected in the following fields like welfare of labour classes, agriculture, irrigation, and preparation of water transport schemes, flood control, river transport and in increasing power production. He suggested for collective farming, equal distribution of land, large scale industrialization, provision of providing money, water, seeds and fertilizers by the government, cultivation of waste land by allotting waste land to landless labour, minimum wages to labours, control and regulation of private lenders of loan to farmers for solving agriculture problem in India. Due to his continuous efforts the 'Land Ceiling Act' was passed after independence.

He knew that development of India was impossible without rapid industrialization. He suggested that government should start large scale industries and smaller industries should be kept in private sector and the insurance and transport companies should be nationalized. He knew that without population control, Indian economy cannot flourish. He forcefully argued for population control and family planning in India and due to his effort only government of India has adopted family planning as a national policy. His thoughts give amazing and constructive insights to the conceptualization the social exclusion of deprived and other excluded groups within India. His thoughts not only conceptualized the social discrimination, but also focused on social emancipation and continuously inspired discussions on the origins of the social injustices within the social, cultural milieu of Indian society. Ambedkar's efforts to eradicate the social evils like untouchablity and caste restrictions were remarkable. Throughout his life he fought for the rights of the Dalits and other socially backward classes. His ideas revolve around the welfare of mankind through social and political action, respect for basic human dignity, human rights and secularization of state. His belief in peace and non-violence, constitutional morality, social justice are some of the most valuable and enduring elements of his political and social philosophy which helps in building up humane in society. His ultimate mission of life was to construct a virtual bridge between the various classes of the society.

Therefore, this national seminar is an attempt not only to evaluate the relevance of Dr. B.R. Ambedkar's thoughts in contemporary India but also to provide academicians and experts from different disciplines to discuss issues, priorities, remedies, action plan, and strategies for social emancipation, economic empowerment, educational advancement and participation of socially, culturally and racially marginalized sections like Scheduled Castes, Scheduled Tribes, Backward Classes and women in India.

UNTOUCHABILITY AND CASTE SYSTEM

Ambedkar underwent a bitter experience of being an outcaste in the society. It had a deep impact on his life and therefore he embarked upon a journey that would lead to eradication of untouchability. Within the Hinduism he took of facts that would favour equality. He spoke in favour of the downtrodden and formed organizations to bring about change in the social life of the suppressed community. He made sure that constitutional and legal provisions in favour of the downtrodden got passed. (Vakil, 1991) By the removal of caste system he was aiming at the taking away of root of all social evils. In rural areas many atrocities were inflicted on the untouchables. He persuaded Brahmins to remove untouchability but they were not interested in it and wanted to be as it is. He sought the help of non-Brahmins but could not succeed in his mission. He therefore favoured conversion to put an end to untouchability. He realized that from within it was difficult to bring about a change because the caste structure has a religious rootedness. It was only an external help that could change the situation and that he called conversion.

For hundreds of years the downtrodden in India remained uneducated. It was with the arrival of the Christian missionaries that they began to go to school and learn. As an educationist he founded the People's Education Society on July 8, 1945 and started Siddharth College on June 20, 1946 in Bombay and Milind College at Auragabad. All this he did to advance the interest of the weaker section of the society. (Jatava, 2008) Ambedkar raised the slogan "educate, organize and agitate" to realize their lost respect and reclaim their humanity. For him education was the main key to open the doors of light, vision and wisdom. He was a great writer who wrote dozens of historic and thought-provoking books. The primary purpose of Ambedkar's life was to encourage people to get educated, know the truth and practice the right path. He recognized that education has a vital force for the individual development and social change. (Jatava, 2004).

POLITICAL AND ECONOMIC THOUGHTS

Ambedkar believed in a democratic system of government and power to the people had been a major concern for him. He was very clear that unless citizens have power in their own hands, there could be no democracy. That is why he says that democracy rests on four premises, where the citizen remains at the centre:

- The individual is an end in itself.
- The individual has certain inalienable rights, which must be guaranteed to him by the Constitution.
- The individual shall not be required to relinquish any of his constitutional rights as a price of any privilege.
- The state shall not delegate power to private persons to govern others.

The core of Dr. Ambedkar's political thinking is contained in two of his statements: firstly the rights are protected not by law but by the social and moral conscience of society; and secondly a democratic form of government presupposes a democratic form of society. Social conscience is the only safeguard of all rights, fundamental or non-fundamental. The prevalent view, that once rights are enacted in a law they are safeguarded, is unwarranted. The formal framework of democracy is of no value. The democracy is essentially a form of society, a mode of associated living. The roots of democracy are to be searched in the social relationship, in the terms of associated life between the people who form a society.

Dr Ambedkar's expertise as a constitutional expert went a long way in enshrining the concepts of political democracy in the Indian Constitution. To him, political democracy cannot last unless there lies at the base of it social democracy. The social democracy is a way of life which recognizes liberty, equality and fraternity as the principles of life. These principles are not to be treated as separate items but in a trinity. They form a union of trinity in the sense that to divorce one from the other is to defeat the very purpose of democracy. Unless there is social democracy, power to the people would remain a distant dream.

Ambedkar knew that mere adoption of a democratic system of government in the Constitution would not be sufficient. Equality in society, equality before law and administration, constitutional morality, lack of tyranny of the majority and developing public conscience are conditions for the success of democracy in India. The foremost condition for democracy, in Ambedkar's opinion, is equality in society as equality is the foundation stone where the notions of liberty and fraternity develop. He remarked that equality is the original notion and respect for human personality is a reflection of it. If equality is denied, everything else may be taken to be denied.

SOCIAL PHILOSOPHY

Dr. Ambedkar was, par excellence, a spokesman of the ignored humanity-the workers, small peasants and landless labourers. He expressed the sorrows of the untouchables and tried sincerely to channel the activities of the depressed classes. In mobilizing them, he created a sense of self-respect and pride in them. He dedicated his life to the cause of removal of untouchability and completely identified himself with the socially segregated section of the Indian society. He launched a life-long crusade for liberating them from their centuries-old enslavement and ostracism. It is this crusade which "lifted him up high from a mere ghetto boy to a legend in his own lifetime". He was born in a family of marginalized community and therefore he had an intense yearning to see that the downtrodden are better placed in social, political and economic fields. He rejected social reforms received as charity and accommodation. He wanted social reforms as of right. He was not so much for peripheral social reforms in Hindu society like widow remarriage and abolition of child marriage. He was for a total reorganization and reconstruction of the Hindu society on two main principles-equality and absence of casteism.

The socially progressive values that Dr. Ambedkar cherished were the basis of his social and political life. Though he was born in the Mahar community, he never represented his own community but represented all those communities which were socially and economically downtrodden. He has been variously described as a crusader for the rights of the depressed classes of India, a literary genius, an eminent educationist, a political philosopher and an able parliamentarian. He was an indefatigable activist who by virtue of his formidable intellectual attributes started a movement for attainment of self-respect for the downtrodden as well as suppressed and depressed classes. He carried on a relentless struggle against the social, political and economic segregation of these classes.

Ambedkar's thinking arose out of his acute dissatisfaction with the anomalous treatment meted out to the people of his community. His mind was preoccupied with the social amelioration, political enlighten, economic well-being and spiritual awakening of the downtrodden. He had a deep faith in fundamental human rights, in the equal rights of man and woman, in the dignity of the individual, in the promotion of better standards of life and, above all, in peace and security in all spheres of human life. He was a champion of a revolution to be brought about by the dynamics of public opinion through a change in the laws of the land. He was not a Utopian, but a realist. He saw a vast difference between a revolution and real social change. A revolution transfers political power from one party to another or one nation to another. The transfer of power must be accompanied by such distribution of power that the result would be a real social change in the relative strength of forces operating in society.

Ambedkar was totally committed to the annihilation of the caste system. According to him, caste system is not merely a division of labour but a division of labourers. It is a hierarchy in which the division of labourers is graded one above other. This division of labour is based on neither natural aptitude nor choice of the individual concerned. It is, therefore, harmful inasmuch as it involves the subordination of man's natural powers and inclinations to the exigencies of social rules. Ambedkar reiterated: the caste system prevents common activity and by preventing it, it has prevented the Hindus from becoming a society with unified life and a consciousness of its own being.

CONCLUSION

The core of Ambedkar's social and political philosophy was liberty, equality and fraternity. To him, a great man must be motivated by the dynamics of a social purpose and must act as the blight and the scavenger of society. These are the elements which distinguish an eminent individual from a great man and constitute his title-deeds to respect and reverence. Indeed, he himself fulfilled all the conditions of being a great man. His title to this dignity rests upon the social purposes he served and in the way he served them. His life is a saga of great struggles and achievements. His message to the people was: by his relevant questions he challenged the divinity and the infallibility of the Hindu *Shastras* which created the society of inequality. According to him a religion which does not contribute to the individual and social wellbeing is of no use. He created rights for the peasants, labourers and untouchables. He fought for their educational and economic emancipation. He can be thus spoken of as the protector of the human rights and an agent of social change for those who were denied of it in the society. Ambedkar's life is itself an inspiration for those who want to be social workers. His life is a journey from slavery to freedom, from inequality to equality and from injustice to social justice.

REFERENCES

1. *Ambedkar and Social Justice*, Vol. I to II, published by the Director, Publication Division, Ministry of Information and Broadcasting, Government of India, New Delhi.
2. *The Hindu* dated December 10, 2006.
3. Jatava, D. R., *B. R. Ambedkar in Modern World*, ABD Publishers, Jaipur, 2008.
4. Jatava, D.R., *Ambedkar: The Prime Mover*, ABD Publications, Jaipur, 2004.
5. Jatava, D.R., *Social Philosophy of B. R. Ambedkar*, Rawat Publications, Jaipur, 1997.
6. Keer, Dhananjay, *Dr. Ambedkar Life and Mission*, Popular Prakashan, Bombay, 1971.
7. Vakil, A.K., *Gandhi-Ambedkar Dispute*, Ashish Publishing House, New Delhi, 1997.
8. Wilkinson, T.S. & M.M. Thomas, *Ambedkar and the Neo-Buddhist Movement*, The Christian Literature Society, Madras, 1972.

9

Ideas and Thoughts of Ambedkar: Their Impact on Indian Politics

– N.V. Aski

Dr. Ambedkar is not a person he is himself of Institution. Ambedkars political views are not evolved around power and authority but his embodiment of social, economic and political thoughts. Ambedkars political thoughts concern with the existing socioeconomic and political order of the society.

Ambedkar was a true and sincere democrat. For him, political democracy without social and economic democracy was a double deception. He warned that as long as there was inequality on the social and economic plane there can be no political democracy, except in name or form. Unlike most of the Indian leaders, he never indulged in unnecessary glorification of the Indian civilization. He frankly pointed out several reasons to the weaknesses from which the Indian society suffering severely. He honestly contended that democracy was a top dressing on the Indian soil which is essentially undemocratic. He believed that constitutional morality is not a national sentiment and it has to be cultivated.

Baba Saheb was a great philosopher of his time. His socio-political philosophy appears in the way of his life. It is a fact that the mahar community and the mahars of Maharastra were known as "a great robust, adaptable, intelligent fighting brave and leading community which he belong to Baba Sahebs socio-political philosophy is based on the philosophy of Mahatma Phooley, Kabir and Budha. He preached this such philosophy viewing that God almighty is one; there is no need for any middleman between man and god and that greatness should not depend on the condition of one's birth. By the inspiration of Kabir, Baba Saheb became a great aversion of casteism and irrational rituals. After suffering from indignities and hatred of untouchability he attracted towards the philosophy of Buddhism in which there was no room for caste discrimination. It was a movement to destroy the gospel of inequality and that it was based on reason, morality and humanity. Baba Saheb inspired so much from the philosophy of Booker T. Washington, a great educator and emancipator, of Negro in America and John Dewey, philosophy of pragmatism which infused a firm believe in Baba Saheb that if man is to enjoy real freedom it is necessary to consider the social conditions conducive to the perpetuation of freedom. He believed that democracy is a way of life which is expounded through the feelings which people have for each other and its success is measured by the effect it has on their lives. Baba Saheb believed in the political philosophy that right is natural and inherent in individual and so individuals have certain inviolable and inalienable rights which built his theory of social and political philosophy further move powerful. In practical life his traumatic experiences of untouchability and his reflection impelled him to make the cause of betterment of the dalits as the mission of his life. He was frank enough to declare, "Whenever there is any conflict of interest, between the country and the dalits, the interest of the Salter will be taken precedence over the interests of the country.... As between the country and myself the country will have precedence, as between the country and the depressed classes, the depressed classes will have the precedence even when Ambedkar entered the Constituent Assembly he was frank enough to admit, "I came into the constituent Assembly with no great aspiration than to safeguard the interest of the scheduled castes." With such supreme commitment to this cause it is no wonder that Ambedkar judged everything and everybody by the standard of their usefulness to the depressed classes.

He has highly affiliation to the western political system which is based on democracy, equality and constitutional morality. He defines democracy not as a form of Government but a way of life that transfers the power or political change without bloodshed. In his writing frequently cited that politics and government should become the platform for social change in which everyone should have equality of opportunity.

His experience as founder of Labor Party as a dethatch in election and as a member of constituent assembly he expressed that "Party and politics should not be a platform for leader worship which we see in our political system that rooted in caste and religious needs."

His political ideas always emblazon the concepts of equality, liberty and fraternity, as the cardinal principles of his political views. He assesses himself as the downtrodden and backwards is still subject to bear with utter discrimination and humiliation due to caste. This glare inequality theep the common people from the sailor of political power. In his political ideas he ascertained reservation in politics for their empowerment and opportunity in politics.

Liberty: According to him, liberty is not merely freedom of speech or expression but free from wants, hungry, unemployment and economic equality with respect to their occupation. So he cited in his writings "economic liberty is the base of equality and democracy."

Fraternity: In his political ideas he gave gravidity emphasis for fraternity. According to him India is a multy layer society based on caste, creed and religion that always cause for imping social harmony and political stability thus nurturing of fraternity should be the duty of individual. Therefore, he added it in fundamental duties.

State Socialism: Means ownership of resources by society, community, everyone should have equal economic resources and economic representation in society.

Democracy: In his political views democracy planned unique nature, he prescribe certain basic principle to sustain of infinity of democracy.

1. Regular periodical Election: According to him election merely not a process for power change and social change. Elections

constitute basic foundation of democracy that should be free from Castism favoritism and repotism that should be based on competency and equality.

2. No tyranny over minority by majority. He advocated tyranny should be removed by majority. To him some less number of caste people also occupied the preview of minority apart from religion.

3. In allied fundamental rights. People should fundament rights in order to presentation, interest, life and dignity in society.

4. Observation of constitutional morality. It means government should give due place to each and every clause of constitution before going to formulate and implement any law, to limit the government and protect rights from arbitrary government.

Women Rights: Dr Ambedkar fought for woman right empowering women with equality, liberty and education. He introduced Hindu code Bill but it is defeated with negative impact on him.

Relevance of Ambedkar Socio-political Philosophy in New Millennium: Dr. Ambedkar was a great emancipator, a supreme social architect and a great social revolutionary. Throughout his life he struggled for the dumb and deaf, the suppressed and the depressed in order to enable them to live with a sense of respect and dignity. He aimed at a great social revolution that would demolish all manmade barriers and would enable all to rise to position warranted by their abilities. He fought for the actualization of "their gradual deliverance from deprivation to development, from social stigma and suffering to social respect solace and equality. The remarkable thing is that he taught his people to self-assert through mass-based action and led many heroic struggles to instill in them a sense of dignity, self-respect and self-assertion. As Narayanan says his whole life was a ceaseless struggle for the attainment of the social objective he had set as his goal for the purpose. He asserted the need of rooting out the idea of inferiority by high or low. He asked them to self elevate, through self-help, self-respect and self-knowledge. He asserted that the inalienable and inviolable nature of rights of individuals and contended that equality meant equal opportunity and making power dependent on inherent qualities. His message to downtrodden was, "be a lion" be your own light." After Maha Tank satyagrah the social and religious struggle of the dalits under the leadership of Ambedkar took a distinct turn. At every depressed class conference, Ambedkar demanded equal rights to untouchables, demanding safeguards for them and denouncing Hinduism Ambedkar invariably exhorted his temple to be manly and to be assertive.

So his political ideas not ideas of politics and power but are convergence of socio-economic women rights. Socialism and above all equality, liberty and fraternity.

REFERENCES

1. V. Dhadra Molwi, "*Dr B.R. Ambedkar: Maand Mission*" Sterling Publication, New Delhi, 1964.
2. Nim Hotilal (ed), "*Thoughts on Dr. Ambedkar*", Siddharth Educational and Cultural Society, Agra, 1969.
3. Chandra Bharill, "*Social and Politcal Ideas of B. R. Ambedkar*" Alekh Publication, Jaipur, 1990.

10

Dr. Bhim Rao Ambedkar

– Dr. M. M. Gondi

Dr. Bhimrao Rao Ambedkar was born in the town of Mhow, Madhya Pradesh (a state in Central India) on April 14, 1891. The Fourteenth child of Ramji and Bhimabai Sakpal Ambavedkar, he belonged to the untouchable Mahar caste. Ambedkar's father was one of the few Mahars who had benefited from colonial rule, and had managed to break away from his traditional caste occupation as a village servant and messenger. At the time of Bhimrao's birth, he was a retired army officer and headmaster in a military school. Thus, Bhimrao was fortunate to receive good education which otherwise would have been denied to him.

Armed with a degree in law and a Doctorate in Philosophy, Dr. Ambedkar now felt fully equipped to fight for the cause of the suppressed classes. In July 1924, he founded the Bahishkrut Hitkaraini Sabha that aimed to uplift the downtrodden socially and politically. The Sabha campaigned for scrapping the caste system from the Hindu religion, started free school for the young and the old and ran reading rooms and libraries. Dr. Ambedkar took the grievances of the "untouchables" to court and got them justice. People affectionately called him "Babasaheb." Dr. Ambedkar firmly believed that education and political organization were the only true avenues for the social and economic upliftment of the suppressed classes.

1920's and 30's represent a turning point in the direction of the Dalit movement. Under the leadership of Ambedkar, the Dalit culture and politics were given a new direction. Ambedkar formed the Independent Labour Party in 1936 and contested the provincial elections. Ambedkar and his candidates won at many places. When India became independent on August 15, 1947, Dr. Ambedkar was appointed Chairman of the Draftingommittee to draft the Constitution of India.

Ambedkar was a leader in the struggle for Indian Independence, the architect of the new nation's Constitution, and the champion of civil rights for the 60 million members of the "untouchable" caste, to which he belonged. He spoke and wrote ceaselessly on behalf of "untouchables," but his passion for justice was broad: in 1950 he resigned from his position as the country's first minister of law when Nehru's cabinet refused to pass the Women's Rights Bill. Ambedkar was committed to maintaining his independence, and many of the positions. he staked out in a long and complex relationship with Gandhi–on the future of Hinduism, for example–remain central to debate within Indian society.

Great Politicians of India and World, 49 Ambedkar received a scholarship to Columbia from the Maharajah of Baroda. He earned his MA in 1915 and then obtained a DSc at the London School of Economics before being awarded his Columbia PhD in 1927. In 1952, Columbia presented him with an honorary doctorate for his service as "a great social reformer and a valiant upholder of human rights." In 1995, a bronze bust of Ambedkar was donated to Lehman Library by the Federation of Ambedkarite and Buddhist Organizations of the United Kingdom.

At Columbia, Ambedkar studied under John Dewey, who inspired many of his ideas about equality and social justice. Ambedkar later recounted that at Columbia he experienced social equality for the first time. "The best friends I have had in my life," he told the New York Times in 1930, "were some of my classmates at Columbia and my great professors, John Dewey, James Shotwell, Edwin Seligman, and James Harvey Robinson.

In September 1920, after accumulating sufficient funds, Ambedkar returned to London to complete his studies. He became a barrister and got a Doctorate in Science. He now considered himself fully equipped to fight the evil of "untouchability." In July 1924, Ambedkar founded the Bahishkrut Hitkaraini Sabha. The aim of the Sabha was to uplift the downtrodden socially and politically and bring them to the level of the others in the Indian society. The Sabha aimed at scrapping the caste system from the Hindu religion. The Sabha started free schools for the young and the old and ran reading rooms and libraries. Dr. Ambedkar took the grievances of the "untouchables" to court and gave them justice. Soon he became a father-figure to the poor and downtrodden and was respectfully called "Babasaheb." On March 19-20, 1927 a conference of the depressed, classes was held at Mahad. Ten thousand delegates, workers and leaders attended. Babasaheb condemned the British for banning the recruitment of "untouchables" into the military.

The next day, the conference decided to implement the resolution passed four years ago to open public places to all, regardless of religion, caste or creed, by drinking from the Chavdar. Taley (Sweet-water Tank)[1]. They walked to the tank and drank from its water. Higher caste Hindus attacked them. They beat the delegates, pulled down the conference pulpit, threw away all the cooked food and broke all the vessels. Ambedkar told his people to stay calm and not to retaliate. Later the Hindus performed rituals to "purify" the "defiled" water. Ambedkar vowed to offer a satyagraha and re-establish his people's right over the water tank.

On December 25 of the same year, thousands responded to Great Politicians of India & World 53 Ambedkar's call. Speaker after speaker spoke, passions rose and the vast gathering waited for the satyagraha to begin with intense anticipation. The satyagraha was deferred when the matter was referred to the court. At the end of conference, a copy of the Manusmruti; the age-old code of the Hindus that gave rise to the caste system was ceremoniously burnt. In a thundering voice, Ambedkar demanded in its place a new smruti, devoid of all social stratification. This act sent shockwaves through the nation. In 1929, Ambedkar made the controversial decision to co-operate with the all-British Simon Commission, which was to look into setting up a responsible Indian Government in India. The Congress decided to boycott the Commission and drafted its own version of a constitution for free India. Unfortunately, the Congress version made no provisions for the depressed classes. Ambedkar became more skeptical of the Congress's commitment to safeguard the rights of the depressed classes. He was invited to the Round Table Conference in London held from November 1930 to January 1931 to represent the depressed classes. He emphatically declared that the before the British came the evil of "untouchability" was rampant and now after 150 years of British rule, this evil had not abated. The British had done nothing to alleviate the status of the depressed classes. He declared that India must have a minimum of Dominion Status. He pressed for a separate electorate for the depressed classes. When a separate electorate was announced for the depressed classes, Gandhiji went on a fast unto death against this decision. Leaders rushed to Dr. Ambedkar to drop the demand for a separate electorate. Ambedkar held fast and did not buckle under the immense pressure. Finally on September 24, 1932, Ambedkar and Gandhiji signed the Poona Pact. According to the pact, the separate electorate demand was replaced with special concessions like reserved seats in the regional legislative assemblies and Central Council of States. On May 27, 1935, Dr. Ambedkar's wife Ramabai died. Ambedkar could not bear the loss of his wife.

He broke down, a shattered man. On October 13, 1935, at conference at Nasik, Dr. Ambedkar reviewed the progress made on the condition of the "untouchables" in the decade since The start of his agitation. Ambedkar declared that their efforts had not borne the kind of results he had expected. He then made a fantastic appeal to the "untouchables." He encouraged them to forsake the Hindu religion and convert to a religion where they would be treated with equality. The nation was shocked. The British Government agreed to hold elections on the provincial level in 1937. The Congress, Muslim League and Hindu Mahasabha started gearing. up for the elections. Dr. Ambedkar set up the Independent Labor Party in August 1936 to contest the elections in the Bombay province. On

February 17, 1937, Ambedkar and many of his candidates won this a thumping majority. Around the same time, the Chavdar Taley water dispute which was referred to the Bombay High Court in 1927, finally handed down its verdict in favor of the depressed classes. Dr. Ambedkar introduced Bills in 1937 to abolish the "khoti" system of land tenure in the Konkan region, the serfdom of agricultural tenants and the Mahar "watan" system of working for the Government as slaves. A clause of an agrarian bill referred to the depressed classes as "Harijans," or people of God. Ambedkar was strongly opposed to this title for the untouchables. He argued that if the "untouchables" were people of God, then all others would be people of monsters. He was against any such reference. But the Indian National Congress succeeded in introducing the term Harijan. Ambedkar felt bitter that they could not have any say in what they were called. On July 15, 1947, the British Parliament passed the act of Indian Independence and on August 15, 1947, India became free[2]. The Constituent Assembly of Independent India appointed a Drafting Committee with Dr. Ambedkar as its Chairman to draft the Constitution of India. Dr. Ambedkar was also invited to join the Cabinet as the Minister of Law. Ambedkar toiled over the Constitution while he took care of his ministry. In February 1948, Dr. Ambedkar presented the Draft Constitution before the people of India. The mammoth effort had taken its toll on Dr. Ambedkar's health. He went to Bombay for treatment and married Dr. Sharada Kabir on April 15, 1948, who worked in the same hospital where he was receiving treatment. The Constituent Assembly adopted the Draft Constitution as the Constitution of India on November 26, 1949 with all its 356 Articles and eight Schedules and Article 11 which abolished untouchability in all forms. In October 1948, Dr. Ambedkar submitted the Hindu Code Bill to the Constituent Assembly in an attempt to codify the Hindu law. The Bill caused great divisions even in the Congress party. Consideration for the bill was postponed to September 1951. When the Bill was taken up it was truncated. A dejected Ambedkar relinquished his position as Law Minister. In May 1956, on Buddha's Anniversary, Dr. Ambedkar announced that on October 14 he would embrace Buddhism. With him his wife and some three lakh followers also converted to the faith. When asked why, Dr. Ambedkar replied, "Why can't you ask this question to yourself and... your forefathers...?" On December 5, 1956, Dr. Bhim Rao Ambedkar died peacefully in his sleep or as the Buddhists would say, he attained "nirvana."

Dr. B.R. Ambedkar completed the writing of the Indian Constitution in February 1948 AD. The discussion was made on this constitution in November 14, 1949. Ambedkar had the moral values like Self improvement, Independence and self confidence which are leads towards the development of society and individual.

REFERENCES

1. Jagadish Gupta, *Biography of grate leaders of India and world,* Bookhive (India), New Delhi, 2006, p.47-55.
2. Basavaraj M and Sanvidhan Shilpi, Dr. B.R. Ambedkar, Kademani, New Delhi, 1978, pp.42-61.

11
Social Philosophical Thoughts of B.R. Ambedkar: A Brief Analysis

– Kartick Chandra Barman

India is a land of many leaders, saints and sages but among them some are remembered as the mission of humanity who lived and died for the cause of mankind. Dr. Ambedkar is one of them who worked for the downtrodden and marginalized tirelessly throughout his life. The Social justice is the fair and just relation between the individual and society. The term social justice is comprehensive having a great social value in providing a stable society and in securing the unity and integrity of the country. In general, social justice may be defined as "the right of the weak, aged, destitute, poor, women, children and other under-privileged persons". This is measured by the explicit and tacit terms for the distribution of wealth, opportunities for personal activity and social privileges.

Ambedkar had strongly argued that social equality, justice and freedom were the pre-requisites for swaraj. Ambedkar produced series of thought provoking writings criticizing social injustice, untouchability and backwardness based on the caste system in India. Social justice is basically a term, which provides sustenance to the rule of law. It has a wider connotation in the sense that it includes economic justice also. The tasks of justice is "just allocation of advantages and disadvantages, preventing the abuse of power, preventing the abuse of liberty the just decision of disputes and adapting to change". The aims of social justice is to remove all kinds of inequalities based on the parameters of caste, race, sex, power, position, wealth and to bring about equal distribution of social justice is a balance between social rights and social controls and providing equal opportunities to all citizens in social and economic affairs. He treated social justice as a grass-root for patriotism and nationalism. According to Ambedkar, the term "social justice" is based upon equality, liberty and fraternity of all human beings. The aim of social justice is to remove all kinds of inequalities based upon caste, race, sex, power, position and wealth.

The social justice brings equal distribution of the social, political and economical resources of the community. Dr. Ambedkar considered that the root cause of social injustice to the Scheduled Castes and Scheduled Tribes is the caste system in Hindu society. He observed, that the castes are enclosed units and it is their conspiracy with clear conscience that compels the ex-communicated to make them into a caste. A civilized society is based on the principles of liberty, equality and fraternity. Dr. B.R. Ambedkar's concept of the ideal society is most relevant to a civilized society and suited to the needs of modern Indian society. Hence this attempts to bring out his contributions towards the attainment of their two human ideas in the society by democratic process. Knowledge about liberty and equality is essential to analyses the social ideology of B.R. Ambedhar and his services to the society.

HUMAN RIGHTS AND SOCIAL JUSTICE

India is one of the largest social democratic countries in the world. Also, its Constitution gives emphasis for the democratic nation and safeguards of the each and every human being. As the constitution of India defines that the marginalized castes must be secured, but, the one section is facing atrocities and exploitation in the various corners of the country in modern period. Further, the violation of human rights and atrocities against downtrodden, it raises question about the government's role and theory of social justice. It is an attempt to identify the reasons for perpetuation of violence on suppressed community in spite of various safeguards provided under the Constitution and legislations enacted by the Parliament over a period of time. In contemporary period, human being reached in 21st century and India has been developed in various perspectives (economic, political, and social). Further the importance of social Justice for development of downtrodden, if Indian Constitution provides Social Justice for all. In this regard, it is imperative to conceptualize the term of social justice. The ideas of social justice applied solely to a particular people or nation with the intention of redressing effects of hierarchical inequalities, particularly inherited inequalities. In other hand, the social justice being a multi-dimensional concept, it has been viewed by scholars of law, philosophy and political science with differences. The term social justice is quite comprehensive. The social justice is a bundle of rights, it is Ambedkar's Vision: Social Justice balancing wheel between upper and down. It is a great social value in providing a stable society and in securing the unity of the country.

The most of moral and political philosophers are treating injustice as the simple absence of justice: as Justice in the time of transition a kind of situation, where the principles of justice are premeditated to manage or eradication of injustice. Plato defined social Justice as, "the principle of a society consisting of different types of men… who have combined the impulse of their need for one another and their concentration on their combination in one society and their concentration on their separate function, have made a whole which is perfect because it is the product of image of the whole of the human mind" it means, his theory of Justice is based upon equal treatments for all human beings but in Indian scenario it is very complex about Justice for the downgraded castes because Indian society is based upon the grading system. In this regard, it is critical to conceptualize the term of Egalitarian society and Hindu Social system. Great people who gave their significant contribution to the welfare of human beings, helped to improve the situation of downtrodden and the oppressed. He fought for human rights. Therefore, Dr. Bhimrao Ambedkar, despite several possibilities has the best excellent in the world because of his unique talent and merit. He also received a law degree.

EDUCATION AND THE BACKWARD SOCIETY

Dr. B.R. Ambedkar was not only the father of Indian Constitution but was a great freedom fighter, political leader, philosopher, thinker, writer, economist, editor, and a revivalist for Buddhism in India. His educational philosophy stresses on development of persons and their environment. Ambedkar strongly believed that education should be provided without any discrimination to all the citizens of independent India. Dr. B.R. Ambedkar, education has the sole purpose to enlighten the depressed classes so as to enhance their cause of social, economic and political upliftment. The social and ethical philosophy of Ambedkar aimed at making the depressed people aware to change their thoughts and old behavior-patterns and to move forward in the direction of unity and freedom through education. The basic theme of his philosophy of education was to inculcate the values of liberty, equality, fraternity, justice and moral character among the boys and girls of all religion, region, class and caste. For Ambedkar, education was the main key to open the doors of light, vision and wisdom. Ambedkar had taken education as the main tool to bring social change. He believed that education can act as a change agent to bring equality in the society. Dr. B.R. Ambedkar had done plentiful to awake the depressed class, to make them aware of their situation, to raise their voice and showed them education as a path for their political, economical and social upliftment. He motivated the Dalits to merge with the upper caste in social, economic and political aspects through the slogan of educate, agitate and organize. Also he ensured educational rights of all sections of Indian society by providing certain rights under the Article 30 and 29 in Indian constitution.

Dr. B.R. Ambedkar wanted an educational system which would serve all. Ambedkar educational model was a socialist one based on Buddhist ideology. According to Ambedkar, the society must be based on reason, and not on traditions of caste system. "The backward classes have come to realize that after all education is the greatest material benefit for which they can fight. We may forgo material benefits, of civilization, but we cannot forgo our right and opportunities to reap the benefit of the highest education to the fullest extent. That is the importance of this question from the point of view of the backward classes who have just realized that without education their existence is not safe." His greatest contribution to the eradication of social evils was fighting for the rights of people called lower castes and untouchables. At the time of preparing the Government of India Act of 1919, advocated independent downtrodden and others from the lowest castes constituencies. He demanded reservation for these communities. Ambedkar started several publications as *Mook Nayak*, a weekly newspaper; *Bahishkrit Bharat*, a newspaper to raise awareness and fight for the rights of low castes and untouchables. He founded Bahishkrit Hitakarini Sabha on July 20, 1924 in Bombay with the aim of creating political and social awareness among the untouchables, and also to make government responsive to their problems; He urged the Dalits and the untouchables "educate, agitate and organize" for their rightful place in society.

He began releasing public movements against discrimination faced by suppressed community as the opening of public water resources for the dalit, burning Manusmriti, an ancient Hindu text that gives sanction the caste system and the rights of people of the lowest to enter Hindu temples. In 1932, after the Third Round Table Conference in Britain, where Dr. Ambedkar part, the British announced the prize infamous community according to which there was a provision of separate electorate in British India to different communities; Therefore, besides also considered as another independent voters; meant that for the choice of seats reserved for dalits only people who could vote were dalits. The scheme is vehemently opposed by Gandhi and other Congress leaders as community and divisive in nature that divides Hindus in two separate groups. But Dr. Ambedkar was in his favor, as it was of the opinion that has more independent voters and would be more number of elected legislators "depressed class". After long and tedious discussions between Ambedkar and congressional leaders Pact Poona was reached on September 25, 1932, according to which the separate electoral system was abolished, but the reservation of seats for the depressed class remains the same; therefore depressed class would not be independent of the Hindus, but the seats are reserved for them. It was an important recognition of the political rights of the depressed class into the fold of Hindu society step. In the same vein, the Constitution of India in 1950 gave benefits reserved for scheduled castes and tribes were referred to earlier as "depressed classes". In Ambedkar's vision of social relations, morality, precisely called as 'Human brotherhood' has been given a prominent place in order to bring men together. Law is important, but it has been given a secondary place. The social and ethical philosophy of Ambedkar encourages the people to organize themselves on the basis of liberty, equality and fraternity. As a humanist, Ambedkar was in favour of imparting the education of human personality.

He had a preference for humanistic education which stands for the effort of man to rediscover himself as a free being rather than as a child of the church or the state. The exercise of one's intellectual powers through education constituted the highest value for man. With the rapid pace of education, Ambedkar saw the nerve of social and moral revolution in the Buddha's religion for the welfare of men in distress. Education would enlighten the depressed classes on the one hand, and on the other, religion would unite them; and that would enhance their cause of social, economic and political revolution. The philosophy of Ambedkar, therefore, is directly related to secular humanistic outlook which is closely linked with liberal education and religious inspiration of non-theistic nature. The social and ethical philosophy of Ambedkar, thus, always aimed at engaging the mind and understanding of the depressed people to change their thoughts and old behavior-patterns and to lift their sight high in the direction of unity and emancipation through education and religion. Education is the process by which man has made the great positive changes in the society and the lifestyle. The importance of education cannot be stated enough. It is a self enlightening process. It is crucial to the overall development of an individual and the society at large. Education for all means has been the most important debate in all stages of society, progress and development.

SOCIAL EQUALITY AND DEMOCRACY

Dr. B.R. Ambedkar held that every citizen of India must be treated equally and should not be deprived of any opportunity and equality based on gender, work and caste differences. Therefore, the social justice for him is associated with social equality and individual rights. He wanted to establish a society in which an individual is the centre of all social purposes, a society which is based on equality, equity of opportunities, liberty and fraternity. Equality is a prominent political ideal of the present day democratic world. It is an essential ingredient for social justice. It constitutes the voice of the oppressed against injustice for changing unfair social conditions. In this sense it is complementary to the principle of liberty. It is essential to understand the nature and essence of equality in order to determine its proper relationship with the principle of liberty. Equality, like liberty, is a prominent political ideal of the present-day world. The French Revolution was fought for "liberty, equality, fraternity". They constitute the voice of the oppressed, the voice against injustice and the voice for changing unfair social conditions. The problem of equality and inequality has figured in political thought since earliest times. Aristotle discovered that inequality was a cause of revolution in many a state.

He defined justice as treating equals equally and unequal unequally. This was a typical statement in that it insisted on recognition and maintenance of existing inequalities in society-between master and slave, between rich and poor, between morally superior and inferior, and so on. The Hindu social order in India has often been accused of being an undemocratic and unjust order wherein a large section of its members are doomed to a permanent degraded life by reason of birth. Ambedkar was a bitter critic of Hinduism. The impact of the principle of inequality is quite apparent and glaring in the Hindu social order. In view of Ambedkar, the Hindu social order does not recognize equal need, equal work or equal ability as the basis of reward for labour. Its motto is that in regard to the distribution of the good things of life, those who are reckoned as the highest must get the most and the best and those who are classified as the lowest must get least and worst. The problem of equality and inequality had figured in political thought since earliest times. Aristotle thought that inequality was the cause of rebellion in many states. The modern idea of equality seeks the correction of the prevailing inequalities insofar as they can be proved to be unjust according to the prevailing social consciousness.

The modern idea of equality is derived from the theory of rights. The term equality has its root in 'Latin'. It refers the sameness in quantity, quality, size and rank for one thing or a person. Equality makes the content of liberty more relevant and substantive. The principle of equality is invoked to prevent some section of society from acquiring unlimited money, power or prestige. It is only intended to restrict the element of 'exploitation' so that other sections of society are not deprived of their due share in these advantages. Further, it aims at widening the base of social benefits lest these benefits are cornered by a small and vocal minority impoverishing the rest of the community. It is evident that liberty and equality are human rights which do not emanate from very different sources. The contribution of Ambedkar towards the upliftment and dignity of the Dalit community is remarkable and phenomenal. The amount of injustice, cruelty, oppression and suppression had given to the Dalits, is simply unbelievable and unforgivable.

He was the only person, who not only tried to wipe out this caste system, but also did his level best to eliminate the hierarchy based caste system. Ideas of high and low had crept into the Hindu society; Ambedkar suffered because of this; he also fought hard against such differences; later he became the first Law Minister in free India. The credit for making a Law and creating the necessary atmosphere to wipe out 'Untouchability' goes to Ambedkar. The 'Untouchables' are Hindus. Therefore, the doors of temples should open to them. If the Hindus can touch the Christians and the Muslims, why should they not touch the people who are themselves Hindus and who worship the Hindu Gods? This was Ambedkar's argument. He gave a call that people who practice and support 'untouchability' should be punished. Some people argue that the 'untouchables' were not yet fit for equality. The Hindus say that they want independence and democracy. Ambedkar is the greatest political thinker. Outwardly this may seem strange that in India, life was the monopoly of the *Brahmin* caste and was completely denied to other castes for thousands of years.

However, here no contradiction is involved. It was the very privileged position assigned to the *Brahmin* that became the cause of the retardation. In Indian society, property, illiteracy, caste distinctions as the positive dangers to democracy. In these situations, educational facilities and economic help should be provided for those who are illiterate and backward on one hand and on the other, who want to wipe on the roots of caste system in order to safeguard the interest of democracy. Ambedkar says, "If you give education to the lower strata of the Indian society which is interested in blowing up the caste systems, the caste system will be blown up". At the moment, the indiscriminate help given to education by the Indian Government and American foundation is going to strengthen the caste system. Giving education to those who want to blow up caste system will improve prospect of democracy in India and put democracy in safer hands. The dignity of the individual, political liberty, social progress and human rights are necessary constitutional safeguards which form Ambedkar's basic decent democratic ideals in the political democracy. To him, the ground plan means the social structure of a community to which the political plan is sought to the applied. Political democracy and liberty are nothing if not beaked and bucked up by equal social patterns, because the political structure rests on the social structure. "Indeed, the social structure," he says "has a profound effect on the political structure. It may modify it in its working. It may nullify it or it may even make a cherry of it." It is therefore, essential that before passing any Judgment on any scheme of political relationship even making plans for economic reforms, the people must consider the ground plan that means social relations; Democracy should be regarded as both a social and a political method.

The constitution of India, chiefly authored by Ambedkar, in its quest of social, economic and political justice offers some special opportunities for the hitherto neglected and oppressed segments of the Indian society such as the SC/STs, socially and educationally backward classes, weaker sections of the people and minorities. Ambedkar firmly defended the inclusion of the Directive Principles of State Policy in the constitution as a great measure for justice. The constitution also provides mechanism to ensure protection of the constitutional rights with a view to creating an egalitarian social order. In order to ensure justice to the most neglected sections of Hindu society, Ambedkar got the untouchability and forced labour abolished and upheld people's fundamental rights. This way the fighter in Ambedkar impressed the builders of new India to recognize the rights of the depressed classes – the shudras and untouchables – to be the respectable human beings in their own homeland. He said, "How long shall we continue to deny equality in our social and economic life? If we continue to deny it for long, we will do so only by putting our political democracy in peril."

THE CASTE SYSTEM AND THE HINDU SOCIETY

The caste system is the result of the Hindu belief in Vedas, Smrtis, Ramayana, Mahabharata and Geeta. The four castes eventually developed into a social assortment of thousands sub castes, with the Untouchables at the end of the list or more precisely outside the grade. Such a rigid caste system is not found anywhere in the world outside India. A person is born into a caste; if born in that caste, his status is determined and absolute. Ambedkar proceeded to offer his own concept of caste. The essence of the caste, according to Ambedkar, is endogamy; caste is not merely a division of labour. It is a hierarchy in which division of labourer is graded one above the other. Caste system involves an attempt to appoint tasks to individuals in advance, selected not on the basis of trained original capabilities, but on that of the social status of the parents. i.e. absence of intermarriage. The birth decides one's status and this cannot be altered irrespective of any talent that a person may develop or wealth a person may collect. The Hindu social system is based up on the tow pillars, first is that caste, and second major pillars that known as Chaturvarnya. It means Hindu social system is based upon the grading which is doing one thing divided to the human society that based on the caste system and killing human spirit.

Further, B. R. Ambedkar argues that the social justice means equal opportunity for all and no discrimination based on caste, sex, religion, gender and region. However, Indian society is based upon the Varnadharma. According to Ambedkar, "..My ideal would be a society based on the liberty, equality and liberty and fraternity... what objection can there to be fraternity? I cannot imagine any. Ideal society should be mobile, should be full of channels for conveying a change taking place in one part to other parts". Further, he especially emphasis on rationality of Hindu social order, which completely negated equality, liberty and fraternity, and also justice for the marginalized groups. Ambedkar argues that Hindu society does not have the specification to be called as a society, because Hindu social system is based upon the caste system and laws of 'Manusmartis'. So, the main problem is the caste system that preventing common activity and it has prevented the Hindu from becoming a society with a unified life and consciousness of its own. Hindu society based upon the isolation and exclusiveness and this is a main feature of the Hindu social system and its main objective is that to prevent to the solidarity of human-hood. In this regard, the caste system only is creating discrimination, violence, crime and inferiority between human beings. In other word, the Hindu Social system is destroying the spirit of welfare and sprit of humanity. Even in modern India, those problems are continuing in different forms.

It is only favour in inequality and exploitation of society and no space for humankind and social justice for human beings. Subsequently, the Hindu social system is deciding work basis on birth neither quality of human and also doing narrow-down rights of women and Dalits. Although, Indian Constitution is based upon on equal participation and social justice for all and no discrimination on the basis of caste, religion, birth, language and place etc. But, reality is totally different, if we examine on the grassroots level, there are many social problems for one section which based on caste and religion. Indian Constitution is describing rights for citizen as freedom of speech, equal treatment, right to religion, right to education and right to vote, etc. there are emphases on the humanity and also maintain socioe--conomic & political participation for all.

It is common experiences that discrimination and crimes going on one section which are associated with Hindu social system. Because, it philosophy is based upon the hierarchy which is fixed by the birth. Subsequently, Ambedkar argued that Hindu Law is established the Brahmanical philosophy. The suppressed class had nothing to do and accept and respect it. They have no right against the upper castes. For them there is no equal right, no justice, which due to them and nothing is allowed to them excluding what the dominant castes are prepared to grant. He believed that liberation of depressed classes is based on education as an educated person can assert their rights and be motivated for development. It not only trains the human mind to think but also to take the right decision to ensure social justice.

According to Dr. B.R. Ambedkar, "It is the education which is the right weapon to cut the social slavery and it is the education which will enlighten the downtrodden masses to come up and gain social status, economic betterment and political freedom". This deep sense of injustice energized Dr. Ambedkar to mount a challenge on the existing social institutions, which he felt, were oppressive in nature. He was passionately critical of the Hindu caste system, which he realized, was at the basis of social, cultural, economic and political subjugation of those who were considered "lower castes". Ambedkar had campaigned against social discrimination and also criticized orthodox Hindu politicians for their discriminatory practices and the perceived reluctance of the Indian political community to fight caste discrimination in our society.

CONCLUSION

Bharata Ratna Dr. B.R. Ambedkar was a man of versatile personality, the great economist, constitutional, social reformer, political thinker, defender of the oppressed and, above all, a great humanist. Throughout his life he fought to establish the basic principles - liberty, equality and fraternity in all areas of life in society. To achieve these use their mental caliber and followed constitutional methods. His whole life was a struggle for the emancipation of the exploited. He had taken the utmost care to write the liberal Constitution so that the citizens of this country to enjoy fundamental rights without discrimination of caste, color and creed, place of birth, religion or sex. His notion of democracy made him stand unique among modern thinkers of democracy. For him, democracy is "a way of life in which the revolutionary changes in the socio-economic code of life of people who are taken without bloodshed`. This it is a testament to his belief in the establishment of a system liberal democratic. This system must end all forms of discrimination and thus establishing a casteless society believes that caste is an obstacle to the growth of the person and the democratic system.

Ambedkar was one of the pioneers of social justice in India. It was Ambedkar who provided new dimensions to the concept of justice. We regard him as the 'Champion of social justice.' He was himself a victim of social injustice, faced its difficulties; and he was not tolerated the injustice, but boldly fought against them. Ambedkar had a liberal concept of justice. Like Gandhi, for Ambedkar, justice is simply another name of liberty, equality and fraternity.' In this sense, the core value of Ambedkar concept of justice is human equality, equal distribution of the welfare materials and discrimination less society. Thus, the spirit of social justice, according to Ambedkar, gives a significant place to mutual sympathy and respect. Due to his commitment to the cause of freedom and social justice for all sections of society and particularly to that of the socially marginalized and much exploited section of our population, i.e., the Scheduled castes, Dr B. R. Ambedkar by his political activism and scholarly work has left an indelible mark, unparalleled so far on our Indian polity as well as our society. Even though much is claimed to be known about his political, social and economic contribution towards public life, yet there has been not a rigorous attempt made at understanding and spread of the philosophical underpinnings and theoretical backgrounds of his world view, which was influenced not only by a scholarly interest but also his personal experience of discrimination and marginalization in Indian society.

In his struggle against such caste based discrimination, Ambedkar had emphasized that emancipation of Dalits in India can be possible only through a three-pronged approach consisting of education, agitation and organization. Hence his writings focused on the secular and modern understanding of human society, besides influenced by a very strong sense of humanism and a firm belief in human dignity and worth. The ideas of Buddha, Kabir, Jyoitba Phule and John Dewey have inspired his revolutionary thinking. Central to Ambedkar's worldview, was Buddha's realist portrayal of the world. This led Ambedkar to show commitment towards the betterment of the material conditions of the Dalits. The concentration of land in the hands of the upper caste had become a mean of that of continuation and furthering of caste hierarchy. This was realized to be responsible for presence of inequality and increased incidence of poverty for the deprived masses. Ambedkar was acutely aware of the contradictions within the Indian society.

REFERENCES

1. Ambedkar, B.R., Caste in India: Their Mechanism, Genesis and Development, Speeches of Ambedkar, Bombay, 1916.
2. Sudershan Aggarwal (ed.), *Dr. B.R. Ambedkar – The Man and His message*, Princeton Hall of India Private Ltd., New Delhi, 1991.
3. D.R. Jatava, *B.R. Ambedkar – Study in Society and Politics*, National Publishing House, Jaipur, 1998. B.S. Murthy, Depressed and Oppressed, S. Chand and Co. Pvt. Ltd., New Delhi, 1994.
4. V.R. Krishna Iyer, '*Dr Ambedkar and the Dalit Future*', B.R. Publishing Corporation, Delhi, 1992.
5. K. David Pandyan, '*Dr. B.R. Ambedkar and the Dynamics of Neo-Buddhism*', Gyan Publishing House, New Delhi, 1985.
6. Raj Kumar, *Ambedkar and Politics*, Commonwealth Publishers Pvt. Ltd., New Delhi, 2011.
7. Nanak Chand Rattu, "*Last Few Years of Dr. Ambedkar*", Amrit Publishing House, New Delhi, 1997.
8. Prem Parakash, "*Ambedkar Politics and Scheduled Castes*", Ashish Publishing House, New Delhi, 1990.
9. Ambedkar, B. R., '*Dr. Babasaheb Ambedkar Writing and Speeches*', Vol.III, Bombay, Department of Education, Government of Maharashtra, 1987.
10. Keer, Dhananjay, '*Dr. Ambedkar: Life and Mission*', Popular Prakashan, Bombay, 1971.

12

Vedic Philosophy and Ambedkar's Social Philosophy: A Comparative Study of Indian Social Construction

Mala Laha

India is a country where different kind of religions are followed for their own spiritual life. Equality in diversity is the main key word of Indian culture. So that we can call India is a secular country. The social construction of India is based on equality, tolerance and national integration. Indian constitution is one of the important parts of our social construction. Dr. Ambedkar was the architect of our constitution. At the end of the nineteenth century Indian society enriched with the birth of a noble person who is well known as Babasaheb, Dr. Bhimrao Ramji Ambedkar. Dr. Ambedkar was born to Bhimabai Sakpal and Ramji on 14th April in Madhya Pradesh. In childhood he was a victim of caste discrimination. He belonged to Hindu Mahar Caste which was created as 'untouchable' by the upper caste. Due to this, Dr. Ambedkar had to face severe discriminations from every corner of the society. Such discrimination experience called Dr. Ambedkar devot his life for the removal social evil like untouchability. According to Ambedkar a society where religion is the motivator of overall human development is called an ideal society. Humanity is the father of all religions. At that time the Hindu caste system was polluted by the narrow minded self centered upper class. Due to this upper class The Hindu caste system was fixed by the law of father identity. In that time lower class always was dominated by the upper class of The Hindu society. But if we minutely observe to the history of our past Indian culture and tradition of Vedic era, any can clearly see that quality and work are the source of social class division.

THE VALUE OF EQUALITY IN *THE UPANISAD*

The Upanisad is the ultimate source of Knowledge of all Vedas. Each and every Upanisad of all vedic branches ultimately believe the path of equality in every part of a society. In The Isopanisad author said that a person who can see himself in the every part of the world is able to achieve the real happy in the world:

यस्तु सर्वाणि भूतान्यात्मन्येवानुपश्यति।
सर्वभूतेषु चात्मानं ततो न विजुगुप्सते।६। ईशोपनिषत्
यस्मिन् सर्वाणि भूतान्यात्मैवाभूद्विजाननः।
तत्र को मोहः कः शोकः एकत्वमनुपश्यतः।७। ईशोपनिषत्

Yastu sarvāṇi bhūtānyātmanyevānupaśyati |
Sarvabhūteṣu cātmānaṁ tato na vijugupsate||6||
Yasmin sarvāṇi bhūtānyātmaivābhūdvijānanaḥ|
Tatra ko mohaḥ kaḥ śokaḥ ekatvamanupaśyataḥ||7||

(Īśopaniṣat)

On the another side we also find the same theory of equality in The Vrihadaranyakopanisad:

पृथिवी सर्वेषां भूतानां मध्वस्यै पृथिव्यै सर्वाणि भूतानि मधु यच्श्चायमस्यां पृथिव्यां तेजोमयोऽमृतमयः पुरुषो यच्श्चायमभ्यात्मं शरीरस्तेजोमयोऽमृतमयः पुरुषोऽयमेव स योऽयमात्मदममृतमिदं ब्रह्मेदं सर्वम्।।१।।

(वृहदारण्यकोपनिषदि द्वितीयाध्याये चतुर्थब्राह्मणम्)

मानुषं सर्वेषां भूतानां मध्वस्य मानुषस्य सर्वाणि भूतानि मधु यच्श्चाऽयमस्मिन्मानुषे तेजोमयोऽमृतमयः पुरुषोऽयमेव स योऽयमात्मेदममृतमिदं ब्रह्मेदं सर्वम्।।१३।।

(वृहदारण्यकोपनिषदि द्वितीयाध्याये चतुर्थब्राह्मणम्)

pṛthivī sarveśāṁ bhūtānāṁ madhvasyai pṛthivyai sarvāṇi bhūtāni madhu yaścāyamasyāṁ pṛthivyaṁ tejomayo'mṛtamayaḥ puruṣo yaścāyamabhyātmaṁ śarīrastejomayo'mṛtamayaḥ puruṣo'yameva sa yo'yamātmadamamṛtamidaṁ brahmedaṁ sarvam ||1||

(Vṛhadārṇyakopaniṣadi dvitīyādhyāye caturthabrāhmaṇam)

mānuṣaṁ sarveṣāṁ bhūtānāṁ madhvasya mānuṣasya sarvāṇi bhūtāni madhu yaścā'yamasminmānuṣe tejomayo'mṛtamayaḥ puruṣo'yameva sa yo' yamātmedamamṛtamidaṁ brahmedaṁ sarvam ||13||

(Vṛhadārṇyakopaniṣadi dvitīyādhyāye caturthabrāhmaṇam)

THE THOUGHT OF VEDIC SOCIETY ABOUT SOCIAL CLASS DIVISIONS

In the Purusa Sukta the four types of social class were mentioned. They are Brahmin, Kshatriya,Vaishya and Sudra.

बाह्मणोऽस्य मुखमासीद्वाहु राजन्यः कृतः।
उरु तदस्य यद्वैश्यः पभ्द्यां शूद्रो अजायत।।

Brāhmaṇo'sya mukhamāsīdvāhu rājanyaḥ kṛtaḥ|
Uru tadaśya yadvaiśyaḥ padbhyāṁ śūdro ajāyata||

(Rig-veda 10/60/12)

According to this mantra The Brahmin was his (God) face,the two arms made (by) the Kashatriyas, the two thights of it were the vaishya and from his two feet was born the Sudra.The important theory which is behind this mantra is the original meaning of four words like 'Brahmin' means not a caste but a person who is enriched with the real knowledge about the Brahm.In the Rgveda Samhita we also observe that a synonims of 'Brahmin' is 'Bipra' which means an intellegent person.

विप्रं विप्रासोऽवसे देव मर्तास उतरे।
अग्निं गीर्भिहवामहे।।

Vipraṁ viprāso'vase deva martāsa utare|
Agniṁ gīrbhihavāmahe|| (Rig-veda 8/2/6)

In this above mantra 'Bipra' which means intelligent person is the pronoun of Agni. On the other hand in the vedic literature the word Kshatriya means physically strong person. For example we can present many mantras from The Veda for evidence.

आ राजाना मह ऋतस्य गोपा सिन्धुपती क्षत्रिया यातमर्वाक्।
इलां नो मित्रावरूणोत वृष्टिमव दिव इन्वतं जीरदानु।।

(Rig-veda 8/64/2)

मो षु वरूण मृन्मयं गृहं राजन्नहं गमम्।
मृला सुक्षत्रा मृलय।। (Rig-veda 7/89/1)

यदेमि प्रस्फुरलिव दृतिर्न ध्मातो अद्रिवः।
मृला सुक्षत्र मृलय।। (Rig-veda 7/89/2)

क्रत्वः समह दीनता प्रतीपं जगमा शुचे।
मृला सुक्षत्र मृलय।। (Rig-veda 7/89/3)

अपां मध्ये तस्थिवांसं तृष्णिविदज्जरितारम्।
मृला सुक्षत्र मृलय।। (Rig-veda 7/89/3)

ā rājānā maha ṛtasya gopā sindhupatī kṣatriyā yātamarvāk|
Ilāṁ no mitrāvaruṇota vṛṣṭimava diva invataṁ jīradānu||
(Rig-veda 8/64/2)

Mo ṣu varuṇa mṛnmayaṁ gṛhaṁ rājannahaṁ gamam|
Mṛlā sukṣatra mṛlaya||(Rig-veda 7/89/1)

Yademi prasphuraliva dṛtirna dhmāto adrivaḥ|
Mṛlā sukṣatra mṛlaya||(Rig-veda 7/89/2)

Kratvaḥ samaha dīnatā pratīpaṁ jagamā śuce|
Mṛlā sukṣatra mṛlaya||(Rig-veda 7/89/3)

Apāṁ madhye tasthivāṁsaṁ tṛṣṇividajjaritāram|
Mṛlā sukṣatra mṛlaya||(Rig-veda 7/89/4)

In those mantras the word sukcatra means the suprim powerfull person in four time by the Rishi. In the Vedic society persons were involved in diffirent work which indicate thier different castes, not castes conformed thier work in the society.For example a mantra which is devoted for Somdeva in the Rgveda Samhita indicates this process of living in the vedic society.

नानानं वा उ नो धियो वि व्रतानि जनानाम्।
तक्षा रिष्टं रुतं भिषाग्ब्रह्मा सुन्वन्तमिच्छतोन्द्रायेन्दो परि स्त्रव।।
इमे ये नार्वाङ्ग परश्चरन्ति न ब्राह्मणासो न सुतेकरासः।
न एते वाचमभिपद्य पापया सिरीस्तन्त्रं तन्वते अप्रजज्ञयः।।

Nānānaṁ vā u no dhiyo vi vratāni janānām|
Takṣā riṣṭaṁ rutaṁ bhiṣagbrahmā sunvantamiccha-
tondrāyendo pari srava||(Rig-veda 9/112/1)

Ime ye nārvāṅna paraścaranti na brāhmaṇāso na sutekarāsaḥ|
Na ete vācamabhipadya pāpayā sirīstantraṁ tanvate
aprajajñayaḥ|| (Rig-veda 10/71/9)

In the mean time we also see that after the creation of the birth oriented caste system nobody can chose their occupation as per to their own wish.

Kāruraham̐ tato bhiṣagupalaprakṣiṇī nanā|
Nānādhiyo vasūyavo'nu gā iava tasthimendrāyendo parisrava||
(Rig-veda 9/112/3)

THE CONCEPT OF SOCIAL ORDER ACCORDING TO *GITA*:

Bhagavad-gita is also known as Gitopanisad. It is the essence of vedic knowledge and one of the most important Upanisad in vedic literature. The spirit of Bhagavad- gita is like a medicine which removes the pain of our human society. But at the same time we must remind that if we want to take a particular medicine then we have to follow the direction written on the level. We cannot take the medicine according to our own whim or the direction of a friend. It must be taken according to the direction on the label or the direction given by a physician. Similarly, Bhagavad-gita should be taken or accepted as it is directed by the speaker himself. The speaker of Bhagavad-gita is Lord Sri Krishna. In the fourth chapter of The Gita Lord Krishna also supports the vedic society, four division of the society on the basis of quality of work.

चातुर्वर्ण्यं मया सृष्टं गुणकर्मविभागतः। (श्रीमद्भगवतगीता ४/१३)
Cāturvaṇyam̐ mayā sṛṣṭam̐ guṇakarmavibhāgataḥ|
(Śrīmadbhagavadgītā 4/13)

Here Lord Krishna is the creator of everything. Everything is born of him, everything is sustained by him and everything after annihilation rests in him. He is therefore, the creator of four divisions of social order, beginning with the intelligent class of men technically called Brahamanas due to their being situated in the mode of goodness. Next is the administrative class, technically called the Ksatriyas due to their being situated in the mode of passion. The mercantile men, called the Vaisyas, are situated in the maxed modes of passion. The Sudras, or the labouer class are situated in the ignorant mode of material nature. The tendency of a particular man toward work is determined by the modes of material nature which he has acquired. In the Mahabharata we also observe this same law of social order.

न योनि नापि संस्कारो न श्रुतं न च सन्ततिः।
कारणानि द्विजत्वस्य वृत्तमेवात्र कारणम्।। (महाभारतम्)

Na yoni nāpi saṁskāro na śrutaṁ na ca santatiḥ|
Kāraṇāni dvijatvasya vṛttamevātra kāraṇam||(Mahābhāratam)

THE VIEW OF *THE SUKRANITI* ABOUT FOUR SOCIAL DIVISIONS

Sukraniti's view also matched with the Veda and the Mahabharata. In this text author says that quality and work are the most powerful condition of social order.

न जात्या ब्राह्मणश्चात्र क्षत्रिया वैश्य एव वा।
न शूद्रो न च वाऐ श्लैच्छो भेदिता गुणकर्मभिः ।। (शुक्रनीति)

Na jātyā brāhmaṇaścātra kṣatriyā vaiśya eva vā|
Na śūdro na ca vāai ślaiccho bheditā guṇākarmabhiḥ||
(Sukraniti)

If we follow the path of Veda, the faith of Srimad Bhagavad Gita and the concept of Sukraniti, then a complete reconstruction of society is possible. In this point of view equality is the main key word of a society. Every caste is equal contribution to build up a society. Everyone deserves respect from that society which they belong to. If we avoid this path many social problems will arise in the society. Dr. Ambedkar had to face several discriminations from every corner of the society. This type of harmful caste system must be abolished from the society. In the construction of Indian constitutions Dr. Ambedkar wanted to eradicate this type of social disease. For that reason Right to Equality is one of the most important and powerful fundamental right of Indian citizens is incorporated in the Indian Constitution. Actually religion is one of a part of a society. It never spoils the society. But some type of narrow minded people polluted their own religion as well as the whole society. Yet a man professes to belong to a particular time and circumstance and thus claims to be a Hindu, Muslim, and Christian, Buddhist or any other religion. Such designations are non-sanatana-dharma. A Hindu may change his faith to become a Muslims or a Christian and both of them may change their as well rendering. But in all circumstances the change of religious faith dose not effect the eternal occupation of rendering service to others. The Hindu, Muslim or Christian in all circumstances is a servant of someone. Factually we all are related to the Supreme Lord in service. The Supreme Lord is the supreme enjoyer and we living entities are his servitors. We are created for His enjoyment and if we participate in that eternal enjoyment with the supreme personality of God head, we become happy.

REFERENCES

1. A.A. Macdonell, Hymns from the Rigveda, London, 1962.
2. A.A. Macdonell, Vedic Mythology, Varanasi, 1963.
3. Anirbana, Vedamimansa (tritya khanda), Sanskrit College, Kolkata, 1965.
4. A.C. Bhaktivedanta Swami Prabhupada (Ed.), 'Bhagavad Gita As It Is', The Macmillan Company, New York, 1964.
5. Anilacandra Basu (ed), Abhijñanasakuntalam, Sanskrit Book Depot, Kolkata, 1999.
6. Dr. B.R. Ambedkar, Hindu Dharma ki Ridal, Goutam Books, Delhi, 2008.
7. Dr. D.R. Jadav, Dr. Ambedkar ka rajneeti darshana, Samata Sahitya Sadan, Jaipur, 1996.
8. Gobindagopala Mukhopadhya, Vedic Sahitya Sankalan, Bardhman, 1965.
9. Hermanu Grassman, Dictionary of the Rigveda, Weisbaden, 1955.
10. K.C. Chatterjee, Vedic Selections, Calcutta University, 1944.
11. Paritosa Thakura, Vedagranthamala, Kolkata,1971.
12. Rameshcandra Datta, Rig-veda Samhita (sastha khanda), Kolkata, 1885.
13. Sitaram Sastri (ed), Rigveda Samhita (sastha khanda), Kolkata, 1933.

13

Ambedkar and Social Justice

– N.P. Koti

The Social Justice is one of the principal concerns for Ambedkar; and this gets clearly reflected in his understanding of the minority issue. Dalits constitute the real minority in Indian society, and there was consequently, a genuine need to safeguard their interests against the Communalism practiced by the Hindu majority. We also looked at the reasons given by Ambedkar to support his claims. We discussed the nature of these safeguards, if Dalits have to live in communal harmony with a Hindu majority. He believed that the rights of a minority can only be secured in a democratic setup and a democratic society. If society is not democratic enough then the violations of the minority rights will go unchecked. He also believed that Indian society due to the dominance of Hindu or Brahmanic values is gravely undemocratic to the core. Hence, there is a need to democratize Indian society.

In resent paper we discuss, Ambedkar's understanding of Indian society in detail. To get clear ideas, it is important to rise the following questions: what are the characteristic features of Indian society that make it undemocratic?; How can Indian society be reformed?; What is Ambedkar' s conception of reform, and how is it different from that of others?

TOWARDS SOCIAL JUSTICE

In response to the highly discriminatory caste-ridden social system that utterly devalued human dignity of Sudras and untouchables, Ambedkar stood determined to eradicate social, educational, and cultural disparities of the lower castes. He was of the view that as long as there was a caste system, there would be outcastes too. He mobilized them with the motto: "educate, agitate and unite." He inculcated in their minds the values of self-respect, dignity, and an urge to fight for their rights. Hinduism, the predominant religion in India, never taught the virtues of liberty, equality and fraternity and, consequently, it could never unite the entire Hindu society.

Ambedkar's first ever public struggle led him to drink water from a public tank named, Choudar-Talab, which was out of bounds for the untouchables. This was an effective agitation because it helped to disrupt the brutal everyday inequality that the untouchables had to suffer as they were not allowed to drink water even from a public tank reserved for the upper castes.

To restore human dignity of the untouchables in society, he sought them a religion that could free the depressed classes from the bondage of caste hierarchy. As he sought to unleash individual human potential, he had to search for a religion that taught the value of liberation. For him, a true religion was one that enabled the upliftment of the individual, irrespective of caste, creed, sex, etc. But the Hindu religion, instead of according equality to all, treated people, especially the untouchables, unjustly. It did not safeguard their interests. Hence this religion did not appeal to Ambedkar. As W.N. Kuber writes, "On 13 October 1935, a provincial conference of the depressed classes was held at Yeola in Nasik district. In his presidential address he announced his decision to leave Hinduism and said, "I was born in Hinduism but I will not die as a Hindu'. After analyzing the Varna mode of Hindu social system, he put forward an appropriate alternative by which the untouchables in Indian society could attain socio-political strength. He proposed Buddhism as the best option which, in his opinion, could shoulder the responsibility of the depressed classes: "Buddhism teaches *prajna* (understanding) as against superstition and supernaturalism, *karuna* (love) and *samata* (equality)... neither God nor soul can save the society... it's a revolt against "parasitic luxury".

He aimed at restoring the untouchables to their rightful status. For that, he rigorously criticized the social negligence of the depressed classes and blamed the British for political and economic backwardness of his community. He was of the view that before considering their political empowerment, it was necessary to extricate them from the bondage of caste system. In the beginning of his fourteen years long struggle against Brahminism, he was deliberately pro-British, as he argued that oppressions within the society should be first eradicated before entering into a freedom struggle. He felt a fight against the foreigners would be shallow if inequality within the society couldn't be eliminated. For national integration, he rightly pointed out "the urgent need of fulfilling the social aspiration of these people for maintaining the unity of India, which can be preserved only through recognizing its diversity." He was the first to recognize this and incorporate it into the Constitution of India. S.R. Bakshi elaborates that" as Babasaheb Ambedkar was well conversant with the socio-economic condition of the backward community of the subcontinent, he wished enthusiastically to do something substantial for them through legislation and social pressure. The way he acted and showed his dedication to the common man who had only an insignificant social position. By his incessant hard work, he took up their cause, gave a severe jolt to the social structure and achieved success in the existing circumstances."

The attitudes and approaches of different leaders were extensively divergent and dissimilar in this regard. Gandhi once stated vigorously that "to destroy caste system and adopt Western European social system means that Hindu must give up the principle of hereditary occupation which is the soul of caste system" (*Navajivan*, 1921). Although Gandhi himself challenged existing caste system in his own way – for example, by asking the members of his ashram to clean toilets – Ambedkar's analysis of caste system and struggle against it was much more radical.

AMBEDKAR VISION OF SOCIAL JUSTICE RELATING TO WOMEN

Dr. B.R. Ambedkar, being a philanthropic, kind and generous social reformer was much moved with the pitiable and pathetic condition and low status of women in society and he was a torch bearer in the direction of social upliftment of women generally and Hindu women specially. Ambedkar chooses his social reform approach only after understanding the reality of the status of women.

Dr. Ambedkar had of the opinion that the Hindu women are tied up with bandage of superstitions which contineous untill their death. They are also responsible for inculcating these wrong notions learnt by them through baseless traditions and preaching of the Shastras in the budding mind of their off spring. Otherwise the women in India have also remained a matter of joy and a source of amusement at such she was used and misused by men guest to serve their evil ends. She has been used just like a machine for procreation. It has also been mentioned in Hindu Shastras that women is the bond slave of her father when she is young, to her husband when she is middle aged and to her son when she is mother.

The reforms introduced by Dr. Ambedkar through 'Hindu Code Bill' have been adhered to and have been accepted by and large. He by codifying Hindu law in respect of marriage, divorce and succession, rationalized and restored the dignity to women. It is needless to say, the Bill was a part of social engineering via law, sharp criticism of this Bill in and outside parliament led many to belief that it might inflict heavy damages on the Hindu society.

Even the president of India Dr. Rajendra Prasad got scared and issued a threat that he would with hold his assent even it had been passed by the parliament. Justice P.B. Gajenedrgadkar while congratulating Dr. Ambedkar for the role he had played in drafting and piloting the Bill said, "If Dr. Ambedkar gives us Hindus our code, his achievement would go down in history as a very eloquent piece of poetic justice indeed". The whole story of Hindu code bill presents the determination of Dr. Ambedkar to bring about the changes in the society. He was the one who just not talked on things; but really worked on them. His concern for women is unquestionable. It is not wrong to say he was a great feminist of his day. Because women's rights form a part of human rights and Babasaheb can rightly be termed as the champion of it.

Dr. Ambedkar says that the women education was denied by the Manu and he caused both an insult and an injury to the women in India. It was an injury because without any justification she was denied the right to acquire knowledge which is the birth right to every human being. It was an insult because after denying her the opportunity to acquire knowledge she was declared to be allowed to take to 'Sanyas' which was regarded as the path to attain the Brahmin. Not only she was denied the right to realize her spiritual potentiality by the Brahmins but she was also declared to be barren of any spiritual potentialities.

According to Ambedkar, women were treated as mere tools to bear the burdens of the family, restricted to the role of bearing children and fulfilling duties of a wife or mother. Division of labour is not in their favour, as a result Indian women have lost their identity. They have to face discrimination on gender basis and because of this availability of equal opportunity for remains a dream of them. Poverty, illiteracy, lack of health and inequality of class of status and powerlessness, degradness are associated with them. Weight of traditional attitudes that regard them as physically, intellectually and socially, inferior to man subject them to male exploitation and unjustified division of labour. A society where women, i.e., the half of the population, enjoy a low status of women in Indian society is primarily due to the fact that they have no control over material and social resources. This is further compounded by lack of participation opportunities in the decision making process of the family.

Ambedkar impartially concentrates on Muslim women also. He starts with the reference to Mother India which created an impression throughout the world that while Hindus were groveling in the mud of social evils and conservative, the Muslims in India were free of them and as compared to the Hindus, were progressive people. Babashaheb Ambedkar takes the help of census report and other data and proves Indian Muslims are equally harsh on their women; of course Muslim law has better provisions for women. But no Muslim girl has the courage to exercise them; there is latitude in their matter of divorce. The wife cannot escape marriage even if it's risk save, the husband can always do it without having to show any course. This destroys the sense of security which is fundamental for a happy life. The right of polygamy and concubine which the Muslim law gives to its men worsens the plight of Women. Ambedkar comments are sharp in saying "Purdah" deprives Muslim women of mental and moral nourishment. The segregation from the outer world makes them engage their minds in petty family quarrels which develop narrow outlook.

In 1936 Dr. Babasaheb Ambedkar delivered a speech at Damodar Hall and addressed to Devadasis, Muralyas and Jogathinis. He gave them a call to come out of their nasty occupation. "Our society has been put to shame because of you, Women are respected in our society, and every society honour's the women of character. Therefore you should forsake this dirty occupation, bring good names to yourself and your society.

Many Devadasis, Muralya's and Jogathinis were impressed by his speech and approached him saying that they wished to come out of their occupations, their marriages were arranged. Ambedkar had a great visionary, he always thought far ahead his contemporaries, he rightly identified that the progress of the community is measured by progress of women. He said so in his address in the All India Depressed Classes women's conference held at Nagapur on July 20, 1942. He identifies that marriage is a liability and says "let each girl who marries stand up to her husband claim to be her husband's friend equal and refuse to be his slave. These words hold good even today, even after passage of six decades.

At present we find a number of women empowerment programmes, concern for women is show-up by all political parties, even though some time just lip service. Whatever is the issue Babasaheb Ambedkar had totality in his views and sixth sense, perhaps because he did not consider himself belonging to these religions. His arguments were without bias and always probed deep and deep in to the real problem center. His reasoning is fine in all this, whether it is the problems of Hindus or Muslims, women of the religion were just dice in their play. This is clearly presented by Ambedkar in his all emancipatory effort.

CONCLUSION

The fundamental meaning of this concept of "Social Justice" is to bring a radical social change in the unequal practice. The main objective of this concept is to uplift the women, Scheduled Castes and Scheduled Tribes and pull them to the main stream of the society. This concept also prevents unjust enrichment at the cost of the weaker sections. So far as Dr. B.R. Ambedkar vision of 'Social Justice' is concerned, he is real earnest, sacrificed his whole life for the amelioration of the women, Scheduled Castes and Scheduled Tribes in the society. He strongly fought against the prevalent caste system and gender discrimination in the society and ventured to secure social justice to these sections of the society. His struggle for social justice could be visualized in the ideals and philosophy of the Indian Constitution. Thus the Constitutional ethos of the social revolution running through the 'preamble', Fundamental Rights and the directive principles expressly emphasize the establishment of an egalitarian social order and based on human values of justice, social, economic and political, equality of status and of opportunity and fraternity assuring human dignity. Thus Dr. Baba Saheb Ambedkar created a social revolution by awaking the women, Scheduled Castes and Scheduled Tribes and breaking all social values based on Hindu Social System.

REFERENCES

1. Mahbal Ram, "*Changing Economic Scenario and Social Justice on India*", Dominent Pub, Delhi, 2003.
2. Article 44 of the Constitution of India.
3. Purohit, B.R., Sandeep Joshi, "*Social Justice in India*", Rawat Pub, Jaipur, 2003.
4. Mohamed Shabbir, "*Ambedkar on Law, Constitution and Social Justice*" Rawat Pub, Jaipur, 2005

14

B.R. Ambedkar's Mission on Radical Social Change

– Dr. T. Chandrasekaran

Dr. B.R. Ambedkar emerged as the leader with outstanding abilities from among the downtrodden classes. He made good use of his opportunities to advance his career and to rise to great heights in national arena. He obtains his doctorate degree from Columbia University and in 1923 became a Barrister in London. On account of his personal achievements and success, he could impress upon his people the need of development in their potentialities for greater achievements in life rather than remain sweepers and scavengers in the society.[1] He instilled in his people a faith to prove their capacity worth and be entitled for equal status and opportunities as other men. He became a symbol of the highest aspirations of the low castes and a guiding sprit of the liberation movement of the downtrodden. He decided to improve the lot of his people through education, agitation and organization. Working for within the ranks of the untouchables he aimed at arousing them to gain self-respect and self evaluation. He became the Lincoln of India.[2]

In order to bring socio political awakening to the depressed classes, he started *Mook Naik*, a fortnightly in Marathi from Bombay on 31 January 1920.The first All India Conference of the depressed classes was held at Nagpur on30, 31 May and 1st June 1920, it was presided by delegates from Bombay and Central Province, Madras and Bengal. The conference resolved among other to have representatives of the depressed classes in Legislative.[3]

Ambedkar realized that words alone would not overcome the tremendous obstacles of social and religious prejudices. Organization was necessary to achieve the goals and impress upon the rest of society, the sincerity of these people who wanted to grow and learn and live like human beings with dignity and equal opportunity in society. These inert and dormant masses lacked courage and needed a vision and a leader. Ambedkar became their messiah and inspired them to struggle for securing their human rights. His whole movement is divided into three phases: social, political, and economic. In July 1924 he organized *Bahishkrit Hitkari Sabha* with a view to secure civil rights for the untouchables by law. In 1923 the government of Bombay issued notification allowing free access of all public places to the untouchables.[4]

Ambedakar founded a Depressed Classes Education Society at Bombay on June 14, 1928. The Bombay Government sanctioned to build five hostels at Panvel, Thane, Nasik, Pune and Dharwad for the special benefit of higher school students belonging to the depressed classes.[5] His main aims were to discus and decide the nature of future constitution of India and to resolve the communal problem. The British Government convened the Round Table Conferences in Londón and invited Ambedkar, as representative of the depressed classes to the said conferences. This was of course, the first occasion when the British Government recognized the depressed classes as a separate element in Indian Politics, which could rightly be attributed to the strenuous effort of Ambedkar. Ambedkar participated in the Round Table conferences.[6] The British Government conceded the demand for separate electorate to the depressed classes put forth by him in the first and second conferences. However due to Mahatma Gandhiji's epic fast against it, he had to accept the Poona pact of 1932, which envisaged joint electorate with reserved seats. During this period he submitted his note on the Indian franchise committee known as Lothian Committee on 1st May 1932. He was trying to prove that depressed classes were not the part of Hindu and thus as a separate class they should be given a separate statutory and constitutional recognition likes Muslims and Christians.[7] When he did not succeed in his mission, he exhorted the depressed classes to convert to Buddhism so that they may have separate recognition as a religious minority for the purpose of representation. In order to protect the political interests of the Scheduled Castes and other weaker sections, he founded the Independent Labour Party on 15 August 1936, when general elections were declared under the Act of 19A, he filled his candidates for certain reserved and non-reserved seats in the Bombay presidency and in central province and Berar.[8] In order to spread higher education among the Scheduled Castes in particular among other. He founded "Peoples Education Society" in Bombay on 8 July 1945,[9] to get social rights to make poor has guaranteed by the constitution of India. In his later life, Ambedkar devoted his intellectual energy towards securing political rights for the depressed classes. Therefore, government should recognize them as a separate entity and grant them special representation so that they might secure rights and better conditions of life through legislation. In a democracy, such a group must be entitled to the right to protection and improvement of its living conditions.

The Independent Labour Party was the first All India political party which comprised exclusively for the Scheduled Castes. Its laws founded by Ambedkar in a national convention of the Scheduled Castes held at Nagpur in 1942. Cripps proposals were condemned because it failed to consider the interests of the depressed class. The separate identity for depressed class and special provision should be given to higher education for the Scheduled Caste people. The untouchables should get adequate representation in the Central and Provincial Ministries. Certain seats should be reserved in the Government services, including separate electorate, separate settlement for Scheduled Caste.[10]

In order to find out the solution to the Indian problem the Cabinet Mission came to India on 24 March 1946. The representatives of various political organizations including Ambedkar on behalf of town trodden community met the cabinet mission. The Cabinet Mission declared its plan on 16 May1946, which contained no reference to the demands of the Scheduled Castes. It was proposed the constituent assembly consisting of 210 members selected by the general electorate would be formed to frame the new constitution. It was proposed that there would be an inter Government composed of the Congress and the Muslim League. Finally both the major parties however accepted the Cabinet Mission Plan.[11]

The role played by Schedule Caste Federation in political and legal fields is of great importance. It could enlist the participation of the Scheduled Castes in politics. It had branches all over the country. Ambedkar was appointed as chief Labour Commissioner along with necessary field staff in 1945. All the activities were done for the development of the Scheduled Caste through this scheduled caste federation. Ambedkar argued that he wanted to secure basic rights for the untouchables in order to establish a healthy and strong society.

Ambedkar got another unique opportunity of being nominated as the first Law Minister of free India in the Cabinet of Pandit Jawarhalal Nehru. Further he was elected as Chairman of the Drafting Committee of the Constituent Assembly on 29 August 1947. He drafted the constitution and presented it to the constituent Assembly on 25 November 1949 for its acceptance. The same constitution after having been accepted with certain modifications by the Constituent Assembly came into force on 26 January 1950. His death on 6 December 1956.[12]

He made provision for the abolition of the untouchability in Indian Constitution. The constitution of the Indian Republic has abolished untouchability and forbidden its practice in any form, while reservation of seats for Scheduled Castes and Scheduled Tribes in the Lok Sabah and State Vidhan Sabah's apart from reservation of seats for them in the services are steps in the right direction. Caste disabilities are fast crumbling under the new democratic setup and economic pressures and the Scheduled Caste are increasingly playing their due role in the national life.[13] He announced the three principles viz liberty for the upliftment of the downtrodden This principles seems to be very simple and apparent; but it is actually complex and comprehensive in its ramifications. It has its own historical background and new meaning and values emanate from it in new circumstances. Each part of this principle is different from the other. Yet all the three are closely related to one another. Each one is dependent on the other and in the social context; the relevance of all the three parts is universal and perpetual. They have their own limitations; yet their implications are varied and valuable. Therefore, before knowing when and why Ambedkar had adopted the first trinity principles it is necessary to understand its background and circumstances, which made the principle of liberty, equality and fraternity possible as a password of social change.[14]

CONCLUSION

We may assert that Ambedkar was very much concerned to bring the ideals of liberty, equality and fraternity in to peoples practical life, not because out of any political expediency, but genuinely as the governing principle in the context of rampant caste inequalities and severe economic disparities in the Indian society. The ideals of democracy and secularism that we have accepted in our constitution would be strengthened only when the people and their representatives recognize and accept the need of constitutional morality as was emphasized by Ambedkar fifty years ago. Practically, we may face many hurdles, harsh and hostile facts; yet sooner or later we have to recognize and practice the tenets of liberty, equality and fraternity, if we want radical changes in our social life in order to solidify the roots of our political system based on democracy, socialism and secularism, which stand as Ambedkar visualized, respectively for freedom, equality and fraternity all leading at the same time towards unity and solidarity of our nation in this highly competing and complex world.[15]

The noble impulses as Ambedkar conceived are the altruistic feelings supported by intelligence, which gain mastery over selfish interests. For Ambedkar the family is a social entity. Intelligence is the leading principle for progress. The progress consists in the development of the human relations, which distinguish man from the brute in the advance of reason and the higher, or nobler impulses. From Ambedkar point of view the nobler impulses lead society to its positivistic stage or to the newer aspects of the progressive stage of humanity. Ethics also play a very important role in establishing right relations between man and man and as such, morality and religion cannot be ignored in sociological and religion cannot be ignored in sociological perspective. Ambedkar was the social thinker to emphasize that everything must be related to humanity that is love, liberty, equality and fraternity that may help individuals to live for others, so humanity is the great being worthy of appreciation that is the central tenet of Ambedkar's sociological thoughts.[16]

According to Ambedkar all phenomena of society are phenomena of human nature generated by outward circumstances to influence the masses of human beings. He did not believe in supernatural governance as the Hindu society is supposed to be governed by the fourfold division of social structure of *Varna* system which was created by *Prajapati*, the supreme creator. In fact Ambedkar rejected such a notion of society. To him there is a progressive change both in the character of the human race and in its outward circumstances. This means that only the human beings determine the social life, which changes from time to time to safeguard the human rights and values. The term "progress" means the development of the consciousness of freedom, equality and fraternity.[17]

Ambedkar's sociological thoughts emphasize that the constitution of the state must be adapted to the conditions and requirements of its people. It is just when it canters equal rights on the people in so far as they are equal. No doubt citizens differ in personal capability in proper qualifications in birth and freedom. Yet the moral sense demands that they be treated equal in-terms of law and opportunity. Ambedkar did not justify "slavery" in any form as the Aristotelian view stood for it. He believed that since man is a social being he can realize his true self (personality) in society based on equal rights. The aim of society must be to produce good individuals who make the aggregate of social life. Its purpose must be to enable the individual members to live a life of social respect and moral responsibility of mutual trust and friendship. Ambedkar as a democrat and humanist stressed the need of "social democracy" where in the freedom and dignity of individual is safeguarded in terms of social mobility and progress. Another aspect of Ambedkar's sociological thoughts is that social facts and values are co-ordinate each other.[18]

Rationalism means the type of philosophy that regards reason as the Chief instrument and test of knowledge. Rationalism in philosophy is primarily a theory of knowledge as opposed to empiricism, which holds that all knowledge comes from perception; it maintains that the most important part of knowledge comes from intellectual insight. At the same time rationalism is that system of philosophy, which asserts that human reason unaided is competent to attain objective truth. One man of the middle classes learned to shape life rationally on the basis of his own foresight. Reasons come to play a new role in political and social life. It was first explicitly formulated by Plato and it reached its highest development in the 17th century. The humanists of renaissance asserted the intrinsic value of man's life before death and the greatness of his potentialities.[19]

Humanism had its roots in the earlier period; but become dominate in the renaissances. With the growth of urban society the ecclesiastical leadership of intellectual, aristocratic and even religious life declined. A literate found the values of monastic culture to restrictive scholasticism was a theology that did not speak of the human conditions. Education was the preserve of ethics and humanism was a revolt against all this. Broadly speaking, liberalism in its classical sense stood for the liberty of the individual's democratic institution and free enterprise. Various 'ism' and western thought like rationalism, individualism, humanism, etc.[20] B.R. Ambedkar concentrated on the implementation of the western thought rationalism, humanism and individualism in his social struggle for the emancipation as the inequality.

The socio-religious awakening of the 19th century was a remarkable feature of modern Indian history. It was a slow process in the beginning. The contact with the West acted as an important stimulus to the awakening movement. According to Sri Aurobindo the Renaissance in India is as inevitable as the rising of tomorrow's sun and the renaissance of a great nation of three hundred millions with so peculiar a temperament, such unique traditions and ideas of life, so powerful an intelligence and so great a mass of potential energies cannot but be one of the most formidable phenomena of the modern world. Ambedkar thus did much to improve the conditions of the untouchables and to incorporate some guarantees within the Indian constitution for securing social, economic and political justice for them.

REFERENCES

1. *Thammukku,* February, 1997, p.1.
2. R.C. Majumdar, et. al., *Modern India,* Bombay, 1986, p.178.
3. *Ibid,* pp.4-5.
4. R.C. Majumdar, *op.cit.,* p.179.
5. *Marutha Malar,* July 1998, p.8.
6. *Dalit Murasu,* August 1997, p.7.
7. Kshirsagar, R.K, *Dalit Movement in India and its Leaders Bliss 1857-1956,* New Delhi, p.160.
8. Bhatia, K.L, *B.R.Ambedkar Social Justice and the Indian Constitution,* New Delhi, 1995, p.163.
9. Chachreak, K.C., *B.R.Ambedkar Patriot, Philosopher, Statesman,* Economic Writing, 1982, p.20.
10. Raja Sekhariah, A.M., *Ambedkar -The Quest for Social Justice,* New Delhi, 1989, p.18.
11. Chaudhary, S.W, *Changing Status of Depressed Castes in Contemporary India,* Delhi, 1998, p.11.
12. Ahir, D.C, *The Legacy of Ambedkar,* Delhi, 1990, p.13.
13. Grover, B.L., Grover, S., *A New Book at Modern Indian History,* New Delhi, 2003, p.410.
14. Jatava, D.R., *Ambedkar and Humanism,* Jaipur, 1999, p.20.
15. *Ibid.* p.39.
16. Idem.
17. Nanda, S.P., *Economic and Social History of Modern India,* New Delhi,1999, p.28.
18. *Ibid,* p.29.
19. Nanda, S.P., *op.cit.,* p.28.
20. Thiyagarajan, J., *Socio -Cultural History of India,* Madurai, 1997, pp.140-141.

15

Dr. B.R. Ambedkar Views on Women Empowerment

Dr. Mustak Ahammad

INTRODUCTION

Women's empowerment is priestly related to the caste system. If we want to empower of women it is necessary to abolish their caste system. It is also necessary to free women from slavery. Because of patriarchy and fundamentalism women are still enjoying secondary position in India. It means they are made slaves by the social set up. We have accepted persistence of inequality that tends to killing of daughters before birth. This is one of the big social problems. So, it is essential to study the thought of Dr. B.R. Ambedkar's on women's empowerment.

Dr. B.R. Ambekar spent his life for the betterment of women who even involve in bad practices like professional thieves or prostitutes. Dr. B.R. Ambedkar created awareness among poor, illiterate women and inspired them to fight against the unjust and social practices like child marriage and devdasi system. Dr. B.R.Ambedkar adequately tried for the inclusion of women's right in the political vocabulary and constitution of India. He insisted on Hindu code bill suggesting the basic improvements and amendments in assembly. He also insisted and evoked all the parliamentary members to help to pass the bill in parliament. Eventually, he resigned as the Law Minister from Nehru's Ministry for the same. Thus, his deep concern and feelings for all round development of women is expressed from his sentence and word.

FIGHT FOR GENDER EQUALITY

Dr. B.R. Ambedkar's approach to women's empowerment is entirely different from other social reformer like, Mahatama Gandhi, Joytiba Phule, Raja Ram Mohan Roy, Panchanan Barma, Iswar Chandra Vidyasagar and others who tried to reform the Hindu society of certain outdated customs and practices without questioning the hierarchical social order. His approach also differed from Bhakti Movement which preached brotherhood without attacking the iniquitous Hindu social order that was based on grade system of caste hierarchy.

Dr. B.R. Ambedkar's mission in life was to challenge the ideological foundations of graded system of caste hierarchy that denied equality, freedom and human dignity to women in Hindu society. He believed that society should be based on reason and not on atrocious tradition of caste system. Therefore, in order to reconstruct Hindu society along with modern democratic ideas of liberty and fraternity he suggests in "The Annihilation of Caste System" that Hindu minds should be purged from thralldom of the shastras. To quote him make every man and woman free from the thralldom of the shastras.

Dr. B.R. Ambedkar began to voice his concern about the low status of women's in Indian society while he was still studying in Columbia University. He perceived education as a catalyst for accelerated change. He began to raise his voice for the liberation of women through his newspaper *Mooknayak* launched in 1920 and *Bahishkrit Bharat* in 1927. Through his writings in these new papers, he raised the issue of gender inequality prevalent in Hindu society and the need of women's education to raise their social status. He involved women in his social reform movements against social evils and demanded socioeconomic and political rights for depressed classes and women.

IMPORTANCE OF WOMEN'S EDUCATION

Dr. B.R. Ambedkar gave importance to women's education. An educated man according to Ambedkar meant a lot of difference to his family, but an educated women would see the progress of two families at a time. Ambedkar "while he had been pursuing his higher studies in America, wrote a congratulatory letter to Jamdar Jadhav of Sangali for having begun to educate his daughter. He further stated in the letter that the parents must share the duty of schooling their children". During the 1927 satyagraha of Mahad Ambedkar appealed to the assembled women that they must realize the significance of education and educate their daughters. He proclaimed that knowledge and education are not the property of men only. He allocated special space for women's education in the objectives of the Bahujan Hitakarani founded in the year 1924 and in the manifesto of the Independent Lab our party set up in 1936

OPPOSITION TO CHILD MARRIAGES

Dr. B.R. Ambedkar was totally against the practice of child marriage. "He thought that child marriages were neither in the interest of men nor women, since they were unscientific. He asserted if the next generation to be healthier, the marriages intended age must be precluded.

One of the important resolution at the satyagraha of Mahad organized under the leadership of Ambedkar between 19th and 20th March 1927, was the demand for the marriage of a male at the age of 20 and that a female at 16.

The impact of the child marriage can be felt in the present situation also. The issues of growing population, malnourished children, diseases among women are some of the result of the age-old unscientific practices in India.

ENCOURAGED PARTICIPATION OF WOMEN IN THE MOVEMENT:

Dr. B.R. Ambedkar motivated the practice of women in all the agitations he undertook in his life time. Women worked along with in all the fight organized by Ambedkar in the interests of the rights of the socially backward communities in India. It all started with the movement for the water of Chavadaar Lake in Mahad. It was followed by the agitations launched for temple entry of the backward communities. The struggles in social participation were also shared by the women under the guidance of Ambedkar. This is also quite sufficient to declare Ambedkar to be a social revolutionary. The suffocated breath of the Dalit women was given relief by his efforts. Women began to attend the public meetings. They started to express themselves by adopting different means of writings. In the Bombay and Vidarbha regions, there came into existence a class of women activists as a result of the work done by Ambedkar, Ramabai Kamble, the women's leaders who organized the mill workers Jaibai chowdhary, the founder of the girl school Virendrabai Teerthkar undertook the task of disseminating education among the deprived and underprivileged people are some of the examples of women who had been essentially inspired by Ambedkar's creed, words and deeds.

HINDU CODE BILL AND EMPOWERMENT OF WOMEN

As the chairman of the Drafting Committee of Constitution Ambedkar did a pioneering work to raise the status of women by granting the fundamental rights to all the citizens irrespective of cast creed, race and sex. Also, as the Law Minister of the Nehru's Cabinet, he introduced on 5th February 1951. The Hindu code Bill. The main aim was to bring about basic change under law in the frame work of the Hindu society on more liberal patterns suited to modern conditions and times through the Hindu code Bill.

It is important to note that Ambedkar's Hindu code Bill was the first attempt to persuade Hindu society to accept its own power and its responsibility in moldings its own destiny. This Bill introduced some important features like women's right to property from parent's property and provision for divorce and abolition of doctrine of the rights by birth. The Bill also insisted on the consent of the wife for the adoption of a daughter by the husband.

There have been concerted attempts at enhancing the status of women in India right from Buddha and Vardhaman Mahaveer and several social reformers and men of learned like Raja Ram Mohan Roy and Mahatama Gandhi. However, Dr. B.R. Ambedkar through the formulation of the Hindu code Bill is supposed to have unprecedentedly contributed to the development of Indian women by virtue of fundamental constitutional provisions. He was of the opinion that women must have the financial rights, which happen to be the only way for benefiting then from the other rights. In addition, the women must be allowed the rights to seek divorce, alimony, adoption, registered marriage, inter-caste marriage and inheritance Ambedkar incorporated in the Hindu code Bill. The women, who had been deprived of for ages together, were to get their due rights through the Hindu code Bill. The manu, the code of Hindus had deprived women of their fundamental rights. Dr. B.R. Ambedkar was all set to help the women in India to overcome centuries, old misery by means of the creation of Hindu code Bill. His sole intention was to revive the glorious status of women, but the Bill was not passed in the parliament. As result, Dr. B.R. Ambedkar resigned as the central minister.

CONCLUSIONS

In the condolence message, on Ambedkar's death in Parliament, Prime Minister Jawaharlal Nehru said "Dr. Babasaheb Ambedkar was a symbol of revolt against all oppressive features of Hindu society". His dream of society, based on gender equality is yet to be realized and therefore his thoughts are important for the social reconstruction that favors women empowerment. Dr. Babasaheb expressed his views on the state of life of all women. He stated that women must be treated equally and given equal prestige. He insisted on Hindu Code bill suggesting the basic improvements and amendments in assembly. He also insisted and evoked all the parliamentary members to help to pass the bill in parliament. Eventually, it was happened. The teachings and thoughts of Dr. Ambedkar are useful not only women but also all the Indians even today. His deep concern and feelings for all round development of women is expressed from his each sentence and word. In his last speech in Indian Parliament we can know his feelings and respects showed towards women. He quoted the famous thoughts of an Irish Patriot Daniel O Connal as, "No man can be grateful at the cost of his honour, no woman can be grateful at the cost of her chastity. And no nation can be grateful at the cost of her liberty." In his famous book "*Pakistan and Partition of India*" he expressed his views about Muslim women and their religious traditions, about wearing veil, their marriages and so on.

Muslim women were suppressed under various religious traditions. Towards all women, irrespective of their religion, casts and class, Babasaheb had a particular humanitarianism view. He frequently raised his voice against all sorts of injustice towards women.

REFERENCES

1. Ambedkar, B.R., '*Dr Babasaheb Ambedkar writing and speeches*', Govt. of Maharashtra, Education Department, Vol. 1 to 21.
2. Ambedkar, B.R., '*Babasaheb Ambedkar ka Sampurn Vangmaya* (Hindi)', Govt. of India, Welfare Department, New Delhi, 1993.
3. Ambedkar, B.R., '*Budha Ki Karl Mart*', Sugava Prakashan, Pune, 1992.
4. Ambedkar, B.R., '*Mazzi Aatmakutha*', Gajendra Raghvansi, Pune, 2008.
5. Ambedkar, B.R., '*The Rise and fall of Hindu women*', Bhim Patrika Publication, Jalandhar, 1974.

16

B.R. Ambedkar: Champion of the Women Empowerment

– Sanjay Prasad

INTRODUCTION

It is believed that in Ancient India, women enjoyed equal status with men in all aspects of life. It is a culture whose only words for strength and power are feminine-"*shakti*" means "power" and "strength", male power comes from the feminine. In Vedic times, women and men were equal as far as education and religion was concerned. However, with the passage of time, position of women went down. With the expansion of Vedic religion in Northern India and possibly also under the impacts of threats from the outside, a new definition of the place of women in the Aryan society emerged, which amounted to increasing restrictions of their independence and a clear dominance of patriarchal rule. It appears from *Smritis* that on the whole, women were respected. But we also find that certain restrictions were also being imposed on them. Medieval India was considered the "Dark Age" for Indian women. The status of women in Modern India is a sort of paradox. If on one hand, she is at the back of ladder of success, on the other hand, she is mutely suffering the violence afflicted on her by her own family members and society. In such a situation, Dr. B.R. Ambedkar and other social reformers like Raja Rammohan Roy, Iswar Chandra Vidyasagar, Swami Vivekananda, Jotiba Phule raised their forceful voices in favour of women. The present paper is an attempt to highlight the efforts undertaken by Dr. Ambedkar for the empowerment of women in India.

STRUGGLE FOR GENDER EQUALITY

Dr. Ambedkar was an educationist, economist and administrator. Besides this, he was a social reformer, political thinker, parliamentarian and constitution expert of high order. He possessed many rare qualities of head and heart.[1] As far as Dr. Ambedkar's approach to women's empowerment was concerned, it was entirely different from other social reformers like Raja Rammohan Roy, Vidyasagar, Mahatma Gandhi, who tried to reform the Hindu society of certain outdated customs and practices without questioning the hierarchical social order. He believed that society should be based on reason and not on atrocious tradition of caste system. Therefore, in order to reconstruct the Hindu society along modern democratic ideas of liberty, equality and fraternity, the ideological foundations of the graded system of caste hierarchy must be defied.[2] In "*The Annihilation of Caste System*", he writes, "Make every man and woman free from the thralldom of the *Shastras*, cleanse their minds of the pernicious notions founded on the *Shastras* and he or she will inter-dine and inter-marry without your telling him or her to do so." He referred to education, inter-caste marriage and inter-dinning as tools by which caste and patriarchy maintained through endogamy can be eliminated.

Dr. Ambedkar demanded separate electorate and reserved seats for the depressed classes in proportion to their population. After fifty years of the implementation of the Indian Constitution, the demand of the Indian women for political reservation and the lower and poor status of other non-privileged sections prove that this theory is correct. Dr. Ambedkar launched his movement in 1920. He said, "We shall see better days soon and our progress will be greatly accelerated if male education is persuaded side by side with female education". He started fierce propaganda against the Hindu social order and launched a journal *Mook Nayak* in 1920 and *Bahishkrit Bharat* in 1927 for this purpose. The journals also aimed to upgrade the social status and to motivate women to participate in social reform movements against social evils and demanded for their socio-economic rights as the societal positioning of the women were not at par with men and were deprived from the basic rights, and were equated with animals and put to the lowest position of humanity.[4]

Dr. Ambedkar championed the cause of women as well as the miserable plight of Scheduled Castes and Scheduled Tribes throughout his career. He discussed a number of problems of Indian women and sought for their solutions in Bombay Legislative Council in the Viceroy's Assembly as the champion of the Drafting Committee and also in the Parliament as the first Law Minister of independent India. He was sworn in as a nominated member of the Bombay Legislative Council in 1927. He advised Indians to participate in the world war on behalf of the British Government. He argued for the Maternity Benefit Bill and birth control which were quite relevant to recognize the dignity and honour of the women. He stated, "It is in the interest of the nation that the mother ought to get a certain amount of rest during the pre-natal period and also subsequently, and the principle of the Bill is based entirely on that principle." He was a great believer of women's organization and in their strength of improving the condition of the society. In his movement of 1920, women actively participated and started acquiring confidence to voice their issue on various platforms by participating in Satyagrahas and setting up women's association for dalit women to spread education and awareness.[5] He exclaimed, "I strongly believe in the movements run by women. If they are truly taken into .confidence, they may change the present scene of society which is very miserable. In past, they have played a significant role in improving the condition of weaker section and classes". In 1927, Dr. Ambedkar launched the Mahad Satyagraha. In this historic march, thousands of men and women were accompanied to assert their rights to take water from Chawdar tank at Mahad. The movement aimed to liberate society from outworn traditions and evil customs imposed ruthlessly and upheld religiously by a vast majority society upon to its weaker and helpless constituent and to restore human rights and dignity to women.[6]

In January, 1928, a women's association was established in Bombay with Ramabai, Ambedkar's wife as its president. Along with the Depressed Classe's Conference in Nagpur in August, 1930, women also held their separate conference. In the famous Kalaram temple entry movement at Nashik, a non-violent styagraha launched in March, 1930, about five hundred women participated in it and many of them were arrested along with men and ill-treated in jails. To face tortures along with their men, women also organized their Samata Sainik Dal. When Dr. Ambedkar returned to India after attending the Round Table Conference in 1932, hundreds of women were present for joining the committee meetings. At various places, depressed classes women's conferences were held and they began to present their demands assertively. This encouragement by Dr. Ambedkar caused empowered women to speak out boldly their feelings. In a press conference held in 1931, Radhabai Vadale said, "We should get the right to enter the Hindu temples, to take water at their water sources. We call these social rights. It is better to die a hundred times than to live a life full of humiliation. We will sacrifice our lives but we will win our rights". The credit for this self-respect and firm determination of women goes to Dr. Ambedkar.[7]

Dr. Ambedkar believed in the strength of women and their role in the process of social reforms. He said, "I measure the progress of community by the degree of progress which women had achieved. Let every girl who marries stand by her husband, claim to be her husband's friend and equal, and refuse to be his slave. I am sure if you allow this advice, you will bring honour and glory to yourselves." Under the leadership of their savior, the downtrodden, the dehumanized and dumb millions opened a new chapter in the annals of India. They not only voiced their age-old grievances but also took on themselves energetically to mitigate them. They now summoned up courage and showed the right spirit in standing boldly and shaking off the dust from their feet, faces and future.[8] The All India Dalit Mahila Conference was organized on 20th July, 1942, wherein 25,000 women attended under the Presidentship of Sulochanabai Dongre. Ambedkar was highly pleased with the awakening and activities of women. On 6th January, 1945, the All India Untouchable Women's Conference was held in Bombay.[9] Gaining inspiration and encouragement from Ambedkar, many women wrote on topics like gender equality, planning, Buddhist philosophy and others. The extent of awakening achieved among the women of downtrodden classes was visible from the fact that the Women's Conference demanded abolition of polygamy and urged institutions to provide pensions and leave with pay for women workers.

Since Ambedkar was well aware of the status of women as the Chairman of the Drafting Committee, he tried in adequate inclusion of women's rights in the political vocabulary and constitution of India. Therefore, by considering women's equality both in formal and substantial senses, he included special provisions for women, while all other general provisions were applicable to them, as to men. His key work in the preparation of the Indian Constitution made it to be known as a New Charter of Human Rights. He looked upon Law as the instrument of creating a sane social order in which the development of individual should be in harmony with the growth of society. As the Law Minister, Dr. B.R. Ambedkar introduced the Hindu Code Bill in the Parliament in 1951 so as to codify the Hindu Laws pertaining to marriage, divorce, inheritance that sought to give equal rights to women as well men in these aspects. However, the Bill was strongly opposed by orthodox Hindus opining that it would lead to break-up the Hindu social order, if the Bill was passed in that form. The government lacked political will to pilot the Bill through the Parliament and decided to withdraw it. To register his protest against government inaction, Dr. Ambedkar resigned from the Union cabinet. His explanations for resignation show how the parliament of independent India deprived its women citizens of even basic rights.[10] He proved that he was champion of social justice. His economic ideas were based on the state of socialism which he has reflected in Indian Constitution at different places. It has been pointed out that social justice is a part of governance reflected in Indian Constitution.[11]

The strong disagreements of Dr. Ambedkar with Hindu ideals compelled him to embrace Buddhism as his religion. In a speech at Nagpur in 1956, he said that according to the tenets of Hinduism, only the so called higher castes have been benefitted. *Sudras* and dalits have nothing much to gain from it. As soon as the wife of a Brahmin conceives, she thinks of the High Court, whether any post of a judge has fallen vacant for the foet in womb but when our woman become pregnant, she cannot think of anything better than a sweeper's post under the Municipal council. He concluded that the Hinduism would ruin the Hindus and ultimately India. The *Mahaparinirvan* of Dr. Ambedkar, who was recognized internationally as a crusader against caste system, a vigilant fighter for the human rights of all the oppressed and enslaved and the emancipator of humanity from social and economic injustices, took place on 6th December, 1956. In the condolence message on Ambedkar's death, the then Prime Minister, Jawaharlal Nehru remarked in the Parliament, "Dr. Baba Saheb Ambedkar was a symbol of revolt against all oppressive features of the Hindu society". His dream of society based on gender equality is yet to be materialized and therefore his thoughts are important for the social reconstruction that favours women's empowerment.

CONCLUSION

Dr. Ambedkar was one of the greatest intellectual and social reformers of modern India, who stood throughout his life for the emancipation of Indian women from the bondage of different social institutions of Hinduism. Not only the women society, rather all the people of India can take pride for the tremendous steps undertaken by Dr. Ambedkar for the empowerment of women. It may be noted in this connection that Dr. Ambedkar was not averse to Hinduism, rather he was against un-religious acts in the name of Hinduism. Dr. Ambedkar's feelings about the women of Indian society can be understood from his following statement, "Unity is meaningless without the accompaniment of women. Education is fruitless without educated women and agitation is incomplete without the strength of women."

REFERENCES

1. Chanchreek, K.L., *Dr. B. R. Ambedkar*, H. K. Publishers & Distributors, Delhi, 1991, p.11.
2. Barnawal, Bijay K., Dr. B.R. Ambedkar's Quest for Gender Equality-It's Relevance in Contemporary Feminist Discourse, *Online International Interdisciplinary Research Journal*, Bi-Monthly, Vol. IV, Issue- II, March-April, 2014. p.393.
3. Ambedkar, B.R., "*The Annihilation of Caste*", Text of the Presidential Address to Jat-Pat-Todak Mandal Annual Meeting, Lahore, 1935, p.17.

4. S. Mohammad, Azad, Dr. Ambedkar and Gender Equality, *Proceedings of Third International Symposium (SEUSL)*, pp.117-121.
5. More, Vijay G., Dr. B. R. Ambedkar's Contribution for Women's Rights, Variorum, *Multi-Disciplinary e-Research Journal*, Vol. 02, Issue-I, August, 2011, pp.1-8.
6. Bharati, T., Ambedkar and Uplift of Women, published in an edited book, "*Ambedkar and Social Justice*", Vol. II, 1992, p.264.
7. Singariya, M.R., Dr. B. R. Ambedkar and Women Empowerment in India, Quest Journals, *Journal of Research in Humanities and Social Science*, Volume 2, Issue-1, 2014, pp.1-4.
8. Keer, Dhananjay, *Dr. Ambedkar: Life and Mission*, Popular Prakashan, Mumbai, 1990, p.77.
9. Limaye, Champa, *Women: Power and Progress*, B.R. Publishing Corporation, New Delhi, 1999, pp.57-61.
10. Haksar, Nandita, *Demystification of Law for Women*, Lancer Press, New Delhi, 1986, pp.56-57.
11. Rao, R.V.R. Chandrasekhara, *Indian Constitution and Polity*, Sterling Publishers Pvt. Ltd., New Delhi, 1991, p.34.

17
Ambedkar on Human Society

– Soumyajit Sen

B.R. Ambedkar is one of the prominent mythological wishing gem and social reformer of India. Ambedkar was born on 14th April, 1891 A.D. in a family of mahar community of lower caste of Mahau region in central India. The full name of Ambedkar is Bhimrao Ramoji Ambedkar. His ancestors were the original residents of village Ambabhate of Ratnagiri district. His ancestors took the surname as 'Ambedkar' from the name of this village. He was the 14th and youngest son of father Ramji Maloji Ambedkar and mother Bhimabai. His father was a salaried worker of the British. Ambedkar was very much attentive in his education from his childhood. He became graduate in Parse and English in the year 1913 A.D. from the Elphinstone College of Bombay.[1] He got Doctorate degree from the Colombia University and got D.Sc. degree in Economics from the London School of Economics. He took education not only in Economics but also in Law. He died on 6th December, 1956 A.D.

Ambedkar was not a bookworm. He tried to make practical application of his knowledge that acquired from book in a reality. He protested against the caste-distinction. He faced opposition from caste-system since his boyhood. His place was outside his class-room at the time of learning in School as he belongs to a lower caste family. The teachers of his School did not touch his books. He could not drink water from pots those used by others. Though he had great intention he was deprived from getting education in Sanskrit for the reason that he come from a lower caste family. An indomitable intention was grown in his mind due to the problems he faced in his life. He decided to unearth the roots of those problems. As such he attentively engaged himself as a social reformer after completion of his education.

Ambedkar never agreed with the caste-system of Hindu religion. He struggled against it throughout life. He would think that four caste-system of the Hindu society is nothing but strike of a strong on a weak. He believed that it is immoral and inhuman to make divisions of men into four castes on the basis of their occupation. He believed that there is no such caste system in any religion. Shudras, the lowest level position holder of caste system were untouchable. They had no opportunity, advantage and dignity in the society. Ambedkar tried to show that there is no separate caste as Shudra in Rig Veda. They enjoyed the same right like Kshatriya at that time.[2] Ambedkar told about the untouchability of the Hindu society, "The Hindu civilization could hardly be called a civilization. It is diabolical to suppress and enslave humanity."[3]

Ambedkar did not accept the explanation given in the Hindu scriptures about family, community, race and caste. He told that it is totally wrong to make an effort to show Shudras as non-Aryan. He told that the works those we don't like in our society and the persons who do these works are not in our likings. So we place them as lower caste in our society. But it is a matter of thinking that whether the work too is not as important as the other works in our society. All works (professions) were same important to him. He believed that it is great harmful for our society to make division of society by the division of caste. He wanted awakening of men by proper humanity, morality, free from superstation by keeping faith on science amongst the people. He tried to break the wall that built in the Hindu society to make divisions amongst men by caste-system. He understood that the logical principle had to be adopted amongst the men. Good fraternal loves amongst the people have to be grown.

Ambedkar understood that social balance is not possible without the economic equality. He watched the poor economic shape of lower caste family of the Hindu society. In one side the British imperialist and on the other side the upper caste people of our country were amongst that extortion. He believed that the British administration is very much harmful for the people belonging to lower caste. The rate of extortion was too much upon the lower caste due to lack of education amongst them which caused them could not causes to identify their enemy. As such they were cheated several times. The British repeatedly enhanced their tax amount as a weapon of extortion and the people belonging to lower caste endured that without any objection. People belonging to upper caste able to realize some advantage in their favour but the people belonging to lower caste people could not do that out of their fear. Also, the contribution of lower caste in the national movement had no recognition while only the upper caste people got recognition for it.

Ambedkar protested against the economic extortion upon the people of lower caste. He represented for this people throughout his entire life. He watched the landlords imposed the burden of enhanced tax on the farmers and lived in perfect health when the British enhanced the tax on cultivated land. He protested against the system of land lordship and ownership of a proprietary over a vast area of agricultural farm. He strongly expressed his views in favour of farmers about giving up of agricultural land to them.

Ambedkar formed 'Bahiskrut Hitkarini Sabha' in the year 1924 in order to uphold the demand of lower caste people. Not only that he took the responsibility of editing of a Patrika named '*Bahiskrut Bharat*' in order to bring about the state of people of lower caste for the knowledge of all.

INTUC, led by Congress labour organisation could not be able to influence him much. So, he formed Independent Labour Party (ILP) in the month of August, 1936, in order to fight against the caste system of the Hindu society and the capitalistic system that makes extortion to the labourers.[4] The main objectives of this organisation were:[5]

(i) Giving more stress on national industrialisation.

(ii) Enacting strong labour law for the worker of a factory. Ascertain time period of work (8 hours work a day) and holiday.

(iii) To end the system of Jagir.

The political concept of Ambedkar was driven by his social concept. He never looked at the state as like as anarchist concept of Gandhiji. Also, he never agreed that the state as a weapon of an extortion of caste like the persons who believe in Marxism. In his opinion the state should be the sympathetic guardian of people of the country. The state should bring happiness, peace, prosperity for her people. Also stringent measures have to be taken by the state for the practice of extortion by the upper caste upon the lower caste. State must protect the weaker at the time of oppression upon them by the stronger. In his opinion the intention of laws of a state is to awaken the social animate and morality.[6]

Ambedkar had some different ideas about democracy. He did not like customary administration process in democracy by the wining party. He believed that the people of lower caste with a few elected representatives subjected to extortion it in the society repeatedly. The number gives political advantages to one community over another and the Indian National Congress is not very conscious of advancing the lower caste minority he added. He had an idea that our majority is essentially caste majority, similar minority is caste minority. So majority is a permanent majority and minority is a permanent minority.' He made it clear that democracy admits people's representatives with a political majority. Communal majority of born not made.

Ambedkar played the most important role as the maker of Indian constitution. The Colombia University awarded him L.L.D., the highest honour of law for his important role for the composition of constitution of India. He mentioned untouch-ability is unlawful in the manuscript of constitution and made arrangement for the reservation through 'Directive Principle' in government institution for education and employment.

The entire thinking (social, economic and political) of Ambedkar was about the deriving of equal dignity of people of lower caste with the others in the society. For the benefit of the people belonging to lower caste he formed Schedule Caste Federation, a republican group in the year 1956, and he tried to realize the demand of the people belonging to lower caste by bringing them in this group.

He had disgust in his mind for the caste system of the Hindu religion. He was attracted by the Buddhism as it has no caste-system. So, he along with his wife and 5 lakh supporters (approx.) embraced Buddhism in a historical gathering at Nagpur in the year 1956.[7] According to Sekhar Bandhyopadhyay, this event is often celebrated as an ultimate public act of dissent against Hinduism that was beyond reform.[8]

Ambedkar was a socialist. Social balance is more important to him than economic balance of Marx. He wanted to establish social balance and to abolish difference amongst men by the abolition of caste and religion. He believed that social extortion is the root of economic extortion. So, social extortion must have to be removed. Then there could be the abolition of economic extortion. Otherwise abolition of economic extortion is not possible. According to him, "Without the reform of the social order no economic reform is possible; caste is a monster that crosses your path. You cannot have political reform; you cannot have economic reform unless you kill this monster."[9]

If we look at the time of Ambedkar, we can understand that most of his education, work and life he devoted during the British India for the cause of casteless and classless society in India. But he was at a great distance from the freedom movement of India. The degree at which he was vocal for the freedom of India is too little with respect to his protest against caste system of the Hindu religion and its conservativeness. His arrangement for reservation for the minor community is participating till now since their problems alive even today. In spite of that it can be said that his heart would cry for the people belonging to lower caste as his feelings attempts, efforts and struggles he devoted for the freedom of lower of layer of people throughout his life.

REFERENCES

1. Banerjee, Dube, Ishita, *A History of Modern India*, Delhi, 2015, p.356.
2. Dr. B.R. Ambedkar, *Who were Shudras*, Bombay, 1970, pp.121-144.
3. Ibid, *A History of Modern India*, p.357.

4. Mendelson, Olive, Marik, *The Untouchables: Subordination, Poverty and the State in Modern India*, CUP, 1988, p.115.
5. Mahendra Prasad Sing and H. Roy, *Indian Political Thoughts: Themes and Thinkers*, Pearson Education India, New Delhi, 2011, p.228.
6. S. Bandhopadhyay, *Plassey Theke Partition*, Kolkata, 2011, p.418.
7. https://en.wikipedia.org/wiki/B._R._Ambedkar
8. S. Bandhopadhyay, *From Plassey to Partition*, Delhi, 2006, p.357.
9. Ambedkar, *Annihilation of Caste with Reply to Mahatma Gandhi*, Bombay, 1935, p.122.

18

B.R. Ambedkar's Idea on Economic Development: An Indian Perspective

– Bedadyuti Barman

> "I know today we are divided politically, socially and economically. We are in warring camps and I am probably one of the leaders of a warring camp. But with all this I am convinced that, given time and circumstances, nothing in the world will prevent this country from becoming one, and, with all our castes and creeds, I have not hesitation in saying that we shall in some form be a united people".
>
> – Dr. B.R. Ambedkar

INTRODUCTION

Whenever any country faces difficult situations, challenges, whether it is a political or economic, the intellectuals and politicians at some point or another need to search their own country's history for the solutions. Dr. Babasaheb Ambedkar is one such great thinker, leader and intellectual of his time in India who has not only changed the life of millions of untouchables but shaped India as a biggest democratic nation by writing its constitution. What is well known about Dr. Ambedkar is his fights against Caste system in India, But what is not known is how Dr. Babasaheb Ambedkar had also Impacted the Indian economy.

Dr. B.R. Ambedkar, the architect of Indian Constitution, came at the appropriate moment in British ruled India to assume the natural leadership of his kinsmen and participated in social movement and got involved in founding the constitutional edifice of the country.

In contemporary India, the Society is undergoing a very rapid transformation at all levels. While establishing an ideal society based on equality, justice, liberty and fraternity, the ideas, thoughts and contributions of Bharat Ratna Dr. Baba Saheb Bhimrao Ramji Ambedkar are indispensible. Therefore, in the context of contemporary Indian scenario ridden with colossal corruption, Baba Saheb Ambedkar as a Bodhisatva becomes a necessity for thorough debate, discussion and application of his thoughts and ideas of *Prabudha Bharat* (Enlightened India).

Ambedkar's legacy as a socio-political reformer had a deep effect on modern India. In post-Independence India, his socio-political thought is respected across the political spectrum. His initiatives have influenced various spheres of life and transformed the way India today looks at socioeconomic policies, education and affirmative action through socioeconomic and legal incentives. His reputation as a scholar led to his appointment as free India's first law minister, and chairman of the committee for drafting the constitution. He passionately believed in individual freedom and criticised caste society. His accusations of Hinduism as being the foundation of the caste system made him controversial and unpopular among Hindus.

Due to his role in economics, Narendra Jadhav, a notable Indian economist, has said that Ambedkar was "the highest educated Indian economist of all times. Amartya Sen said that Ambedkar is "father of my economics", and "he was highly controversial figure in his home country, though it was not the reality. His contribution to the field of economics is marvelous and will be remembered forever. President Obama addressed the Indian parliament in 2010, and referred to Dalit leader Dr. B.R. Ambedkar as the great and revered Human Rights champion and main author of India's constitution.

Ambedkarism is of great relevance to Indian society even today in achieving social justice, removal of untouchability, in establishing equality and freedom and true democracy. Democratic socialism is the key note of his political thought and constitutionalism is the only way to achieve it. Ambedkar was the first Indian to pursue a doctorate in economics abroad. He argued that industrialization and agricultural growth could enhance the Indian economy. He stressed investment in agriculture as the primary industry of India. Ambedkar advocated national economic and social development, stressing education, public hygiene, community health, residential facilities as the basic amenities. His D.Sc. thesis "*The problems of Ruppee, its origin and solution (1923)*" examines the causes for the Rupee's fall in value. He proved the importance of price stability over exchange stability. He analyzed the silver and gold exchange rates and their effect on the economy, and found the reasons for the failure of British India's public treasury. He calculated the loss of development caused by British rule.

In 1951, Ambedkar established the Finance Commission of India. He opposed income tax for low-income groups. He contributed to Land Revenue Tax and excise duty policies to stabilize the economy. He played an important role in land reform and the state economic development. According to him, the caste system divided labourors and impeded economic progress. He emphasised a free economy with a stable Rupee which India has adopted recently. He advocated birth control to develop the Indian economy, and this has been adopted by Indian government as national policy for family planning. He emphasised equal rights for women for economic development. He laid the foundation of industrial relations after Indian independence.

Ambedkar was trained as an economist, and was a professional economist until 1921, when he became a political leader. The Reserve Bank of India (RBI) was based on the ideas that Ambedkar presented to the Hilton Young Commission.

Here are some of Dr. Ambedkars ideas of Economic Development on Indian perspective:

Agriculture and land reforms: Dr. Babasaheb Ambedkar had made in-depth study of Indian Agriculture, wrote research articles, organised Seminars and Conferences in order to solve the problems of agriculture and farmers, also led farmer's movement. His thoughts on agriculture are found in his article "Small Holdings in Indian and their remedies"(1917) and also in "Status and minorities"(1947).

He mentioned that holdings of lands by few people is an acute problem of Indian agriculture which has various disadvantages, like difficulties in cultivation and utilization and resources, increasing cost, low productivity, inadequate income and low standard of living. According to Dr. Ambedkar, productivity in agriculture is related to not only with the size of holdings of land but also with other factors such as capital, labour and other inputs. Therefore if capital or labour etc are not available in adequate quantity and quality, then even a large size land can become unproductive. On the other hand small size land become productive if these resources are available in plenty. With this thought the 'Land Ceiling Act' is passed after Independence.

He also mentioned about the slavery and exploitation of labour bound under caste system is extremely bad for economic development and fought for its abolition.

His other suggestions for solving agriculture problem are collective farming, economic holding of land or equal distribution of land, Large scale Industrialization, Provision of money, water, seeds and fertilizers by the government, cultivation of waste land by allotting waste land to landless labour, minimum wages to labours, control and regulation of private lenders of loan to farmers.

India's Currency Problems: Dr. Babasaheb Ambedkar's thoughts have a great impact on current Indian currency system. Under British rule when India Govt. was struggling with falling value of Indian Rupee, Dr. Babasaheb Ambedkar In 1923 wrote '*The Problem of Rupee, its origin and solution.* He focused his studies and research on the condition of Indian currency during British India. He wrote research thesis on it. In his thesis, he argued that the gold exchange standard does not have stability. The developing country like India cannot afford gold exchange standards, and besides this, it also increases the risk of inflation and price rise. He proved with statistics data and reasons how the Indian Rupee has lost its value and hence the purchasing power of Rupee is falling. He suggested that govt. deficit should be regulated and money should have a circular flow. He also suggested more attention should be given on price stability than exchange rate stability. This book eventually leads to the establishment of Reserve Bank of India.

Views of Taxation policy: Dr. Ambedkar expressed his views on taxation in the manifesto of 'Swatantra Majdur Party' in 1936. He opposed Land Revenue and its system and their taxes as significant burden on the poor sections of the society. He suggested some taxes as follows:

- Tax should be imposed on payer's capacity and not on income.
- Tax should be less on poor and more on rich.
- Tax exemption should be given up to certain limit.
- There should be equality between different sections in tax imposition.
- Tax should not lead to lowering the standard of life of the people.
- Land Revenue tax should be more flexible and it should not be levied on agricultural land.
- He suggested that Indian tax system at that time was based on discrimination and inequality.

Nationalization of Industries: Dr. Babasaheb Ambedkar thought that fast development of India is impossible without Industrialization. According to him creating large scale employment produces essential goods for mass consumption. It utilizes raw materials, reduces foreign dependence and increasing security to labour, and ultimately leads to the overall economical development of the country. The private sector industries cannot make big industries for want of large scale investments. So, government should come forward to start large scale industries. The smaller industries should be kept in private sector. The insurance and transport companies should be nationalized. Rights to strike should be given to labourers. After the independence the industrial policy of the Indian government is in keeping with Dr. Ambedkar's expectations.

Strategy for economic development: Dr. Ambedkar believed that the strategy for India's Economic development should be based on Eradication of poverty elimination of inequities and ending exploitation of masses. He emphasized exploitation has many dimensions. In fact in India, social or religious exploitation is not less Oppressive than economic exploitation and it should be eliminated.

Democratic state Socialism: Dr. Babasaheb Ambedkar has presented a Democratic State Socialism to the constitution committee. The main points of it are:

(1) All basic industries should be owned and run by the state.

(2) Insurance and agriculture should be nationalized and managed by the state.

(3) Maintenance of Productive resources by state.

(4) Just Distribution of Common produce.

(5) Provision for compensation of land or industry acquisition in the form of bonds.

(6) The distribution of village and among the families in a village for collective farming

(7) No discrimination as landlord, tenants and agricultural labour.

(8) All agriculture input like capital, seeds fertilizers etc would be provided to collective farming by the government.

(9) Distribution of agricultural income only after payment of land revenue tax.

(10) Punishment according to rules who do not follow.

Dr. Ambedkar wanted this state socialism to be inculded in the constitution so that no legilature could change or reject it. But it could not come into existance as the constitution committee rejected it. It suggested that the conditions of labour, farmers and poor people would have difference if this has not been rejected.

Free Enterprises Economy: Surprising enough Dr. Ambedkar had already suggested free economy, globalization, liberalization and privatization as early as 1923; Recently Indian government has adopted this policy. In this respect Dr. Ambedkar was a century ahead. He had stressed that the value (Price) of a rupee must be kept stable if the policy of free economy is to be successful.

Population Control-Family Planning: Dr. Babasaheb Ambedkar said that the control of the country's economy is impossible if the population is not controlled. Hence he forcefully argued for population control and family planning in India. Later on in keeping with his views the government of India has adopted family planning as a national policy.

Economic Upliftment of Indian Women: Dr. Babasaheb Ambedkars contribution to economic development and progress of women is significant. According to him, participation of women in the economic development is impossible without developing their social status and equality. But due to bad economic conditions of women in India, India's economic progress is hampered. So, it is important to improve the economic condition of women and give them equal rights and freedom of occupation.

Concept of Human Capital: Dr. Ambedkar argued that concept of human capital in india is useless if the poorer and downtrodden (dalits)are not recognized by other classes as human being with equal social prestige and religious basis. It is therefore impossible to use this human capital in the economic development of India.

Opposition to Hindu Economy: Dr. Ambedkar denounced the Indian economy as Hindu dominated economy. He came out with hard hitting critique of this Hindu economy. He showed logical flaws in it. Caste System is not merely the division of labour but a division of labourers also. It is not based on natural aptitudes or skills. It is a major obstacle to economic development. It reduces mobility leading to inefficient production. Untouchability is worser than slavery. It is a system of exploitation.

Hence, it is evident that Dr. Babasaheb Ambedkar's concepts of family planning, uplittment of women and human capital and many others are important contribution to the development of the Indian economy. As the existing laws and reforms land ceiling Act, minimum wages Act, Distribution of surplus land etc are not effective and it is essential to reconsider them in the context of Dr. Ambedkar's perspective. Also as current scenario of Indian economy, inflation, farmer conditions, India's large young labour force not being fully utilised for the economic development, we need to reconsider the thoughts of Dr. Babasaheb Ambedkar and again frame our economic policies towards better economical growth of India.

CONCLUSION

As a part of India's present socio-political-economic scenario, the political leaders are misusing the name of Dr. B.R. Ambedkar for their political interest and playing the dalit sentiment in destructive way.

This is a high time to understand Dr.Ambedkar's socail, economic, political thoughts and let everyone know how they are beneficial to overall development of people and nation as a whole. The basic needs of any human being is food, shelter and clothing. The Consititution of India provides enough guidelines to provide basic needs to the common man and help them to develop. The duty of the state is to distribute the resources equally among all and see that no injustice is done to them. If India wishes to become a super power and a strong economy the must implement the constitutional provisions then only this country will grow, this nation will stand tall. The principles of liberty, equality, fraterntiy and justice will remain strong.

REFERENCES

1. O.P. Gauba, *An introduction to Political Theory,* 4th. edition, Delhi, 1978.
2. Baws, *Annihilation of Caste,* Vol.1, p.47. & Vol. 2. Kolkata,1999.
3. Ibid.
4. Baws, *Annihilation of Caste,* Vol.1
5. Baws, *The Hindu Social Order: Its Essential Principles.* Vol.III, Kolkata, 1991.
6. S.N. Busi, *Mahatma Gandhi and Babasaheb Ambedkar- Crusader Against Caste and Untochability,* New Delhi, 1978.
7. Keer, Dhananjay, *Dr. Ambedkar: Life and Mission,*Popular Prakashan, Bombay, 1971.
8. Kuber, W.N: *B.R.Ambedkar – A Critical Study,* Publication Division, Ministry of Information and Broadcasting, Government of India, Newdelhi, 1987.
9. Lokhande, G.S, *Bhimarao Ramji Ambedkar: A study on Social Democracy,* Intellectual Publishing House, New Delhi, 1982.

19

Dr. B R Ambedkar as an Economist:

The First Neo-liberal Thinker of Indian Economy

– Aloke Bhowmik

Unlike many of his great contemporaries, Ambedkar was professionally trained in "political economics", as it was then known. In 1918, at the young age of 27, he became Professor of Political Economy at Sydenham College of Commerce and Economics in Bombay. Ambedkar studied a wide range of economic issues such as international trade and commerce, the Indian currency, provincial finance and planning, small holdings and agricultural productivity. Apart from many research articles published in professional journals, his four theses submitted–for two Master's degrees and two doctorate degrees–were replete with insight and analysis.

In 1915, he completed an M.A. in economics with a thesis on "*Ancient Indian Commerce*" at Columbia University in New York. In 1916, he submitted another thesis, "*National Dividend for India: A Historic and Analytical Study*", for a Ph.D. degree in Economics, and Columbia awarded him a doctorate in 1917. This thesis was later published as a book, *The Evolution of Provincial Finance in British India*, in London. Further, in 1921, Ambedkar also received an M.Sc. in economics from the London School of Economics (LSE) for his thesis, "*Provincial Decentralisation of Imperial Finance in British India*". In 1922 he completed his now famous thesis, "*The Problem of the Rupee: Its Origin and its Solution,*" submitted for his D.Sc. degree in Economics to the London School of Economics, both published as books in London.

Armed with these four postgraduate degrees, two from an Ivy League University in the U.S. and two from a top university in the U.K., Ambedkar could not be taken lightly by his upper caste, anglicized peers in the Indian establishment. Further, the prolific Ambedkar produced at least three scholarly contributions to economics, in which he made many original arguments. These are:

(1) "Administration and Finance of the East India Company" (1915);

(2) "The Problem of the Rupee: Its Origin and Its Solution" (1923), and;

(3) "The Evolution of Provincial Finance in British India: A Study in the Provincial Decentralisation of Imperial Finance" (1925).

The second and third of these works contain many pro-market ideas which were hardly known then but later gained currency in the second half of the twentieth century. What's more, through his writings Ambedkar pioneered original ideas like "economic and political decision making in an environment of dispersed knowledge" and "alternative monetary systems (and the) denationalized production of money", the sort of ideas that one might have found in the writings of the great Austrian economist, Friedrich von Hayek, but which were virtually unknown in India and Britain at the time.

Ambedkar wrote extensively on finance, monetary economics, banking systems, and interstate financial relations. He had expertise on Indian currency and banking in the second half of the 19th century and the early decades of the 20th century. He was trained under great scholars like Edwin Cannan, Edwin Seligman, John Dewey, James Robinson, and James Shotwell.

A keen student of economics, Ambedkar was an advocate for private property rights, the gold standard, "free banking" or multiple competing currencies, and decentralized planning. Always a champion of individual liberty and freedom, he was a vehement critic of Maynard Keynes, and his views were much more in consonance with the great architect of libertarian thought, Hayek.

Ambedkar even aged 17, clearly understood that no one person or institution could possess all of the information and knowledge needed to plan for the whole country. This original argument for the weaknesses inherent in a centralized economy can be found in *The Evolution of Provincial Finances in British India*, published in 1925, but written in 1917 where he says: "by centralisation all progress tends to be retarded, all initiative liable to be checked and the sense of responsibility of local Authorities greatly impaired" and "centralisation conflicts with what may be regarded as a cardinal principle of good government".

Ambedkar went on to argue: "Centralisation, unless greatly circumscribed, must lead to inefficiency... there must come a point at which the higher authority must be less competent than the tower, because it cannot by any possibility possess the requisite knowledge of all local conditions. It was therefore obvious that a Central Government for the whole of India could not be said to possess knowledge and experience of all various conditions prevailing in the different Provinces under it. "It's striking to think that Ambedkar wrote these ideas decades before Hayek published his classic article, "*The Use of Knowledge in Society*" (1945). One might even say that Ambedkar was a Hayekian before Hayek!

The Problem of the Rupee was Ambedkar's magnum opus, in which he emphasized the need for a sound monetary system for trade and its nexus with private property rights. Writing in the first chapter (1947: 1-2) he mentioned "Trade is an important apparatus in a society, based on private property and pursuit of individual gain; without it, it would be difficult for its members to distribute the specialized products of their labour...With money as the focusing-point of all human efforts, interests, desires, and ambitions, a trading society is bound to function in a regime of price, where successes and failures are results of nice calculations of price-outlay as against price-product."

If Ambedkar were alive today, it's evident where he would stand on the "Sen-Bhagwati debate" – firmly on the side of free markets and not redistributive, socialist welfare schemes.

The Royal Commission on Indian Currency and Finance, chaired by Hilton Young in 1924-25, was instrumental in establishing India's central bank, the Reserve Bank of India. While defending before the Commission the idea of multiple or competing currencies issued by individual banks instead of the government's monopoly of legal tender, Ambedkar said (1926):

> "A managed currency is to be altogether avoided when the management is to be in the hands of the Government. When the management is by a bank there is less chance of mismanagement. But the chance of mismanagement is greater when it is issued by Government because the issue of government money is authorised and conducted by men who are never under any present responsibility for private loss in case of bad judgement or mismanagement." If Ambedkar's words had been heeded in the last few years, they might have helped avoid the global financial crisis.

More specifically this is as an important contribution to the discussion of currency problems in India or elsewhere. These ideas are also core beliefs of the Austrian School of Economics, exemplified by Carl Menger whose work was familiar to Ambedkar. However, Ambedkar articulated the idea of multiple or competing currencies inspired by the works of the great liberal thinker, Gopal Krishna Gokhale, who wrote independently of the Austrians. Contrary to what his followers claim, Ambedkar vehemently criticized Keynes and other supporters of the "gold exchange standard" and argued in favour of a modified gold standard. To quote Ambedkar:

> "How can she become a gold-standard country? The obvious answer is, by introducing a gold currency. Prof. Kenyes scoffs at the view that there cannot be a gold standard without a gold currency as pure nonsense. He seems to hold that a currency and a standard of value are two different things. Surely there he is wrong. Because a society needs a medium of exchange, a standard of value, and a store of value to sustain its economic life, it is positively erroneous to argue that these three functions can be performed by different instrumentalities."

In one of his earliest scholarly papers, from 1918, Ambedkar opined that India needed to help people migrate from agriculture to industry:

> "A large agricultural population with the lowest proportion of land in actual cultivation means that a large part of the agricultural population is superfluous and idle...this labour when productively employed will cease to live by predation as it does today, and will not only earn its keep but will give us surplus; and more surplus means more capital. In short, strange as it may seem, industrialization of India is the soundest remedy for the agricultural problems of India."

This is still relevant today and would be great advice to the government on why we need to reduce surplus non-productive employment in agriculture.

In light of all of this, it's evident that, as an economist, Ambedkar was closer to free-market economics and no advocate of socialism or Marxism, as he is often painted by his dubious followers who would gladly erase this important facet of their icon's legacy. Indeed, it was Ambedkar who strongly opposed inserting the word "socialism" in the preamble of the Indian Constitution. Would he do this if he supported Marxist economics?

It's clear that there is not a single political party in India, including the "Ambedkariate" parties, which has taken seriously the economic ideas of Ambedkar. It was Ambedkar who famously said "Educate, Agitate, Organise". But it seems that the trend today is for all manner of people to organise movements and start agitating without bothering to educate themselves! It's a great pity that Ambedkar's Dalit followers are apparently unaware of their hero's free market – even libertarian – views on economics and individual liberty and prefer to hold him hostage to a narrow conception – he as a Dalit leader – that suits their political ends and ideology.

In his article "*Dalit Capitalism and Pseudo Dalitism*" (5 March 2011, pp. 10-11), the civil rights activist Anand Teltumbde makes several dubious claims, one of them being Ambedkar's opposition to capitalism/free market economics "*throughout his life*". In reality, Ambedkar was one of the first-generation economists in India and a leading free-market economist in the early decades of 20th century. He was a trained economist with degrees from Columbia University in U.S.A. and the London School of Economics before moving on to law and social theory and practices.

REFERENCES

1. Ambedkar, B.R., "*History of Indian Currency and Banking*", Vol.1, Thacker and Company Ltd, Rampart Row, Bombay, 1947.
2. Ambedkar, B.R., "*The Evolution of Provincial Finance in British India: A Study in the Provincial Decentralization of Imperial Finance*", Chapter IX, P. S. King and Son Ltd, Westminister, 1925.
3. Ambirajan, S, "Ambedkar's Contribution to Indian Economics", *Economic & Political Weekly*, 20th November, 1999.
4. Jadhav, Narendra, "Neglected Economic Thought of Babasaheb Ambedkar, '*Economic & Political Weekly*', Vol.26, No.15, 1991.

20

Dr. B.R. Ambedkar: Father of Dalit and Relevance of His Thoughts on the Contemporary Indian Politics

– Mantu Barai

Dr. B.R. Ambedkar popularly known as Babasaheb, was a unique character of India in twentieth century. He was an Indian jurist, economist, politician and social reformer. He was an extraordinary scholar in various subjects. He thought that British rules and regulations were much harmful for India and Indians. This is true, but Indian society has met more injury by misguidance of history and culture and religious decomposition. He found that our nation was internally multi-divided. It was very difficult to establish a self-revelation for India. Under these antagonistic circumstances prevailing in India, he applied himself in favour of social, religious and economic equality. Common people found a new expectation in this eminent person. He was like an angel to the numerous downtrodden people of India. He has fought whole life for the realization of equality for the downtrodden community. He played an important role for framing the constitution of India.

HIS LIFE

Bhimrao Ramji Ambedkar was born on 14 April, 1891 in the town and military cantonment of Mhow in the central provinces (now in Madhya Pradesh). He was the fourteenth child of his parents. Ambedkar's father was a Subedar in the Indian Army and posted at Mhow cantonment, Madhya Pradesh. After the retirement of his father in 1894, the family moved to Satara. Shortly after, his mother passed away. Then his father remarried and the family shifted to Bombay where he passed matriculation in 1908.

Ambedkar was born into a poor low Mahar (dalit) caste, who were treated as untouchables and subjected to socioeconomic discrimination. Due to this, Ambedkar had to face severe discriminations from every corner of the society. The discrimination and humiliation haunted Ambedkar even at the Army school, run by the British Government. The teachers would segregate the students of lower class from that of Brahmins and other upper classes. The dalit students were often asked by the teacher to sit outside the class. He was required to sit on a gunny sack which he had to take from home with him. When he needed to drink water, someone from a higher caste had to pour that water from a height as they were not allowed to touch either the water or the vessel that contained it. This task was usually performed for the child Ambedkar by the school peon, and if the peon was not available then he had to go without water; the situation he later in his writings described as "No Peon, No Water".[1] After shifting to Satara, he was admitted to a local school, but the change of school did not change the fate of young Bhimrao. Discrimination followed wherever he went. In 1908, Ambedkar got the opportunity to study at the Elphinstone College where he cleared all the examination successfully. He has passed graduation from the Bombay University in 1912 on Political Science and Economics. He was awarded honors of D.Sc. by the London University.

His original surname Ambavadekar comes from his native village 'Ambavade' in Ratnagiri district. His teacher, Mahadev Ambedkar, who was fond of him, changed his surname from 'Ambavadekar to his own surname Ambedkar in school records.[2]

DALIT MOVEMENT

Bhimrao Ambedkar fought against the caste discrimination that almost fragmented the nation. Ambedkar opined that there should be separate electoral system for the dalits and lower caste people. He also favored the concept of providing reservations for Dalits and other religious minorities.

Ambedkar began to find ways to reach the people and make them understand the drawbacks of the prevailing social evils. He launched a newspaper called '*Mooknayaka*'. As a result, there was created a huge uproar in the socio-political arena of the country.

Dr. Ambedkar emphasized the anti-social, anti-progress character of an unjust social order as well as its vital connection, through networks of force and ideology, with political power. The caste system, in his analysis, militated against fraternity, "*sanghatan* and co-operation for a good cause", public charity and broad based virtue and morality. When critics challenged him to specify his "Ideal Society" in lieu of a caste based order, he replied "My ideal would be a society based on liberty, equality and fraternity". He specified that his ideal society would be mobile, there would be 'Social endosmosis'; there would be fraternity, which was only another name for democracy and democracy was primarily a mode of associated living, of conjoining communicated experience and breeding an attitude of respect and reverence towards fellow human beings.[3]

Dr. Ambedkar represented, in the truly national sense, the profound side of the socio-political struggle which formed an irrepressible part of the nationalist movement, although it was not often understood (by conservatism and orthodoxy in politics) to be such. Politically moderate, he tended towards radicalism and uncompromising struggle in the social arena in which he led many battles. His lifelong concern with religion, morality and justice in the idealistic sense was marked by a restlessly serious attempt to get the intellectual, social and political measure of these things. He did not believe in class analysis, but intuitively and intellectually grasped the link between caste and class in India.

Ideologically, Dr. Ambedkar occupied the centre, frequently the space right of centre, but at times he moved sharply the other way, to the radical side. This happened especially when his ideas, campaigns and political organizational work were backed by powerful mass movements. He was the founder of the Independent Labour Party, which did not take off in an all India sense, but yielded some valuable political, ideological and organizational lessons to the opposition around the nation.

Ambedkar's legacy as a socio-political reformer had a deep effect on modern India. In post Independence India, his socio-political thought is respected across the political spectrum. His initiatives have influenced various spheres of life and transformed the way India today looks at socio-economic policies, education and affirmative action through socio-economic and legal incentives. He passionately believed in individual freedom and criticized caste society. His accusations of Hinduism as being the foundation of the caste system made him controversial and unpopular among Hindus. His conversion to Buddhism sparked a revival in interest in Buddhist philosophy in India and abroad.

INDIAN SOCIETY

In Ambedkar's view the stratification of Hindu society has been created in the perspective of caste system in India. The nature of the caste system of Hindu society has proved to be too much unfortunate for the nation. There is religious and ethical approval behind the caste distinctive society. The causes of the weakness of the Hindu society were imbibed within it. A major group of Hindus has been deprived of all human rights because of this caste system and they were burdened by social liabilities imposed on them. They have been denied of all civilian privileges due for a human being. According to Hindu laws, the '*Achchyut*' (untouchable) were not accepted as human beings. Though the 'untouchable offences act, 1955' has been passed, yet Ambedkar has mentioned of numerous facts of inhuman behaviours in his books. He has pointed out in his book that doctors who belonged to higher caste did not give treatment to the lower caste patients; boys who belonged to the untouchable group could not enter the '*Dharmasala*'; nobody helped the Dalit wretched women. The conservative Hindu society imposed many restrictions on the food habits and clothing of the downtrodden people.[4]

One day B.R. Ambedkar reached the Mandu rail station with his elder brother Balaram because they will go to Gurgaon, the service place of their father. He did not know have the ledge of their arrival; naturally he did not come at the station to attend them. After that they hired a cart. In the way the carter came to know that they belonged to Mahar cast (low caste). At the very moment, the carter threw the luggage from the cart and abused them.[5] This inhumanity towards fellowmen is unheard from any part of the world.

Naturally upper class people of the society availed all privileges and rights. According to Ambedkar, the nature of Hindu religion is liberal, but a major proportion of the people have been kept fully alienated from the society and they were named as '*Achchyuts*'. Caste division of Hindu society has proved to be very miserable and unfortunate.

Equality and fraternity is absent in the Hindu Society. The social organization of the Hindus is based on inequality. Society was established on the Varna and caste system, where lower class people (Untouchable) were deprived of the right of education and they were unable to protest against injustices. They did not have any opportunity of criticism. Soon after birth, some social bars were incurred on the dalit community which they had to ascribe for lifelong.

SOCIAL MOVEMENT

While practicing law in the Bombay High Court, he tried to promote the education of dalits and uplifted them. His first organized attempt was his establishment of the central institution Bahishkrit Hitakarini Sabha, intended to promote education and socioeconomic improvement, as well as the welfare of "outcastes' at the time referred to as depressed classes. For the defense of Dalit rights, he started many periodicals like *Mook Nayak*, *Bahishkrit Bharat* and *Equality Janta.*

By 1927, Ambedkar had decided to launch active movements against untouchability. He began with public movements and marches to open up public drinking water resources. He also began a struggle for the right to enter Hindu temples. He led a satyagraha in Mahad to fight for the right of the untouchable community to draw water from the main water tank of the town. In a conference in late 1927, Ambedkar publicly condemned the classic Hindu text, the Manusmriti (Laws of Manu), for ideologically justifying caste discrimination and untouchability and he ceremonially burned copies of the ancient text.

He wanted that Hindu religion must be reformed and made the religion of humanity deleting the concept of graded inequality. But it could not happen in his life time. He declared in frustration on 13th October 1935, "Unfortunately I was born a Hindu. It was beyond my powers to prevent that, but I solemnly assure you that I will not die as a Hindu."[6] He fought same way against the class divided Hindu society.

Ambedkar's work and ideology remained in dormant stage for too long. Everybody came to know that Babasaheb single handle drafted constitution of India and hence started labeling him as father of Indian constitution. Now the Governments are projecting Babasaheb as the father of Indian constitution in various advertisements published through Ministry of Information and Broadcasting, Government of India. The hard work he put on emancipation of Indian women through Hindu Code Bill, labour laws (minimum wages Act 1946), Registration of trade unions, Maternity leave and workman's Compensation Act has also not been highlighted in desired manner. Few years ago University Grants Commission has given status of Epoch thinkers of India to Dr. Ambedkar, others are Buddha, Gandhi and Nehru.

In 1937, Dr. Ambedkar introduced a Bill to abolish the "khoti" system of land tenure in the Konkan region, the serfdom of agricultural tenants and the Mahar "watan" system of working for the Government as slaves. A clause of an agrarian bill referred to the depressed classes as "*Harijans*," or people of God. Bhimrao was strongly opposed this title for the untouchables. He argued that if the "untouchables" were people of God then all others would be people of monsters. He was against any such reference. But the Indian National Congress succeeded in introducing the term *Harijan*. Ambedkar felt bitter that they could not have any say in what they were called.

In 1947, when India became independent, the first Prime Minister Pt. Jawaharlal Nehru, invited Dr. Bhimrao Ambedkar, who had been elected as a Member of the Constituent Assembly from Bengal, to join his Cabinet as a Law Minister. The Constituent Assembly entrusted the job of drafting the Constitution to a committee and Dr. Ambedkar was elected as Chairman of this Drafting Committee. In February 1948, Dr. Ambedkar presented the Draft Constitution before the people of India; it was adopted on November 26, 1949.

In October 1948, Dr. Ambedkar submitted the Hindu Code Bill to the Constituent Assembly in an attempt to codify the Hindu law. The Bill caused great divisions even in the Congress party. Consideration for the bill was postponed to September 1951. When the Bill was taken up it was truncated. A dejected Ambedkar relinquished his position as Law Minister.[7]

Dr. Ambedkar was the most prominent speaker of Dalit community of India. The Brahmins have taken the policy of injustice, exploitation on Dalit community since long years ago. Ambedkar condemned severely against the said behaviour of the Brahmins. We are owed to Ambedkar because he tried his best to make the Hindus aware of the social crisis or communal conflict. He played an important role for the consciousness of political thought of Dalit community by the skill of compositions, lectures, leadership and creative activities. Practically, he was the father of untouchable, backward Dalit communities.

RELEVANCE OF 125TH BIRTH ANNIVERSARY OF AMBEDKAR

Dr. Ambedkar's thoughts and ideas have same percent relevancy after 69 years have passed of india's independence. The situation of Dalit people has more depredated after the following of Neo-liberalism during last two and a half decade in India. The incidents of injustice and attacking are increasing on the lower classes. Untouchability is a dangerous disease of Hindu society. The burning example is the suicide incident of Rohit Vemula, Ph.D scholar of Hyderabad University[8]. Not only that, Patel movement of Gujrat, Jat movement of Haryana have to make more relevancy of Dalit movements.

There was absolutely no enthusiasm about Dr. B.R. Ambedkar in the popular political parties of India during the last decade of twentieth century. The perspective changed with the rise of regional political parties (Bahujan Samaj Party and others). On the 125th birth anniversary of Ambedkar, the most important political parties of India (Congress, B.J.P) announced their activity and their reverence to the great leader. Before that, regarding him there has been nothing worthwhile. Prime Minister Narendra Modi paid homage to Ambedkar at Mhow cantonment in Madhya Pradesh. R.S. Quril, the Vice-Chancellor of Ambedkar Social Science University' on the occasion commented that, Modi is the first prime minister of India who came at Mhow and paid reverence to Ambedkar. Modi claimed that, the way in which Ambedkar has improved upon the life of the poor and farmers, is being followed by him. The Prime minister launched a nationwide '*Gram Uday* say *Bharat Uday*' campaign on the occasion.[9] He uttered the slogan "*Jai Hind*" at the end of the programme. It has been found that the propensity of BJP increased with the helping hand of Ambedkar in Bombay. In the 'Maritime India Summit' 2016, Modi remarked that Ambedkar was not only the frame maker of the constitution of India but also the framer of new policies on sea route. Modi opened the e-platform of National Agricultural Market at Science Bhawan. On the other hand, Congress high command Sonia Gandhi paid reverence to Ambedkar. Even she commented that, Ambedkar was the 'icon of modern India'. Sonia Gandhi claimed that his contribution has spread in every sector of India.

There were other objectives behind the reverence programme. The main objective of the political parties was to bring the Dalit votes in favour of their control. Bharatiya Janata Party (BJP) has started to build up the statue of Dr. Ambedkar in Mumbai and in other places in the country. The Congress Party known about the technical politics of BJP. Naturally Congress party has also announced their activity of paying reverence to Ambedkar. Leader of Bahujan Samaj Party, Kumari Mayavati joined the said activity. She would like to lead the Dalits. All political parties are fraud and they always aim to ensure the vote of dalits to fulfill their narrow political interests.[10]

Now days every political party is trying to inhibit Ambedkar as their icon. Because the election of Legislative Assembly of Uttar Pradesh is ahead, so situation has become extreme. The Congress party is trying to capture the dalit vote for them. On the other hand BJP is trying to come close with dalit community in order to get votes. Mayavati is single mindedly devoted to capture the vote of the dalits. That is to say, political parties are suffering from existence crisis without Ambedkar. Because they know that the result of election would not be according to expectation without dalit votes.[11]

The socio-political arena got agitated by the report of the 'Mandal Commission' in India. Bindyoswari Prasad Mandal has recommended for the reservation and quota system for the upliftment, development and for the provision of Govt. opportunities to backward classes. This principle of life was the motto and ideal of Ambedkar. He has shown us the right way to pursue research, observation and he standard for the traditional slogan "Educate, a organize and agitate".[12]

But we have seen that, India is divided into two parts, one is 'Mandal' (Dalit) and other is 'Koumandal' (conservative). Left and democratic groups were supported by the Ex-Prime minister of India V.P. Singh and on the other hand extremist fanatic group did not support him. Sangha Pariwar played an offensive role against the dalit community. As a result, there was man created riots in India and there was huge bloodshed.

So, the philosophy of Ambedkar by which he tried to construct the nation is yet to accomplish. According to Rajshekhar Basu (Dept. of History) of JNU, 'Ambedkar took several steps to evict the practice of untouchability and poverty of the Dalit community. After a long time of independence all the laws related to Dalit community are not satisfactory, but as far as letter is concerned makes Dalit people aware of it). So, it can be said that for the attitude of Indian society and politics, we need more Ambedkar to fulfil the desire of the nation'.

REFERENCES

1. Ayan Kumar Dutta, Bartaman News Paper, 24 April, 2016, p.7.
2. Deshitaishi-Bengali Patrika, Edited by Ashok Bandhyopadhyay, Kolkata, 2015, p.17.

3. Frontline, Volume 27, 2010.
4. Mahapatra & Banyopadhyay, Bharatio Rashta Darshan (Bengali), Kolkata, 2009, p.24.
5. Deshitaishi-Bengali Patrika, Edited by Ashok Bandhyopadhyay, Kolkata, 2015, p.6.
6. Ayan Kumar Dutta, Bartaman News Paper, 24 April, 2016, p.7.
7. http://www.iloveindia.com/indian-heroes/br-ambedkar
8. Ayan Kumar Dutta, Bartaman News Paper, 24 April, 2016.
9. Anandabazar Patrika, 15 April, 2016.
10. Abhijit Das, Bartaman News Paper, 24 April, 2016.
11. Ibid.
12. Deshitaishi-Bengali Patrika, Edited by Ashok Bandhyopadhyay, Kolkata, 2015, p.17.

21

Dalit Scenario in Indian Subcontinent and the Role of B.R. Ambedkar

– Uday Sankar Sarkar

The study of 'Dalit' history is considered as one of the major research areas in the field of different branches of humanities and social-sciences. It can be said that, the Dalit research is one of the most complex and emerging issues in recent historical trends. In fact in the field of research it can be attributed that the Dalit history is being considered as subaltern approach. In fact, in post-colonial period the research areas have widely opened in every sector. From the historical and social-scientific view it can be said that the Dalit research is being a great attraction among the research fellows and dalit history was come out widely from subaltern point of view in the research world. Regarding the issues on dalit history it can be noticed that, the many interpretations have came out from different angles in recent socio-historical research and historians, anthropologists and social-scientists have made their focus on Dalit history and issues and they have contributed many aspects like Dalit identity, social crisis of Dalits, Indian social structure and caste system, education and economic conditions of Dalits in recent scenario, Dalit and upper-caste conflict, struggle for existence of Dalit in society, etc. Generally the concept of Dalit includes those who are designated as socially and economically backward, like Scheduled Casts, Scheduled Tribes and Other Backward Classes. But, in common political view, the term Dalit is so far mainly designated to Scheduled Castes. The term 'Scheduled Caste' was first time used by the British Administration and in 1935 Government of India Act, the term 'Scheduled Caste' was first time referred by them. Mainly we designated the Dalit as untouchable castes and M.K. Gandhi designated them as Harijan, Dr. B.R. Ambedkar was came out from Dalit society and he took various initiative regarding dalit awareness by politically and socially. Of course, Undoubtedly, the Dalit issues is a "by–product" of the Ambedkar's movement in Indian society (B.K. Nagla, Indian Sociological Thought, p.307). He took different approach for the emancipation of untouchable castes. Undoubtedly in historical point of view, it is true that, the Scheduled Castes' were neglected by the upper-castes' from the ancient time. In Hindu caste structure generally the Scheduled Castes' group belongs to the lowest level. Ambedkar raised his voice for Dalits and he said that the Dalits should come forward in Indian society by and largely politically, economically and socially. He indicates three crucial matters for emancipation of Dalits, i.e. education for dalits (only the education can play a key role in society for emancipation of dalits), second one is organize them (every dalits or untouchables should organize them like other communities) and the last one is agitation for demands (they should come forward to achieve their social rights through their social movement). He believed in self-awakening and obviously the self awakening could provide Dalits to take necessary power to fight against so-called caste Hindu.

The 'Masiha' of dalits, Bhimrao Ramji, was born on 14th April in the year of 1891 at Mhow, which is situated at Central Province of Indian sub-continent. He died in Delhi on 6th December in the year of 1956. He was an eminent Indian jurist, economist, politician, principal constructor of the Indian constitution and obviously social reformer, and he was a multi talented personality, inspired the marginalised community. Babasaheb strongly campaigned against social injustice not only that, also strong supporter of the social rights of women and labour class. In post Colonial period he was the first law minister of India. In the year of 1956 Babasaheb was converted to Buddhism. He gained a remarkable attention in Indian society regarding his campaigning against the social inequality and social freedom for the untouchables. Edwin Bryant said that, 'actually he believed that the Shudras as originally being part of the Kshatriya Varna in the Indo-Aryan society, but gradually they became degraded socially after inflicted cruel and oppressive rule on Brahmins' (Edwin Bryant, The Quest for the Origins of Vedic Culture, Oxford, 2001, p.50).

Caste system and untouchability both are inter-connected with each other in Indian politics and Indian freedom struggle movement. In Indian social structure the caste is social distribution, the entire society is divided into different segments. Actually in Indian society we can say that, socially by birth a man can get his own identity. From the beginning of the Hindu society the caste system is being continued for a long time and still it is same as before. In this context the castism and untouchability is a dark corner of Hindu society. The so called upper caste people of Hindu society has thrown away the dalits by socially from different angles, i.e., social amalgamation, marriage or any kind of social gathering. It is no question that in Indian social context the dalits are truly untouchables although M.K. Gandhi called them as Harijan or the son of god and the general view remain unchanged. Actually the centralized feudal mind was organized by the Manusmriti and we can not ignore the laws of Manu. The Hindu caste system was centrally organized by the Manusmriti and obviously on the basis of Manusmriti the so-called upper caste people created the theory of untouchable concept. There is no justification the concept of untouchability regarding the dalits, because the every people is son of god and obviously this particular cast should not be untouchable. But the concept of castism is still in our feudal mind and from the very beginning this concept we got from our society. Professor Prangobinda Das told "hereditary specialization, hierarchical organization, reciprocal repulsion" (Prangobinda Das, Vharatiya Rastrachinta O Jatio Andolan, p.452) which are strongly attached with Hindu society. It is no doubt that the castism is an evil practice and unfortunately this practice by the so-called upper caste people was spread over the Hindu society very rapidly. Prof Dr. Sumit Sarkar told about Caste consciousness and he wrote, "...sociological work on caste has increasingly emphasized that the meaningful units here are not the somewhat abstract varnas but the mass of diverse local jatis, united by a varying degree of occupational identity, common rites and customs, and taboos on marriages or eating outside the group" and he also told that "the old assumption of an absolutely rigid and unchanging hierarchy of castes has also been rejected" (Dr. Sumit Sarkar, Modern India 1885-1947, p.54). Dr. Sarkar told that, "the net result has often been the expression of socio-economic tensions through a kind of false – consciousness of caste solidarity, caste rivalry, and movements for Sanskritization" (Dr. Sumit Sarkar, Modern India 1885-1947, p.55).

Ambedkar always tried to promote education and social justice to dalits and always worked for uplift them. In 1924 he established Bahishkrit Sreni Hitakarini Sabha, to promote education and socio-economic improvement for depressed classes. He always promote for the defense of Dalit rights and he organized the movement for the improvement of socio-economic conditions of depressed classes. In 1927 he established Samaj Samata Sangha & Samata Sainik Dal and opened a Marathi publication, i.e., "Bahishkrit Bharat". In 1928 he established Depressed Classes Education Society at Bombay and started remarkable periodical like '*Samata*' (Dr. Basabi Chakraborty, Bhimrao Ramji Ambedkar 1891-1956, pp.162-163). In 1936 he established the 'Independent Labour Party' and in the year of 1942 the party converted in to 'All India Scheduled Castes Fedaration'. Three years later in the year of 1945 he established another organization,i.e., People's Education Society'. In 1947 he was appointed as first law minister of independent India and this year he took charge over as a president of the Drafting Committee of Indian Constitution (Ibid, p.163).

In the year of 1927 Ambedkar organized active movement against untouchability. He started mass movement to open up water resources for drinking and also started a struggle to entry Hindu temples for Dalits. He began satyagraha in Mahad to struggle for the right of the Dalits to collect water from the principal water tank of the town. Ambedkar could not believe the Manusmriti and he strongly believed that ideologically the classic Hindu text, i.e., Manusmriti was created caste discrimination and the concept of untouchability was came out from this classical text. He decided to burnt the copies of the illogical ancient text and on 25th December in the year of 1927 the illogical copies of Manusmriti was burnt by him and his followers. He led this such great movement and draw the attention among the Hindu society. Ambedkar was started Kalaram Temple movement. In Nasik district the untouchables could not have the right to see the god and not to go in Kalaram Temple because the Brahmin authorities could not allow them to go to temple and not to see the god. Ambedkar took strong initiative against the such cruel custom which was running long time in this temple and he started Kalaram Temple Satyagraha in 1930. By his attempt he wanted to abolish such cruel custom which was created by the Brahmin authorities in this temple. Gradually he became '*Masiha*' of the depressed classes.

Babasaheb Ambedkar realized that only political power can solve the social discrimination of the depressed classes. He took the opportunity when the British Colonial Government announced the formation of a separate electorate for depressed classes in 1932. In this regard he signed Poona Pact on 25th September 1932 and the pact was signed between Babasaheb Ambedkar and Madan Mohan Malaviya. The Poona Pact gave reserved seats for the Dalits in the provisional legislatures and Dalits gained 148 seats in the legislature. Actually the whole depressed classes gained political opportunity by the Poona Pact by Ambedkar's political master stroke. In 1935 Government of India Act was passed by the British Colonial Government and the Depressed Classes got their legal identity in Indian society and by this act they were called as Scheduled Castes and Scheduled Tribes. Obviously the depressed classes got special attention by the Poona Pact and India Act of 1935. Obviously the all credit goes to B.R. Ambedkar. After Independence the question of reservation was come out for the SC, ST and OBC. In this regard Ambedkar got major success. He introduced a system of reservations for SC, ST and Other Backward Classes in different sectors, i.e., jobs in the civil services, in education sectors like schools and colleges. Regarding reservation is concern Ambedkar got support from the Assembly. He believed that the reservation policy can solve the problem of socio-economic inequalities in India. Through these measures he wanted to give more opportunities to depressed classes to uplift their socio-economic conditions.

Ambedkar always tried to raised his voice against the social inequality and always take initiative significant action against the upper caste society. He was the real '*masiha*' of the depressed classes, those who were socially neglected. Regarding this matter, "He introduced a Bill in the Bombay Legislature for amending the Bombay Hereditary Offices Act, 1874, which would have benefited inferior hereditary officers, particularly the Watandar Mahars by freeing them from traditional social bonds and duties and letting them pursue vocations of their choice" (The Essential Writings of B.R. Ambedkar, Oxford University Press, p.10). He wanted social equality by his significant attempt through the legislature. In 1927, Babasaheb Bhimrao Ambedkar was appointed for five years as a member of the legislative assembly of Bombay presidency (Ibid, p.10). This was most significant matter because he used the platform for the depressed classes to gain for their social status in Indian society.

Regarding the improvement of education of depressed classes he took many steps which was got shape in the year 1928. In this year the Depressed Classes Education Society was set up. This society established many hostels in different places and such places are Panvel, Thane, Nasik, Pune and Dharwad for the students of depressed classes. In 1930 he became the president of the All India Depressed Classes Congress in Nagpur. In 1930 Babasaheb Vhimrao Ambedkar attended the first Round Table Conference in London, as a representative of Dalits (Ibid, pp.10-11). From the political outlook, that was the most remarkable situation was created in Indian politics by Ambedkar. The history is we all know that what happened in first Round Table Conference and in second Round Table Conference, i.e., I quote from *The Essential Writings of B.R. Ambedkar*, edited by Valerian Rodrigues, that, "Ambedkar attended the first RTC in London, in 1930 as a representative of the depressed classes. The stand adopted by the representative of various communities and interests, the pressure exerted by several associations of Depressed

Classes in India...the attitude of the Congress and Gandhi towards the Untoucehables drove Ambedkar to change his stance in favour of a separate electorate for the Depressed Classes. It was at the second Round Table Conference that Ambedkar came to a head-on collision with Gandhi. When there was an impasse between contending interests, Ambedkar negotiated with the representatives of the minorities and signed a 'minorities pact'. ..." (Ibid, p.11). The Communal Award of 1932 institutionally granted a separate electorate to the Untouchables (Ibid, p.11). In this regard, again I quote from The Essential Writings of B.R. Ambedkar, (ed) by V. Rodrigues, that Ambedkar said about Communal Award so interestingly, i.e. "the Communal Award was intended to free the Untouchables from the thralldom of the Hindus and the Poona Pact is designed to place them under the domination of the Hindus" (Ibid, p.12). I quote from this book, i.e., "Once Muslim constituted themselves on a separate platform... he saw no alternative to forging an identity-based front to demand a share of power" (Ibid, p.13). In that circumstances, he established Scheduled Castes Federation in 1942 in the month of July and than that time in Indian political scenario he started show to project the Scheduled Castes as a third party other than upper-castes Hindus and Muslims in the constitutional development in India (Ibid, p.13).

Ambedkar always campaign to secure civil rights for depressed classes in Indian society and always raised his voice for depressed classes to get equal social status. He thought that the Government is bound to protect civil rights to the depressed classes and to provide right to equality. The fact is that the Dalits are helpless in our society and the orthodox Hindu society does not allow them to enjoy equal status in society. The real scenario of Dalits in our society, i.e., they are live in under poverty, economically backward and much of them are landless labourers (Ibid, p.361-378). In 21st Century India, the Dalits are not in comfortable position in society and they are still facing social injustice. It is no doubt that the increasing number of incidents of violence against the Dalits by the orthodox Hindu section is so unfortunate. On 31st July, Dalits assemble to protest against the attack on Dalit youths in Una incident on 11th July 2016 and they assembled in Ahmedabad. P.L. Punia, Chairperson, National Commission for Scheduled Castes, told that, "the Una incident is part of the entire setting, the Dalit is not even as important as a dead cow.... there were so many protests all over the country and protests by Dalits a good sign ... it is important that Dalits should organize themselves and raised their voice against all such cases happening anywhere in the country. If they are rising in protest, they are treading in the footsteps of Ambedkar" (*Frontline*, September 2, 2016 & see P.L. Punia's interview in *Frontline*, 2nd September, 2016).

Babasaheb Ambedkar realized that, the Dalits have extremely limited capacity to protect themselves and that's why he realized that, "the Dalits should have the power to influence governmental action by seats in the Legislature and that particular Classes should have the opportunity to frame the general policy of the Government. This they can do only if they can find a seat in the Cabinet. The Depressed Classes therefore claim that in common with other minorities, their moral rights to be represented in the Cabinet should be recognized" (*The Essential Writings of B.R. Ambedkar*, ed., V. Rodrigues, pp.378-380). Obviously the Constitutional power can help the Dalits to protect and improve their socio-political and economical status in society. We must salute Dr. Babasaheb Ambedkar to give reservation to protect the Dalits from such orthodox Hindu society. Now the time has come to say to Scheduled Castes communities that they should come forward and say educate, organize and agitate, which was told by Babasaheb Ambedkar. The purpose of this article is to highlight the Dalit scenario and the role of B.R. Ambedkar in Indian society and also protest against those people who are involve in attack on Dalits in different parts of the country in recent time.

REFERENCES

1. Valerian Rodrigue (ed.), *Essential Writings of B.R. Ambedkar,* Oxford University Press, 2002
2. Sumit Sarkar, *Modern India 1885-1947*, Macmillan, Chennai (23rd. Impressions) , 2011
3. Basabi Chakraborty, (article in Bengali)-*Bheemrao Ramji Ambedkar* (1891-1956), Kolkata, 2008

4. Edwin Bryant, *The Quest for the Origins of Vedic Culture*, Oxford, Oxford University Press, 2001
5. Dhananjay Keer, *Dr. Ambedkar: Life and Mission, Mumbai*, Popular Prakashan, 1991
6. M.L. Ahuja, *Babasaheb Ambedkar, Eminent Indians administrators and political thinkers*, Rupa Publisher, New Delhi, 2007
7. *Frontline*, September 2, 2016
8. Websource: Wikipedia, the article; Dr. Bhimrao Ramji Ambedkar, 2016
9. Prangobida Das, *Bharatiya Rashtrachinta o Jatia Andolan*, New Central Book Agency Limited, Kolkata, Pratham Prakash; May 2008

22

Ambedkar's Thoughts on Dalit's Upliftment and Its Relevance Today

– Tapan Kumar Das

Untouchability in the caste system is one of the cruelest features of the *varna* system. The untouchables had almost no right in the society in ancient times. They were not permitted to touch four *varna* people and they were also not permitted to enter the temples. They were confined to despicable jobs of sweepers, gutter cleaners and scavengers, watchmen and farm labors and so on. At the end of the 19th century, the British began recording caste and untouchables castes based usually on occupation, such as Doms, *Dhobis, Mahar, Bhandis* and *Chamar.* The British granted special political representative to the untouchables, who had become politically mobilized under the leadership of Dr. Bhimrao Ramji Ambedkar (1891-1956).[1] He was one of the greatest jurists, lawyers and political leaders of modern India. During this period, according to various services the Hindu people were divided into three groups: Brahmin and allied castes, the intermediate classes and the backward classes including untouchables.[2] The untouchables were treated in distinct ways in different provinces in India. Thus, Untouchable may in other words be also called as Dalit, officially Scheduled Caste, formerly *Harijan,* in traditional Indian society.[3]

The Indian National Congress wanted to resolve by abolishing untouchability in 1917; here it is need to answer the question of who will lead untouchables. Ambedkar said that this was 'a strange event.'[4] In this respect, it provides us with an entry into the political field upon which elite nationalism constructed untouchables' as a discrete community. At that time, the Congress called for the abolition of untouchability. In this perspective, Ambedkar's pointed out that, the resolution was a 'strange event' because the Congress "forgot the Resolution the very day on which it was passed. The Resolution was a dead letter. Nothing came out of it."[5] He is known as the leader of India's untouchables and his political thought and action was also formed in relationship to his own caste (Mahar caste). He was born in Mhow (now Mahu) in Madhya Pradesh. It seemed that two major events had changed his leadership direction. These events were- the Mahad Conferences of 1927 and the battle with Gandhi over the Communal Award during the Round Table Conferences of 1930-32.[6] The Congress adopted first resolution in 1917 to the early 1930s, the Congress was not involved in organizing anything against untouchability. But Ambedkar pointed out that "Mr Gandhi does not appear to have taken any active steps for the removal of Untouchability or get himself interested in doing any activity beneficial to the Untouchable during this period."[7] P D Kaushik was careful to point out: "from 1924 to 1931 the Congress several times repeated its expression to root out the plant of untouchability."[8] Now, the question comes to our mind that did not the untouchables hear from their would-be benefactors until the early 1930s?

The All Indian Hindu Mahasabha was held at Benares in 1923, the conference proclaimed that "it is necessary to make arrangements for their education on sanitation and religions, also to allow them to read in schools, to draw water from wells, to visit in temples and to sit in public meetings."[9] It was stated that Hindu reform groups had already been working through All India Achhutodhar committee, Panjab Achhbut Udhar Mandal (1926), Shraddhananda Dalituddhar Shabha (1921), Jat Pat Torak Mandal (1922), Dalituddhar Mandal (1923). It seemed that the *Hindu Mahasabha,* the guardians of the untouchables was "a strange event", and Ambedkar felt it was an insult.[10] Here the questions arise were the relationship of the *Hindu Mahasabha* with the untouchables, and why were they more suited to the work of abolishing untouchability than the Congress? From the untouchable's point of view, Ambedkar warned that "not to believe those Hindus *Sanghatanists* who were wooing them because of the rising menace of the Muslim pressure."[11] In this perspective, Ambedkar was bitterly opposed to the *Mahasabha* stand. He asserted that the *Mahasabha* was not a social reform organization but a purely political group. Its main aim was to oppose Muslim influence in Indian politics. He blamed the Congress of shifting its anti-untouchability programmer to the *Hindu Mahasabha.*[12] The Untouchables needed to lead themselves. Ambedkar opposed to the caste system, particularly of Brahmanism and he believed that caste system would have to nothing could emancipate the outcaste except the destruction of caste. He said that the Brahmins were responsible for the degradation of the Sudras.[13]

In this situation, the Round Table Conferences were held in London (1930-1932) to recommend a workable solution to the Indian Constitutional problems. At the end of the Second Round Table Conference of 1932, the British Prime Minister Ramsay McDonald announced Communal Awards[14] (1932) which led to the problems of different communities by various stands. The Poona Pact was signed on 24th September, 1932 which increased the untouchable's representative in the legislative Assembly. This pact guaranteed the reservation seats for untouchables but it showed the differences and tactics between Gandhi and Ambedkar. In the early stage, Gandhi believed that untouchability can be removed by changing minds of the caste Hindus. But Ambedkar seemed that the guarantee of rights, backed up by political power. The separate electorate system was acted in the Reform Act of 1935. From the untouchable point of view, D.D. Kosambi argued that the act of articulating an anti-colonial alliance between the elite nationalists and the subaltern masses. A recent example of this approach is provided by Kosambi who says that "when the 1930 *satyagraha* got out of hand and was about to be transformed into a fundamentally different movement by the no-rent and no-tax campaigns in 1932, Gandhi discovered the need for the uplift of the untouchables, and the whole movement was neatly sidetracked."[15] It may be noted that Gandhi was in no position to launch a radical movement against untouchability giving reassert control over Indian nationalism in the early 1930s. It may be questioned if Untouchables are Hindus then why should they not purify their religion by taking possession of a temple? And why should they wait for it to be 'purified by the trustees and the worshippers recognizing? [16]

Until 1935, B.R. Ambedkar's work took three directions, the most visibly successful was the awakening and organizing of the Untouchables through newspaper of their own and social, political, cultural and widely attending conferences 01 Depressed Classes. He gave petition to the British government for considering political representation for Untouchables. In his last direction he wanted to encourage education among the lower class under the Peoples Education Society. Just, he believed that only Untouchables could lead Untouchables. He never joined or supported any caste Hindu-led group; he invited higher caste Hindu leaders to serve in his institutes and its activities. He seemed untouchable's self-improvement, and continued writings and speeches against bad practices (drinking and the eating of carrion beef) which were ethics as lower caste to leave these practices and get self-respect. It is, however clear that Untouchables believed their inability to participate in the religious life around them, it felt that he never much trust in the ability of Hinduism to reform itself.[17] Once Dr. Ambedkar boldly declared, "I was born as a Hindu, but I will not die as a Hindu' and stated that 'change your religion, reject Hinduism and convert to a religion that does not recognize caste or untouchability. Ultimately, both Ambedkar and Gandhi were right: in order to abolish untouchability."[18] Ambedkar protested against the limits of Gandhianism and he commented that the nation does not exist. His main aims were to attack on the system of political, social and economic structures disruptives.

At that time, Ambedkar funded a political party viz, the Independent Labour Party. He established the Scheduled Castes Federation in 1942 for united Untouchables all over India and waged the state for separate electorates. During the period (1942 -1946), Ambedkar was harshly critical of the Congress. He was elected to the Constituent Assembly in 1946; also nominated for the cabinet post of Minister of Law. The Constituent Assembly was formed under the leadership of Dr. B.R. Ambedkar. But in the early stages of drafting the Constitution, he faced two major problems – Firstly, how to protect the rights of the Untouchables? Secondly, to reject the British Communal Electorate System and how to keep intact the rights of the Dalits in the new electorate system? [19] In this research, a Sub-Committee was formed for solving the problems under the chairmanship of Sarder Patel with the other members such as Dr. B.R. Ambedkar, Pandit Jawaharwal Nehru, Dr. Rajendra Prasad and K.M. Munshi. This Sub-Committee recommended for reservation of Dalit Classes.[20] All these demands became the part of independent India's government policy. It was stated that Dalits were at the bottom of the Hindu caste system and laws trying to protect them, they still face widespread distinction in India. Ambedkar being a prolific writer he wrote '*Who were Sudras?*', '*The Untouchable Castes in India*', '*The Buddha and His Dhamma*', and '*Pakistan or the Partition of India*', etc. Ambedkar's theory did not appear until it was published in the book '*The Untouchables: Who Were They and Why They Became Untouchables*' by 1948 book Ambedkar totally denied a racial, ethnic or occupational basis for the origin of Untouchability. He also mentioned that Untouchables were pushed aside in the struggle for supremacy between Buddhism and Brahminism which was so completely to mould the history of India.[21]

Ambedkar devoted himself in his life of over 40 years to a set of principles, standards and goals relating to the removal of Untouchability in the society. These can be identified as follow:

(i) Untouchables must possess self-respect; disassociate them from the traditional promise of the Untouchable status.

(ii) Untouchables must be represented by their own representatives in social and political aspects. Till the Round Table Conferences of 1930-32, Ambedkar wanted reserved seats in a general electorate only. He believed that Untouchables must be seen as a minority and treated as a separate people.

(iii) All types of caste must be abolished. Ambedkar regarded as true that caste had been created by man and it could be removed by man.

(iv) Untouchables must become educated, not merely to literacy but to get the highest level of education.

(v) The government must take responsibility to promote the welfare of Untouchables', creating special rights for those to whom society had denied education and occupation opportunities.[22]

It was asserted that the Indian Constitution requires the state to treat all het citizens equally, without discrimination on birth, gender or religious aspects. Yet the Constitution provides special care and advancement of the Untouchables. For instance,[23]

Article 15(2) declares: "No citizen shall, on only grounds of religion, race, caste, sex–with regard to- access to shops, public restaurants, hotels and places of public entertainments: or the use of wells, tanks, bathing ghats, roads and places of public resorts maintained."

Article 17 declares: "Untouchability is abolished and its practice in any form is forbidden. The enforcement of any disability arising out Untouchability shall be an offence punishable in accordance with law."

After Independence, the Indian Government constituted various commissions and passed acts as follows–Kalelkar Commission (1953-1955), Untouchability Prohibition Act (1955) and Mandal Commission (1979-1980) etc. But ultimately, these steps failed to remove untouchability in our society; the debate is going on among the scholars. In this connection, a question naturally comes, how far the Untouchability can be removed? Now-a-days, the condition of untouchables is worsening day after day they are annihilated upper caste people. There is no doubt that a dalit child is born with a stamp on his forehead can never get rid of it. It is became that dalit born Dr. Ambedkar became the militant champion of untouchables. He stood for the social liberation, economic emancipation and political advancement of untouchables. Even today, majority of dalits are remaining landless, desperately poor and illiterates. In this connection we may point out that Ambedkar devoted himself to improve the living conditions of the Untouchables. In early stage there was a conflicting opinion between Ambedkar and Gandhi other the issue of untouchables. But ultimately both recognized the means of the term untouchable. At the end of their life, both began to admire each other regarding the problem of downtrodden. Ambedkar ultimately recognized Gandhi's contribution and acknowledged that the opposed had been nearest and dearest to Gandhi. Thus it can be said that Ambedkar's contribution as a scholar, parliamentarian and a reformer was well-known. In conclusion, it is quite clear that the untouchability cannot be removed through laws; but through changing interest of people awareness. Dr Ambedkar's thought regarding untouchability will continue to be of great relevance in the socio-political and cultural fields in India.

NOTES AND REFERENCES

1. See, Dhananjay Keer, *Dr. Ambedkar: Life and Mission,* Popular Prakashan, 3rd edition, 1971
2. G. S. Ghurye, *Caste and Race in India,* Popular Prakashan, Bombay, 1969, p. 227.
3. From website: adaniel.tripod.com/untouchables.htm.
4. Vijay Prashad, "The Untouchable Question", *Economic and Political Weekly,* Vol. 31, No. 9 (March 2, 1996), p. 553.
5. Ibid.
6. Thomas Pantham & Kennth L Deutsch (eds.), *Political Thought in Modern India,* Sage Publication India Pvt Ltd, New Delhi, 1986, p. 163.
7. Vijay Prashad, op. cit., p. 553.
8. P D Kaushik, *The Congress Ideology and Programme, 1920-1985,* Gitanjali Publishing House, New Delhi, 1986, p. 153.
9. For details, see A K Misra, *Hindu Mahasabha. Ek Adhyay,* New Delhi, 1988, pp. 72-85.
10. Vijay Prasad, op. cit., p. 553.
11. Dhananjay Keer, op. cit., p. 87.
12. For details the Communal Award and Poona Pact see, Joya Chatterjee, *Bengal Divided: Hindu Communalism and Partition, 1932-1947,* Cambridge University Press, Cambridge, reprint, 2002, pp. 33-54.
13. V.P. Verma, *Modern Indian Political Thought,* Laxmi Narain Aggarwal Education Publishers, Agra, 1974, p. 512.

14. B.R. Ambedkar, *What Congress and Gandhi Have Done to the Untouchables?* Thacker, Bombay, 1946, p. 22.
15. D D Kosambi, "*The Function of Leadership in a Mass Movement (1939)*", Exasperating Essays, Calcutta, 1977, pp. 7-9.
16. *The Young India,* July 23, 1931.
17. See, Thomas Pantham & Kenneth L Deutsch, op. cit., pp. 161-163.
18. From website: www.wondersandmarvels.com/—dr-b-r-ambedkar-untouchable-reform.
19. T. K. Chakraborty, "*Bharate Sanrakshan: Sanbidhanik Byabasta*", an Article Published in *Jatpat O Sanrakshan: Bharatiya Prekshapat* edited by Sujay Sen, Mitram, Kolkata, 2008, p. 20.
20. Ibid, p. 21.
21. Dr. B. R. Ambedkar, *The Untouchables: Who were They and Why They Became Untouchables?* Amrit Publishing Co., New Delhi, 1948, p. 155.
22. See, Thomas Pantham & Kenneth L Deutsch, op. cit., p. 172-175.
23. See, Susan Bayly, *Caste, Society and Politics in India from the Eighteenth Century to the Modern Age,* Cambridge University Press, 2001, pp. 268-269.

23

Dr. B.R. Ambedkar in Making Up the Indian Constitution

– Abhishek Mitra

An eminent member of the constituent assembly and the first president of independent India, Dr. Rajendra Prasad said that, we could never make a decision which could be ever so right as when we put him on the drafting committee and made him its chairman. This statement proved the position and role and also the contribution of Dr. Ambedkar as the chairman of drafting committee. Dr. Ambedkar was not only the framer of Indian constitution but also the great social reformer of that time. According to Bidyut Chakraborty and Rajendra Kumar Pandy, amongst the galaxy of thinkers of modern India, Ambedkar (1861-1956) stands on a pedestal different from others for a variety of reasons. First, very profoundly, his personality exemplifies the unique saga of dalit able to fight the massive social disabilities by sheer formidable courage an eminent constitutionalist, distinguished parliamentarian, scholar and jurist and above all, the leader of depressed classes. Second, he, in a way, began a social reform movement against untouchability in India by evolving a flexible, well-reasoned and multi-pronged strategy to fight against all those who mattered but resisted the struggle of dalits to secure a dignified and respectful place in the Indian society. Third, recognizing him as an innovator of sorts, Ambedekar may arguably be credited with reconceptualising the whole notion of then emancipation of downtrodden in India by broadening the horizons of the concept of the emancipation to include within its ambit.

Certain other critical aspects of empowerment which remained largely, if not totally of its ambit till date.

Dr. Ambedkar was a name similar to justice, liberty, equality and fraternity. He was the most suitable person to be appointed as the chairman of the drafting committee of the constitution of India mainly on two causes. Firstly, He was amongst the most qualified jurist of India at that time, whose works were recognized by famous legal experts like Ivor Jennings, secondly, Dr. Ambedkar was the best person to know the cruel realities of the caste system of society and suggest reforms for removing social in- equality.

According to Granville Austin, Indian constitution is as first and foremost social document. Today Indian constitution is a real instance of democratic model for all nations. Eminent Indian historian Ramchandra Guha describes the process of drafting of Indian constitution as follows; 'the proceedings of the constituent assembly of India were printed eleven bulky volumes'. Some of which exceed 1000 pages and they are little known treasure-trove, invaluable to the historian, and a potential source of enlightenment to the interested citizen. In them we find many compositing ideas of the nation, of what language it should speak, what political system and economic systems should follow, what moral values it should uphold or disavow.' It is true that there were seven members of drafting committee, but the main responsibility goes to Ambedkar, because, in the mid time of drafting the constitution, one had resigned from the house and was replaced. One died and was not replaced. One was way in America and his place was not filled up and another person was engaged in the state of affairs and there was a void to the extent. One or two members were far away from Delhi and due to health reasons they did not to attend. So it happened that the burden of drafting this constitution fell on Ambedkar and no doubt that he successfully done this job. Our constitution reflects:

Rights of the people: Articulating his views on caste annihilation, Ambedkar expressed a social order based on the ideals of liberty, equality and fraternity. As a firm believer in an egalitarian and democratic political system, he was convinced that such an order could be designed only by having the ideals of liberty, equality and fraternity indissolubly ingrained in the law of the land of the country. In the discussion of rights Ambedkar explains, rights are protected not by law but by moral conscience of society. If social conscience is such that is prepared to recognize the rights which law chooses to enact, rights will be safe and secure, ie, when fundamental rights are opposed by the community, no law, no parliament, no judiciary can guarantee them in the real sense of the word.

Fundamental rights are the very essential parts of Indian constitution which secure individual liberty and rights. Ambedkar in his book '*Ranade Gandhi and Jinnah*' expressed his view that the idea of making a gift of fundamental rights to every individual is no doubt very laudable. In Indian constitution there are basically six fundamental rights, rights to equality, right to freedom, right against exploitation, right to freedom of religion, cultural and educational rights and right to constitutional remedies. But the essential question is how to make up them effective. Ambedkar's answer on this question is, the judiciary parliament and law all together would not come to rescue the fundamental rights if there is an opposition from the community.

Right to constitutional remedies Ambedkar's firm believes were those if the fundamental rights are not been seriously protected then these are valueless things. So, judicial review is another essential part of the Indian constitution. He described these provisions enable an individual to file a writ as 'heart and soul' of the Indian constitution. Article 32 and 226 of the constitution provide for judicial review, such provision of judicial review gives teeth to various rights provided in the Indian constitution. In India constitution is considered to be the supreme, unlike UK. In UK the parliament is considered to be the supreme. This shows in India the will of the 'we' the people of India .... as explained in the preamble of the constitution. Therefore, any law, which goes against the constitutional principles, would be subject to Judicial Review and would be declared null and void by the court. In constituent assembly Dr. Ambedkar defended the provisions of judicial review as being very necessary.

Directive principles of state policy as a liberal thinker, Ambedkar were a strong believer in the value of constitutional democracy having irrevocable elements of social and economic democracies in addition to political democracy. Apart from that he was very much familiar to social democracy. Basically, social democracy means a way of life which recognizes liberty, equality and fraternity which are not to be treated as separate items in a trinity. They form a union of trinity in the sense that to divorce one from the other is to defeat the very purpose of democracy. Social and constitutional values of this trend he had incorporated in himself while studying abroad, and again got reflected in his discussions in the constituent assembly. Ambedkars greatest contribution towards achieving economic democracy is the part 4 of Indian constitution. Directive principles are the constitutional guidelines which the governments both central and state have to keep into consideration while framing laws and policies, although these principles are not directly enforceable by the court of law. He had strong opposition while these directive principles of state policy included in the constitution basically in the case of legal validity and the words state shall strive to. Ambedkar's answer was that we have used it because our intention is that even when there are circumstances which prevent the government, or which stand in the way of government giving effect to these principles, they shall, even under hard and unpropitious circumstances, always strive to the fulfillment of these directives.

Abolition of untouchability: The social thoughts of Ambedkar basically revolves around the idea of understanding the dynamics of caste system in India and waging a tireless crusade against the curse of untouchability. Drawn from his own experiences in being subject to numerous social indignities and discriminations at various stages and different walks of his life, he was convinced of the purposes of his life for which he remained steadfastly committed. Ambedkar himself had to face the evil of untouchability at different stages of his life. Abolition of untouchability was one of the objectives of his entire movement. Article 17 of the Indian constitution abolishes untouchability. The practice of untouchability is considered to be a punishable offence.

Reservation policy/positive discrimination: Reservation policy is now become a subject to million dollar debate, either is right or not. But it is true that the basic objectives of such policy are to establish equality among all castes sections of the society. On the subject of reservation, Ambedkar had a view that, a representative government is much effective than an efficient government. Objective resolution of the draft constitution itself guaranteed equality, basic freedom of expression, with adequate safeguards for minorities, tribal's, backwards and other unprivileged sections of the people. These principles acted as guideline for the draftsmanship throughout the constitution making process and provided a strong foundation for inclusion of reservation for the unprivileged, which was essentially aimed at removing the inequality. So, this discrimination in the constitution of India is treated as positive discrimination.

Quasi Federal Form of Government: Dr. Ambedkar Wanted to establish, India as a unitary state along with some strong federal features, this is a unique combination for its own nececetity. He described Indian constitution in the constituent assembly as follows 'our constitution would be both unitary as well as federal according to our requirements of time and circumstances.' According to K.C. where, a system of government which is quasi federal, a unitary state with subsidiary federal features rather than a federal state with subsidiary unitary features, probably says the Indian constitution of 1950. Dr. Ambedkar, described the working of Indian constitution as follows.' In normal times, it is framed to work as a federal system, but in the time of war or other emergency condition it is so designed as to make it work as though a unitary system. Once the president issues a proclamation, the whole scene can become transformed and the state becomes a unitary state. Ambedkar explained the weakness of pure federal government such as America and Australia. Ambedkar thought a federal government suffers from rigidity. Ambedkar also cleared why India is described as a Union in Article 1 of the Constitution. He explained that the drafting committee wanted to make it clear that though India was to be a federation, the federation was not a result of an agreement by the states to join in a federation and that the federation not being the result of an agreement and no state has the right to secede from it. The federation is a union because it is indestructible. So the constitution of India is flexible by its own nature.

CONCLUSION

The Constitution of India is not only treated as a social document for the members of constituent assembly only, many scholars and experts around the world eulogized it. One of the eminent thinkers, Ernest Barker in his popular book '*Principles of Social and Political Theory* included the preamble of the constitution of India. He was of the view that. ....' I ought to explain, as I end, why the preamble to the constitution of India is printed after table of contents. It seemed to me, when I read it, to state in brief and pithy from the argument of much of the book; and it may accordingly serve as a key-note. I am more moved to quote it because I am proud that the people of India should begin their independent life by subscribing to the principles of a political tradition which we in the west call western, but which is now something more than western. The above statement has shown the acceptability and position of Indian constitution worldwide. Although it is true that, Ambedkar was not the single person who make the Indian constitution alone, but the constitution of India and Dr. Ambedkar are inseparable; therefore, when any provision of constitutions comes up for interpretation, the court heavily relies on what was stated by Ambedkar in the constituent assembly. His ideas on constitutionalism are the touching for the Indian judiciary in deciding any constitutional anomaly. Ambedkar proved himself as a multitalented personality of his time. Eminent writer Eleanor Zelliot... during his lifetime, Ambedkar played three roles : that of a caste leader , a dalit spokesman , and a national statesman. In his first leadership he was a guide and decision maker for his own caste, from the mid twenties of this century until his death. From the early 1930s onwards, he was the chief spokesman of the untouchables in the eyes of the government of India. In his third role, he spoke on all phases of India's development, working of problem on the labour and law, being a member of the government, and even put aside his theories to help create a viable, generally accepted constitution. After seventy years of independence the constitution of India has been amended many times without touching upon the basic frame work or structure of the constitution. Thus, Dr. Ambedkar's contribution to the constitution still continues. In the age of liberalization, privatization and globalization the constitution of India still relevant and the people of India will never forget the contribution of this great personality.

REFERENCES

1. Bidyut Chakrabarty and Rajendra Kumar Pandey, *Modern Indian political Thought; Text and context,* Sage Publication, New Delhi, 2015.
2. A. Appadorai, Political *Thoughts in India* (400 B.C -1980) Khama Publisher, New Delhi, 2002.
3. Eleanor Zelliot, *The Social and Political Thought of B.R. Ambedkar* in Thomas Pantham and K Deutsch (eds*), Political Thought in Modern India,* Sage Publications, New Delhi, 1986.
4. Christophe Jaffrelot, *Dr Ambedkar and Untouchability,* Permanent Black, New Delhi, 2005.
5. B.R. Ambedkar, *Caste In India, Their Mechanism, Genesis and Development,* India Antiquity, New Delhi, 1917.
6. B.R. Ambedkar, *Annihilation of Caste,* Arnold Publishers, New Delhi, 1990.
7. M.S. Gore, *The Social Context of an Ideology: Ambedkar's Political and Social Thought,* Sage Publications, New Delhi, 1983.
8. D.D. Joshi, Dr. Ambedkar and Drafting of Indian Constitution: A see through into the making of ***a*** masterpiece from the eyes of its Architect, *Journal of Law,* Vo.13, 2013.
9. I. Mclean and A. Mcmillan (eds), Oxford Concise Dictionary of Politics, Oxford University Press, New Delhi, 2003.

24

Morning Shows of the Day: An Introspection of the Childhood Days of Bhimrao Ambedkar

– Animesh Raptan

The present scenario of socio-economic discrimination throughout the world is perilous as is apparent from the different media coverage. It is in this context that the name of Bhimrao Ramji Ambedkar flashes in our mind, a personality who wrestled against all sorts of discrimination.

"Life should be great rather than long"- It was the voice of Dr. Bhimrao Ambedkar who proved it from the childhood days. Ambedkar's family had a long history of military service, on both his mother and father side. His grandfather and his father Ramji Sakpal were in British Indian army. Ambedkar was born on 14th April 1891 in the British founded town and military cantonment of Mhow in the central province, now in Madhya Pradesh. He was the14th and last child of Ramji Maloji Sakpal and Bhimabai Murbadkar. His family belonged to the Hindu Mahar caste, who were treated as untouchables and subjected to intense socio-economic discrimination. Born in a socially backward family, Ambedkar was the victim of caste discrimination, inequality and prejudice from his childhood days.

Belonging to the British Subedar Ramji Sakpal encouraged his children to learn and work hard at school from the childhood days. His father also incited his children to read the Hindu classic. Belonging a army man Ramji admitted his children to study at the government school, as they faced resistance owing to their low caste. Ambedkar and other untouchable children were segregated and given no attention or assistance by the teachers. They were not allowed to sit inside the class. Even if they needed to drink water somebody from a higher caste would have to pour that water from a height as they were not allowed to touch either the water or the vessel that contained it. This work was usually performed for the young Ambedkar by the school peon and if he could not be found Ambedkar went without water.

In 1894 Ramji Sakpal retired from the army soon after Ambedkar's birth and settled down at Dapoli in Konkon. It was while Bhim was around 7 years old and attending school at Dapoli that he picked up the name Ambedkar. Brahmin teacher of young boys school changed his surname from Sakpal to Ambedkar to protect him from taunts of so called higher caste bluster, who harried him for belonging to the untouchable. Besides this, there are several incidents topic place where Ambedkar was treated badly for his low caste during his childhood days. Some of them may be worth mentioning. On a rainy day Ambedkar during his journey to the school took shelter outside a house. The lady of that house saw him and got angry. She pushed Ambedkar into the rain. The boy fell into the water and his books were damaged. There was another incident where Ambedkar was denied even the life sustaining needs for his just because of his low caste. One day he felt thirsty and took water from a well for drinking. Some people noticed it and punished him mercilessly. These incidents had profound impact on Ambedkar's mind and led him to advocate for a society free from discrimination in terms of caste, creed and race.

Soon after, Ambedkar's mother death and Ramji Sakpal shifted his lodging house to Mumbai. The whole family lived in a single room. Bhimrao was admitted into the Maratha high school, but seeing his son's interest in academics, Ramji shifted Bhimrao to the more expensive and well considered Elphinstone high school in 1897. Belonging to the first suppressed community student of the school where Ambedkar was taught mathematics, science and various other subjects, but was not permitted to learn Sanskrit due to his caste.

Ambedkar was increasingly disturbed by the isolation and discrimination that he faced. Overcoming numerous social and financial obstacles, Ambedkar passed matriculation examination (1907) becoming one of the first person of Dalit origin to enter a college in India. This success provoked celebration in his community and after a public ceremony he was presented with a biography of the Buddha by his teacher Krishnaji Arjun Keluskar. This biography named "Life of Gautam Buddha" played a role in introducing Ambedkar to the teaching of the Buddha, and would later influence him into converting to Buddhism.

In 1908 Ambedkar entered Elphinstone College and obtained a scholarship of twenty five rupees a month from the Gayakwad ruler of Borada, Sahyaji Rao III for higher studies in the USA. By 1912 he obtained his degree in economics and political science, and prepared to take up employment with the Baroda state government. A few months later, in 1913 Ambedkar went New York city and admitted at Columbia University with a scholarship. Ambedkar was admitted to the graduate studies programme at the political science department. He completed his MA degree in 1915. His Master 'thesis' title was "*Ancient Indian Commerce*" and he also presented his first academic work on India's caste system, titled '*Castes in India, Their Mechanism, Genesis and Development*,' in 1916. After a few months, he submitted his Ph.D. thesis titled '*The National Dividend of India, a Historic and Analytical Study*'. After the completion of his courses at the Columbia University, he went to London and enrolled at Grays Inn and London School of Economics studying Law and preparing a doctoral thesis in economics. Once again his studies were sponsored by the Maharaja of Borada. The expiration of his scholarship the following year forced him to temporarily abandon his studies and return to India amidst World War I.

Ambedkar reached India on August 21, 1917 and some years later Ambedkar began to practice law at the age of 32. Becoming of highly educated and qualified Ambedkar was still considered as a dalit and upper caste Hindus refused to have anything to do with him. At that time Veer Savarkar the freedom fighter started the Hindu Sanghatan for the upliftment of backward castes. Mahatma Gandhi also began Harijan movement and Ambedkar established a successful legal practice, and also organized the Bahishkrit Hitakarini Sabha to Promote education and socio economic uplifting of the depressed classes. In 1926, he became a nominated member of the Bombay Legislative Council. By 1927 Dr. Ambedkar decided to launch active movements against untouchability. Ambedkar himself travelled from village to village throughout the region of Bombay and Goa to encourage marginalised community to seek out their rights and work for social upliftment. He also attended and presided over the first Provincial Depressed classes conference held at Nipani in Bombay Presidency and the first conference for untouchables at Malwan. Then he also started his second fortnightly Marathi Paper Bahiskrit Bharat on April 3, 1927 to keep the untouchables informed of situations and to attract enlightened Hindus of the upper Castes to his cause. Ambedkar succeeded in many attempts. For example it was due in past to his efforts that in 1931 the Bombay police opened up their recruitment to the depressed classes. He succeeded to open up and share public drinking water resources and also began a struggle to fight for the right to enter Hindus temples.

Ambedkar wanted to abolish the cause of untouchability from the Hindu society. He realized thatthe caste system be left intact while merely wiping out untouchability. That is why, he called or total annihilation of caste system in the society. Annihilation of caste is an undelivered speech written in 1936 by B.R. Ambedkar. The speech was prepared as presidential address for the annual conference of Hindu reformist Jat-Pat Todak Mandal, on the ill effects of caste in Hindu society. Ambedkar criticized the Hindu caste system and its law book. He argued that inter caste dining and inter caste marriage is not sufficient to annihilate the caste system, but that the real method of breaking up the caste system was to destroy the religious notion upon which caste is founded. He realised that the caste system must be abolished if the Hindu society is to be reconstructed on the basis of equality, goes without saying. Untouchability has its roots in the caste system. They cannot except the Brahmins to rise in revolt against the caste system. According to Ambedkar's opinion, we cannot rely upon the non-Brahmins and ask them to fight our battle.

Most of these are more interested in bringing the Brahmins down rather than in raising the level of the suppressed classes. That is why we ourselves must fight out battles, relying on ourselves. Untouchability has ruined the untouchables, the Hindus and ultimately the nation as a whole. At this point, it is pertinent to mention that many so-called upper caste Hindus like Lokmanya Tilak, M.R. Jayakar were supportive of Ambedkar. Ambedkar stressed that people were not responsible for untouchability just because they were upper caste Hindus. He pointed out that there were many enlightened people among the so-called upper castes who were working alongside him, and even quoted profusely from Bhagavad Gita in proving his points that the caste system was never meant to be such an oppressive joke, it was merely begun as an a means of division of labour.

In 1930, the British government considering this sensitive issue and the overwhelming hostility of the Indian people to the British Raj, proposed a round table conference in which they would discuss the framing of a constitution for India. Indian leaders were invited to London to discuss the matters. M.R. Jayakar, Mohammad Ali Jinnah and also Dr. Ambedkar was invited to represent the depressed classes.

India's tryst with destiny, as India's first Prime Minister Jawaharlal Nehru spoke eloquently about all the fateful hour of India's independence, saw Dr. Ambedkar being entrusted with a monumental responsibility, he was appointed chairman of the Constitution Drafting committee on August 29, 1947. Becoming the chairman of Indian constitution Dr. Ambedkar abolished untouchability and all sorts of discrimination. An ardent proponent of the right of women, minorities and the social underprivileged, he argued eloquently and won the constituent Assembly's support for introducing a system of reservations of jobs in the civil services, schools and colleges, for members of Scheduled Castes, Scheduled Tribes and other backward class. This was later reflected in the policies of affirmative action adopted by the Indian government.

So, young Ambedkar faced a lot of problems during academic training, but he surpassed all these. Ambedkar continuously played a key role to eradicate all sorts' discrimination in terms of caste and race and fought for social inequality. Babasaheb as he was fondly called by admirers and followers, braved the walls of prejudice and caste discrimination in early 20th century to emerge as an exemplar and an unflinching crusader against the inequalities of caste system and socio-economic deprivation that afflicted millions of Indians. His life is an inspiration story of achievements despite trying circumstances and the indomitable will to move beyond individual strife for the larger cause of social justice and national integration. The boy who suffered bitter humiliation during his childhood and became the first Minster of Law in free India and shaped the country's constitution. He was a determined fighter, a deep scholar, reformer and ultimately ahuman to the tips of his fingers. Ambedkar has been honoured with Bharat Ratna, India's highest civilian award. As India celebrates the 125th birth anniversary of this national icon, Dr. Ambedkar remains an inspiration for all Indians and proponents of equality and social justice across the globe.

REFERENCES

1. Misra, Kaushlendra, '*B R Ambedkar As a Human Right Leaders*', Bombay, 1925.
2. Ankodia, R.K. & Ankodia, Hemlata, '*B R Ambedkar & His Ideology*', Bombay, 1947.
3. Michael, S.M, '*Untouchable, Dalit in Modern India*', New Delhi, 1999.

25
Bhimrao Ramji Ambedkar and Buddhism

– Sreerupa Bhattacharjee

Bhimrao Ramji Ambedkar (14 April 1891–06 December 1956), popularly known as Babasaheb, was an Indian jurist, economist, politician and social reformer who inspired the Dalit Buddhist movement and campaigned against social discrimination against untouchables (Dalits). He was Independent India's first Law Minister and the principal architect of the Constitution of India.

In his early career Ambedkar was an economist, professor, and lawyer. His later life was marked by his political activities; he became involved in campaigning and negotiations for India's independence, publishing journals advocating political rights and social freedom for Dalits, and contributing significantly to the establishment of the state of India. In 1956 he converted to Buddhism, initiating mass conversions of Dalits.

Ambedkar was born in the town and military cantonment of Mhow in the Central Provinces (now in Madhya Pradesh) into a poor Mahar (dalit) caste, who were treated as untouchables and subjected to socio-economic discrimination. Although they attended school, Ambedkar and other children form marginalized community were segregated and given little attention or help by teachers.

The story of Bhimrao Ramji Ambedkar's life is the story of how exceptional talent and outstanding force of character succeeded in overcoming some of the most formidable obstacles that an unjust and oppressive society has ever placed in the way of the individual.

In 1908 the young Ambedkar passed the matriculation examination of Bombay University and also graduated from the same university with Politics and Economics. After his father's death he left India to continue his studies at Columbia University (USA). Convinced as he was that knowledge is power, he knew that without that power in full measure he had little hope of breaking the bonds that kept millions of marginal community in a state of virtual slavery. At the age of thirty-two he finally returned to India. His first published work, however, was a paper on '*Castes in India: Their Mechanism, Genesis and Development*'. After completing his studies in America, Ambedkar left New York for London and was admitted to the London School of Economics and Political Science and to Gray's Inn. There he completed his thesis 'on the *Problem of the Rupee*', for which the University of London awarded him a D.Sc. Thus the man who returned to India in April 1923 to continue his fight on behalf of the suppresses class and, indeed, all the depressed classes, was uniquely well equipped for the task. While Ambedkar remained sharply critical of British rule, it was to the removal of the social, economic, educational, and legal disabilities of the Depressed Classes that he devoted the major part of his energies. One of his most significant achievements during the years immediately following his return to India in 1923 was the formation of the Bahishkrit Hitakarini Sabha or Depressed Classes Welfare Association, the objects of which were to promote the spread of education and culture among the Depressed Classes, to improve their economic condition, and to represent their grievances. Unpopular as Ambedkar's activities had already made him with the Caste Hindus, during 1931 and 1932 he became more unpopular still. In his own words, he became the most hated man in India – hated, that is, by the Caste Hindus and by the Congress Party, which they dominated. The cause of the trouble was Ambedkar's continued insistence on the necessity of separate electorates for the Depressed Classes. Mahatma Gandhi and the Congress Party were opposed to separate electorates for the Depressed Classes. Ramsay MacDonald published his Communal Award. The Depressed Classes were given the separate electorates for which they had asked. Gandhi's response was to go on a fast to the death for the abolition of separate electorates. Ambedkar eventually agreed to exchange separate electorates for joint electorates and a greatly increased number of reserved seats. This agreement was embodied in a document that became known as the Poona Pact, the signing of which by Ambedkar marked his emergence as the undisputed leader of the Depressed Classes. He also began to think that there was no future for the depresses class within Hinduism and that they should change their religion. These thoughts found dramatic expression at the 1935 Depressed Classes Conference, when he made his famous declaration that though he had been born a Hindu he did not intend to die one – a declaration that sent shock waves through Hindu India.

In 1947 India achieved independence and Ambedkar, who had already been elected a member of the Constituent Assembly, was invited by Pandit Nehru, to join the Cabinet as Minister for Law. A few weeks later the Assembly entrusted the task of framing the Constitution to a Draft Committee which elected Ambedkar as its chairman. Despite his ill health Ambedkar managed to complete the Draft of Constitution by the beginning of 1948 and later that year, when it had been before the country for six months, had the satisfaction of introducing it in the Constituent Assembly. Thereafter he piloted it through its three readings with his usual competence and in November 1949 it was adopted by the Assembly with very few amendments. But though by 1948 Ambedkar had achieved so much, and though today he is most widely remembered as the author of the Indian Constitution, his greatest achievement was in fact still to come. This achievement was an essentially spiritual one, and it came only at the very end of his life, when he had spent several years in the political wilderness after failing to secure the passage of the Hindu Code Bill. Ambedkar was accused of trying to destroy Hinduism and there were angry exchanges on the Assembly floor between him and his orthodox opponents. At last the Bill was dropped after only four clauses had been passed and in September 1951, tired and disgusted, Ambedkar resigned from the Cabinet. Ambedkar's resignation from the Cabinet marked the virtual end of his political career. In the general elections of January 1952 he failed to win a seat in the Lok Sabha or House of Representatives, and was equally unsuccessful when he contested a by-election the following year. Towards the end of March 1952 he was, however, elected to the Rajya Sabha. But while he continued to participate in the proceedings of the Rajya Sabha, and was to do so until the end of his life, from now onwards Ambedkar's energies were increasingly devoted to more important things. Ever since the 1935 Depressed Classes Conference, when he had shocked Hindu India with the declaration that though he had been born a Hindu he did not intend to die one, he had been giving earnest consideration to the question of conversion. The longer he thought about it the more he was convinced that there was no future for the depresses class within Hinduism, that they would have to adopt another religion, and that the best religion for them to adopt was Buddhism. During his years in office it had been hardly possible for him to bring about so momentous a change, but he had lost no opportunity of educating his followers in the issues involved, and it became increasingly apparent in which direction he and they were moving. In 1950 he not only praised the Buddha at the expense of Krishna, Christ, and Muhammad but also visited Ceylon at the invitation of the Young Men's Buddhist Association, Colombo, addressed a meeting of the World Fellowship of Buddhists in Kandy, and appealed to the marginalized community of Ceylon to embrace Buddhism. In 1951 he defended the Buddha against the charge that he had been responsible for the downfall of the Indian woman and compiled the Bauddha Upasana Patha, a small collection of Buddhist devotional texts. Thus when his resignation from the Cabinet, and his failure to secure election to the Lok Sabha, finally left Ambedkar with the time and energy for his greatest achievement, the ground was already well prepared.

In 1954 he twice visited Burma, the second time in order to attend the third conference of the World Fellowship of Buddhists in Rangoon. In 1955 he founded the Bharatiya Bauddha Mahasabha or Indian Buddhist Society and installed an image of the Buddha in a temple that had been built at Dehu Road, near Poona. Addressing the thousands of suppressed classes who had assembled for the occasion, he declared that henceforth he would devote himself to the propagation of Buddhism in India. He also announced that he was writing a book explaining the tenets of Buddhism in simple language for the benefit of the common man. It might take him a year to complete the book, but when it was finished he would embrace Buddhism. The work in question was '*The Buddha and His Dhamma*', on which he had been working since November 1951 and which he completed in February 1956. Afterwards Ambedkar, true to his word, announced that he would be embracing Buddhism in October of that year. Arrangements were accordingly made for the ceremony to be held in Nagpur, and on 14 October 1956 the depressed class leader took the Three Refuges and Five Precepts from a Buddhist monk in the traditional manner and then in his turn administered them to the 380,000 men, women, and children who had come to Nagpur in response to his call. After further conversion ceremonies in Nagpur and Chanda Ambedkar returned to Delhi knowing that the Wheel of the Dharma had again been set in motion in India. A few weeks later he travelled to Kathmandu in Nepal for the fourth conference of the World Fellowship of Buddhists and addressed the delegates on 'The Buddha and Karl Marx'. On his way back to Delhi he made two speeches in Benares and visited Kusinara, where the Buddha had died. In Delhi he took part in various Buddhist functions, attended the Rajya Sabha, and completed the last chapter of his book The Buddha and Karl Marx. On the evening of 5 December he asked for the Preface and Introduction to The Buddha and His Dhamma to be brought to his bedside, so that he could work on them during the night, and the following morning he was found dead. It was 6 December, he was 64 years and 7 months old, and he had been a Buddhist for only seven weeks and His Dhamma to be brought to his bedside, so that he could work on them. But though Bhimrao Ramji Ambedkar had been a Buddhist for only seven weeks, during that period he had probably done more for the promotion of Buddhism than any other Indian since Ashoka. At the time of his death three quarters of a million suppressed communities had become Buddhists, and in the months that followed hundreds of thousands more took the same step – despite the uncertainty and confusion that had been created by the sudden loss of their great leader. So much was this the case that when the results of the 1961 census were published it was found that in the course of the previous decade the number of Buddhists in India had risen by a staggering 1,671 per cent and that they now numbered 3,250,227, more than three quarters of whom lived in the State of Maharashtra. This was Ambedkar's last and greatest achievement, so that even though it was as the Architect of the Constitution of Free India and the Modern Manu that he passed into official history and is today most widely remembered, his real significance consists in the fact that it was he who established a revived Indian Buddhism on a firm foundation. It is therefore as the modern Ashoka that he really deserves to be known, and the statue standing outside the parliament building in Delhi should really depict him holding. 'The Buddha and His Dhamma' underneath his arm and pointing – not for the benefit of the downtrodden only, but for the benefit of all mankind – in the direction of the Three Jewels.

In order to appreciate the nature of Ambedkar's achievement, and thus the real significance of the man himself, it will, however, be necessary for us to take a look at the remarkable way that he sought to deliver the marginalized community, as well as to trace the successive stages of the road by which he and his followers – travelled from Hinduism to Buddhism. It is also necessary to see the journey through which Ambedkar discovered his spiritual roots, explore his thoughts on the subject of the Buddha and the future of his religion, and to survey the historic occasion on which he and 380,000 suppressed community were spiritually reborn more vividly. A glimpse into his posthumously published magnum opus will give a clear idea of his philosophy of Buddhism.

REFERENCES

1. Omvedt, Gail, *Buddhism in India: challenging Brahmanism and caste*, 3rd ed., Sage, London, 2003.
2. Thomas Pantham, Vrajendra Raj Mehta, *Political Ideas in Modern India*, thematic explorations, Sage, 2006.
3. D.C. Ahir, *Buddhism in Modern India*, Satguru, 1991.

26

Dr. B.R. Ambedkar's Revelation of Women's Rights and Perspectives

– Md. Nisaruddin

INTRODUCTION

Dr. B.R. Ambedkar life was a fight of human rights. So clearly he was a great thinker of women equality. Being a pioneer of justice, he always worked for the woman emancipation. His principle aim was to build up a society based on social justice. To secure and fulfill his dreams he thought everybody should be equal irrespective of caste, creed, gender and religion. For that reason he started work for the upliftment of woman and their rights. In this context, the present paper intends and tries to narrate the rights and upliftment of woman in the vision of Ambedkar's women rights. His immense struggled hard efforts for freedom and empowerment of Indian women. He outlined many laws for women rights modern India like; Dearness Allowance, Women Labour Welfare Fund, ESI, Provident Fund Act, Women Labour Protection Act, Maternity Benefit for Women Labour Bill, Divorce Act, Right over Parental Property, Leave Benefit to Piece Workers, Revision of Scale of Pay for Employees, Restoration of Ban on Women Working Underground in Mines etc., No marriage before age of 18 years, Maintenance Allowance from husband on getting legally separation, Widow can adopt a child, Mother can change guardian of minor by Will and Equal pay for equal work irrespective of the sex. Ambedkar's main character for the 'Maternity Benefits' bill in the Bombay Legislature in July, 1928 itself for the factory women workers. In fact it was the first Act passed in 1929 by the Bombay legislature. On this regard he said:

> I believe that it is in the interests of the nation that the mother ought to get a certain amount of rest during the pre-natal period and also subsequently. I am prepared to admit this fact because the conservation of the people's welfare is primarily the concern of the Government. And in every country, therefore, where the maternity benefit has been introduced, you will find that the Government has been subjected to a certain amount of charge with regard to maternity benefit. I think, therefore, the benefits contemplated by this bill ought to be given by this Legislature to the poor women who toil in our factories in this Presidency.

Ambedkar was contributory in bringing the Mines Maternity Benefit Bill for women modern India. Under this act, a woman employed in the mine is permitted to maternity benefit for a period of 8 weeks. This period is divided into two parts, one part preceding delivery and additional part following distribution. Later all the acts of Maternity Benefit of many states were cancelled and a common Maternity Benefit Act-1961 was accepted by the Central Government for all India. He was the first vision who brought *"Equal pay for equal work irrespective of the sex"* in India in terms of Manufacturing workers as a Labour Minister in the Viceroy executive council. On this regard he said:

> We have also taken care to see, and this is an important point, that women shall be paid the same wages as men. It is for the first time that I think in any industry the principle has been established of equal pay for equal work irrespective of the sex.

Ambedkar played main role for personified the Article 39(d) relates the state of the vision to struggle for securing equal pay for equal work of both men and women. His vision was for 'Right to Vote' (Equal for all Women and Men in India). It was "Founding Father of Modern India" Revolutionary Ambedkar who spoken as the first thinker in India for the 'Universal Adult Franchise' before the Southborough Commission. Later before the Simon Commission for all Indians without bias in gender, Caste, Class, literacy and religion. 'Adult franchise' in the Indian social reality i.e. right to vote to every Indian without any discrimination through the Constitution. For this Ambedkar faced the fundamental problem from Sardar Vallabhai Patel. As well as Dr. Babasaheb insisted on the education of girls.

Ambedkar's strong vision for gender especially boy gets education, he is the only person to get educated in a family. Perhaps, if a girl child is educated in a family, the whole family is benefitted this type Ambedkar shaped awareness among poor, uneducated women and inspired them to contest against the unjust practices like child marriages and *Devdasi* system etc. Since Ambedkar was well convinced about the status of women, as the Chairman of the Drafting Committee, his vision apassable inclusion of women's rights in the political terminology and constitution of modern India. So, by considering women's equality both in formal and considerable minds he comprised unusual requirements for women while all other overall provisions are valid to them, as to men. Hence, there are Articles like 15(3), 51(A), and so on. His key vision in the preparation of modern Indian Constitution made it to be identified as a New Charter of Human Rights. He observed upon law as the tool of making a sane social instruction in which the progress of separate should be in agreement with the progress of society. He combined the values of right, equality and fraternity in the modern Indian.

Patriarchy, the growing caste/class divide in feminist political discourses made Ambedkar's vision on women rights and their equality, caste and Hindu social order and philosophy become significant to modern Indian feminist thinking. The contemporary social realities warrant close examination of the wide range of his topics, the width of his vision, and his suggestions for the Indian Women's Movement. He provides a powerful source of inspiration to formulate a feminist political agenda which simultaneously addresses the issues of class, caste and gender. He wrote in that the female sex is the nobler of the two, as it is the embodiment of sacrifice, silent suffering, humility, faith and knowledge. Of all the evils for which man has made himself responsible, none to me is so degrading, so shocking. He realised that the backwardness of woman was a stumbling block in the path of progress.[2] Basically His lectures and writing or thinking all of on the basis of women's rights. After 2500 years his voice only awakened the sleeping millions of people in Indian continent. His path gave the clarion call to the poor and innocent masses to shake off the shackles and break the barriers.[3]

Ambedkar represents the way in which Manu treated women. He pointed out that the laws of *Manu* on the status of women are very important in molding the Hindu attitude and perspective (Indian perspective) towards women, perpetuated and maintained through Hindu personal laws based on shastras, caste and endogamy, i.e. the base of Indian patriarchy. He attacked Manusmriti as a major source, which legitimizes the denial of freedom, self-respect right to education, property, divorce etc., to women by attributing a very lofty ideal to them. Because Ambedkar who was acknowledged universally as a advocate against caste system, a vigilant fighter for the women rights of all the burdened and enslaved and the emancipator of humanity from socio-economic injustice, occurred on 6th December 1956. In the sympathy message, on Ambedkar's death in Parliament, Prime Minister Jawaharlal Nehru said; "Dr. Baba Saheb Ambedkar was a symbol of revolt against all oppressive features of the Hindu society". His vision of society based on gender equality is yet to be realised and so his opinions are significant for the social reconstruction that favours women's empowerment.

MODERN CHALLENGERS

Dr. Ambedkar, many saints like Guru Nanak, Kabir, Ravidas and social reformers like Swami Vivekananda. Dayananda, Raja Ram Mohan Roy, Periyar E.V. Ramaswami, Mahatama Jyotiba Phuley raised their powerful voices in favour of women be given equality in status and chances with man. Ever fated British Rule in modern India came to release of Indian women in a big way, as it barred *Sati* system on the persistence of Raja Ram Mohan Roy. Mahatama Jyotirba Phule and his wife revered Mata Savitribai Phule opened 18 schools for girls in Pune starting from ever first school for girls on 1-1-1848, and adopted son born to a Brahmin widow as their

heir against strict hostility from Hindu clergies. Till half a century ago the girl child was buried alive by some Upper Caste Hindus. Honour killing to overpower female persons to marry as per their choice lasts despite current laws to the contrary. Out of the 20 Congress women MPs (total women members 37) in the 1991-1996 Lok Sabha, none was a Cabinet minister. Rice of Ambedkar:

> Dr. B.R. Ambedkar women got their real emancipator. The Manusmiriti was burnt in full public view by Dr. Ambedkar on 25th December 1927, thus he blew bugle of fight against discrimination and exploitation on the basis of one's caste, creed, sex or place of birth. His principle of life was to speak, work & fight for the just cause of oppressed, depressed, exploited, illiterates, ill fed & ill-treated men & women irrespective of their caste or social status, place of birth affiliations and without caring for his personnel life discomforts. Till then woman was considered lowest of the low in the Indian society, so he fought a very difficult battle for their cause. On March 19 & 20, 1927 he addressed a huge meeting of depressed classes, including women, and gave strong call for liberation of women. He advised them to attend more to their development of mind and the spirit of self-help; He said that education was as necessary for development of women as was for men. He declared "As you are, so shall be your children". While addressing largely attended Depressed Classes Women conference on 18-19 July 1942, he said, "He measured the progress of a community by the degree of progress made by the women of that community. He advised, let every girl who marries, stand by her husband, claim to be her husband's friend and equal and refuse to be his slave. He advocated avoiding early marriage and producing too many children. Give proper education to your children, so that they live a dignified life". Dr Ambedkar advocated for equal wages for equal work without discrimination on the basis of sex or caste, besides grant of paid maternity leave to expecting mothers. While strongly supporting proposed maternity benefits to women in Bombay Legislative Council in 1928 he said "– it is in the interest of the Nation that the mother ought to get a certain amount of rest during the pre-natal period and also subsequently.[4]

Ambedkar observes in the law book of Manu that the killing of a woman is like the drinking of liquor, a minor offence. It was equated with killing of Sudra. Manu even advises a man not to sit in a lonely place with his own sister, daughter or even mother. Some of the other laws Manu prescribed are every time women must be kept if they attach themselves to sexual enjoyments, they must be kept under one's control. Her father protects her in childhood, her husband protects in youth, and her sons protect in old age; a woman is never fit for independence. Nothing must be done independently by a girl, by a young woman, or even by an aged one, even in her own house.

Ambedkar perceived education as a catalyst for a movement for self-respect and self-help. So after fifty years of the working of the Indian Constitution, the Indian women's demand for political reservations and the lower status of other disadvantaged sections proves that his theory is correct. After that Ambedkar started his movement in 1920. He started fierce propaganda against the Hindu social order and launched a journal *Mook Nayak* in 1920 and *Bahishkrit Bharat* in 1927 for this purpose. Through its issues he put due stress on the gender equality and the need for education, and exposed the problems of the depressed as well as women.

Ambedkar's perception of the women question, emphasizing their right to education, equal treatment with men, right to property and involvement in the political process resembled the global feminist demands. As J.S. Mill expressed in the Subjection of Women, the legal subordination of one sex to the other is wrong in itself and one of the chief hindrances to human development; and ought to be replaced by a principle of perfect equality, admitting no privilege or power on the one side, nor disability on the other, Ambedkar also holds the same thoughts for women.

After back to India he devoted his life fully to work for the depressed classes including women. He was firmly committed to the ideals of equality, liberty and fraternity. In 1923, His movement launched from 1920 for women actively participated and acquired the confidence to voice their issues on various platforms. Venubai

Bhatkar and Renubai Shambharakar are worth mentioning. In 1924, Bahishkrit Hitakarni Sabha was formed to work for the socio-political equality of depressed people and promoting their economic interests. Women started participating in satyagrahas and also launched women's associations for untouchable women for spreading education and awareness among them. In the Mahad Satyagraha for temple entry in 1927, even caste Hindus participated. Shandabai Shinde was one such participant. In the Satyagraha it was decided to burn the Manusmriti, which humiliated women, and shudras. In the demonstration after the bonfire of the Manusmriti more than fifty women participated.

Ambedkar advised women to change their style of wearing saree, wear lightweight ornaments, not to eat meat of dead animals. It was upper caste women like Tipnis who taught them proper way of wearing sarees. He empowered women to speak out boldly their feelings. As Radhabai Vadale said in a press conference in 1931, "We should get the right to enter the Hindu temples, to fill water at their water resources. We call these social rights. We should also get the political right to rule, sitting near the seat of the Viceroy. We don't care even if we are given a severe sentence. We will sacrifice our lives but we will win our rights." The credit for this self-respect and firm determination of women, goes to Ambedkar.

On 20th July 1942, All India Dalit Mahila Conference held on 20th July-1942 25,000 women attended. Ambedkar was highly pleased with the awakening and activities of women,On 6th January 1945, the All India Untouchable Women's Conference was held in Mumbai. (Limaye, 1999:57-61). In the movement, his strategy apply philosophical was similar to Gandhian method thoughts he had disagreements on many things with Gandhi on the basis of equality. But upper strata of the society didn't like. His in depth study of Smritis and Shashtras and his experience from the response of upper castes during his temple entry movement crystallized his conclusions on Hindu philosophy and society.

Dalit's women and peasants, to assert democratic rights and urged for a new path of development which legitimizes this warning of the Father of the Indian Constitution, when he submitted it to the nation. Ambedkar's defense for women as the Law Minister of free India appeared in the form of the Hindu Code Bill in Parliament it Bill provided for several basic rights to women. In the bill major argument "demolition of the entire structure and fabric of Hindu Society. First Prime Minister Jawaharlal Nehru dropped the Bill by saying that there was too much opposition. On this issue, the then Law Minister Dr. Ambedkar resigned. His explanations for resignation show how the parliament of independent India deprived its women citizens of even basic rights. His resignation letter dated 27th September 1951 reads as follows:

> I will now deal with a matter, which has led me too finally to come to the decision that I should resign. It is the treatment, which was accorded to the Hindu code. The Bill was introduced in the House on the 11th April 1947. After a life of four years it was killed and died unwept and unsung after 4 clauses of it were passed. While it was before the house it lived by fits and starts. For full one year the Government did not feel it necessary to refer it to Select Committee. It was referred to the Select Committee on 9th April, 1948.The report was presented to the House on 12th August, and 1948.The motion for the consideration of the Report was made by me on 31st August 48. It was merely for making the motion that the Bill was kept on the Agenda.

The discussion of the motion was not allowed to take place until the February Session of the year 1949. Even then it was not allowed to have continuous discussion. It was distributed over 10 months, 4 days in February 1 day in March and 2 days in April 1949. After this, one-day was given to the Bill in December 1949, namely the 19th December on which day the House adopted my motion that the Bill as reported by the Select Committee be taken into consideration. No time was given to the Bill in the year 1950. Next time the Bill came before the House on 5th February 1951 when the clause by clause consideration of the bill was taken. Only three days 5th 6th and 7th of February were given to the bill and left there to rot. This being the last session of the parliament, the Cabinet had to consider whether the Hindu Code Bill should be gone through before this Parliament ended or whether it should be left over to the new Parliament.

This came to me as a great shock – a bolt from the blue. I was stunned and could not say anything. I am not prepared to accept that the dropping this truncated Bill was due to want of time. I am sure that the truncated Bill was dropped because other and powerful members of the Cabinet wanted precedence for their Bills. I am unable to understand how the Banaras and Aligarh University Bills and how the Press Bill could have been given precedence over the Hindu Code even in its attenuated form? I got the impression that the Prime Minister although sincere had not the earnestness and determination required to get the Hindu Code Bill through. In regard to this Bill I have been made to go through the greatest mental torture.

The aid of Party Machinery was denied to me. The Prime Minister gave freedom of Vote, an unusual thing in the history of Party. I did not mind it. But I expected two things. I expected a party whip as to time limit on speeches and instruction to the Chief whip to move closure when sufficient debate had taken place. A whip on time limit on speeches would have got the bill through. But such a whip was never issued. The conduct of the Minister for Parliamentary Affairs who is also the Chief whip of the party in connection with the Hindu Code, to say the least, has been most extraordinary.

The vision of social fairness, like law, changes. It progresses itself into gradually new designs and increases its borders and assumes new dimensions. Social righteousness has import in the background of modern Indian. Which is separated into Castes, Communities and Class they create walls and barriers of exclusiveness on the foundation of advantage and inferiority such inequities pose serious threat to modern Indian democracy. The concept of social justice takes within its sweep the objective of eradicating inequalities and affording equal opportunities to all citizens in social, economic and political affairs. India, while passing through the process of progress is in the quest for finding our ways for a well and just socio-economic directive. The search for a new model of socio-economic order is the need of the hour. Recent trends in globalisation, Urbanisation, Mobilisation of the poor in examination of better life situations and social justice actions compel us to think afresh. Social application of the concept of distributive fairness to the wealth, assets, rights and compensations that accumulate within a humanity or state because the spirit of justice is the achievement of the common goods as famous from the goods of individuals even of the majority.

There have been two main ideas of social justice one exemplifying the nation of merit and desert, the other those of wants and equality. The first formation involves ending of genetic rights and an open society in which societies have the accidental to display their desert. It is uttered in equality of chance and careers open to capacities. The second outset implies that goods should be owed permitting in each individual's diverse needs. As it aims to make people importantly equal, it needs an idea if equality. He denied the specialist of man over woman and man over man. His philosophy distillates its care upon the analysis of the wildlife and causes of social and moral problems. According to him for a long period human society has been devoted to drastically false practice and ideals. "In his philosophy liberty destroys equality and absolute equality leaves no room for liberty. He gives the highest place to fraternity as the only real safeguard against the denial of liberty, equality and fraternity, which is another name for brotherhood or humanity.[5]

Social fairness includes the formation of just and fair social instruction just and fair to one and all. To make the social order just and fair for every member of the public, it may be essential for the advantaged to make some expenses. In this sense, Social justice is a radical ideal. It comprises both the economic justice and social justice. In India, justice is a general term which comprises both practical and practical justices the former if rules of court events and mechanism what is usually known as natural fairness and the latter creation delivery for social help. Profits, services, discounts, freedoms and special rights, to those who merit and want such help defines by the compilation term social justice in modern India. It is unlucky that even sixty years after independence women's societal rights is still a distant vision not within the reach of the masses.

The Scheduled Castes and Tribes women under the traditional Hindu Caste hierarchy had suffered for periods without education and chances for progression in life. Women rights is compensatory justice to offset the accrued incapacities suffered by these factually deprived sections of society and absorb them pedagogically and occupationally in the mainstream of national life. If chances are not given to progress their deserted talents there will be social inequity and tension subsequent in anarchy and defiance to the rule of law.

Ambedkar started his movement in 1920. He started brutal propaganda against the Hindu social order and launched a journal *Mook Nayak* in 1920 and *Bahishkrit Bharat* in 1927 for this purpose. Through its issues he required gender equality and the need for education, and showed the difficulties of women. According to Ambedkar, women were treated as meager tools to accept the burdens of the family, partial to the role of bearing children and fulfilling duties of a wife or mother. Division of labour is not in their favour, as a result Indian women have lost their individuality.

They have to face discrimination on gender basis and shame. The traditional insolences observed them as actually, intellectually lesser to man subject them to male exploitation and unfair division of labour. The low status of women in modern Indian society is primarily due to the fact that they have no control over material and social assets. Dr. B.R. Ambedkar, being a charitable, kind and generous reformer was much moved with the shameful and worthless disorder and low status of women in society and he was a torch carrier in the track of social lift of women usually and Hindu women particularly.

Ambedkar choose his social reform methods only after sympathetic the reality of the status of women. He was of the opinion that the Hindu women are tied up with bandage of fantasies. They are also answerable for teaching these wrong thoughtful learnt by them through indefensible customs and preaching of the Shastras in the promising mind of their off spring. Otherwise also the women in modern India have remained a substance of joy and a source of pleasure at such she was used and distorted by men to help their evil ends. It has also been stated in Hindu Shastras that women is the promise slave of her father when she is young to her husband when she is central aged and to her son when she is mother. The whole tale of Hindu code bill gifts the determination of Dr. Ambedkar to bring about the changes in the humanity. He was the one who just not spoke on things; but truly worked on them. His anxiety for women is indubitable. It is not wrong to say he was a great feminist of his day. Because women's rights form a part of human rights and Babasaheb can rightly be termed as the champion of it in 1936.[6]

VISION OF WOMEN'S RIGHTS AND EMPOWERMENTS

Gender equality, gender main streaming, networking, leaderships, financial freedom are the essential aspects of women empowerment. Dr. Ambedkar realized this at his time and included in the process of social reforms. Dr. Ambedkar started involving women in the struggle, for eradication of caste systems and upliftment of the underprivileged sections. He realized that this could not be achieved without liberating the women themselves. He motivated women and addressed them to participate in struggle against caste prejudices. During the Mahad Tank Struggle, women marched in the procession along with men. He encouraged women to organize themselves. Impressed by the large gathering of women at women's conference held at Nagpur on 20th July, 1942, he told women to be progressive and abolish traditionalism, ritualism and customary habits, which were detrimental to their progress. Empowerment envelops developing and building capacities of individuals, communities to make them part of the main stream society. Education is the only mean by which societies grow out of oppression to democratic participation and involvement. It is a powerful tool for empowerment of individual. Over the generations, marginalized sections and women in Indian society were denied the opportunity to education. Dr. Ambedkar put all his efforts to guarantee the educational opportunities without any discrimination to all the citizens of India.

Empowerment means moving from a position of enforced powerlessness to one; of power, Multi-faceted, Multi-dimensional and multi-layered concept. Women's empowerment is a process in which women gain greater share of control over resources material. According to Ambedkar, I measure the progress of a community by the degree of progress which women have achieved.[7] Ambedkar a first step towards the recognition and empowerment to tried to break down the barriers in the way of advancement of women in India. He laid down the foundation of concrete and code for the Hindus and the principle is capable of extension to other sections of the Indian society. He was a great patriot. He said, 'so long as we have these differences of Hindu, Muslim and others, or Sindhi, Madrasi etc'.[8] women enjoyed a very high position but gradually their position degenerated into merely objects of pleasure meant to serve certain purpose. They lost their individual identity and even their basic human right. That is why Dr. Ambedkar, the father and architect of Indian Constitution, was of the firm opinion that until and unless, we defy the Hindu Dharma-Shastras, nothing much can be changed. In the name of sanskaras, the Hindu women are tied to bondages of superstitions, which they carry till their death. They are also responsible for inculcating certain wrong notions learnt through baseless traditions and preaching of the Shastras, in the budding minds of their offspring.

Since Ambedkar himself was a victim of oppression and discrimination in all its severity, his views about women's oppression and equal rights are more useful than anybody else's theory based on mere observation for the feminist movement to strengthen its strategy for approaching the systemic challenges and contradictions in a more pragmatic way to bring women to the mainstream. To understand Ambedkar's arguments and the ideals for which he stood, it is necessary to know some of his bitter and better life experiences that he underwent at the outset of the socio-political awakening from the time of his birth.[9]

He says "Our is a battle; Not for wealth, nor for power, ours is battle; for freedom; for reclamation of human personality, women placing in the society was not at par with other human beings. She has no rights. She cannot move nor do anything at her will. In Hindu Shastras, she has been branded just like animals or some objects of enjoyment. From the verses of Ramayana as written by Tulsi Das,

Dhol, Ganwar, Shudra, Pashu, Naari - Ye sab tadan ke adhikari". In 'Manusmriti' the ancient Hindu Code-book, the status granted to women is quite visible and she was put to the lowest rug of humanity as she was treated at par with the animals and slave by the proprietors of Hindu Dharma. Such was the placement earmarked to our mothers, sisters and even great grandmothers that humanity was ashamed of. Hindu women are tied to bondages of superstitions, which they carry till their death. Prof. Hanumaiah said that the Hindu Code Bill of 1949, which was drafted by Ambedkar, was the first step towards women's empowerment, as it gave women the right to property. "Ambedkar had worked towards the breaking down of the barriers in the path of women's empowerment, but it is rarely acknowledged today," he said.

Women's empowerment is an important agenda so there has been significant shift in approach of the district administration towards the development of women, especially the poor & the illiterate. The underlying causes of gender inequality are related to social and economic structure and practices, Consequently, the access of women, particularly those belonging to weaker section including Scheduled Caste/Tribes, Other Backward Classes and Minorities. To education, health, and productive resources, among others is inadequate. Therefore, they remain largely marginalised, poor and socially excluded. Capacity Building and Skill formation improved by the entrepreneurial ability and skill of the women, Government has been imparting various types of training and provide self and wage employment as well as *Skill Up-gradation Training Programme* to women to start their own income as well as start secured accommodation to the working women Hostel since 1996.[10]

The vision of Dr. Ambedkar about women is openly portrayed in Indian Constitution. Equality of sexes is strongly backed by the composition through articles 14, 15 and 16. The principle of gender equality is preserved in the modern Indian Constitution in its Introduction, Important Rights, Fundamental Duties and Directive Principles. He laid down the foundation of justice and there can be no social justice without gender equality. Enforced widowhood and girl marriages just to maintain strict endogamy in a caste. The social ills about women in Hindu religion as well as in Muslim society were highlighted by him. As an investigator, He widely studied the position of women in both the religion and thrown light on disavowal of rights to her and finally the status of separate. He specified that the penalties of *purdah system* on Muslim women were that it deprives her of mental and moral nourishment. He sought that Buddhism awards women, position equal to men and considered women skilled of reaching devoutness. By accepting Buddhism, Dr. Ambedkar barred in just for deprived sections including women and patient the distinguished equal status. So he denied worshiping Hindu deities, ultimately freed women from inhumane duties, rituals and fallacies and made the way for her freedom.

VISION OF WOMEN'S POLITICAL RIGHTS

Political equality to all children regardless of birth, sex, colour, etc is one of the basic premises of democracy. Political equality includes not only equal right to franchise but also more importantly, the right to access to the institutionalised centers of power. Thus, political participation of women means not only using the right to vote but also power sharing, co-decision making and co-policy making at all levels. The active participation of women in political sphere is integral to empowerment of women and helps to build a gender-equal society as well as to speed upthe process of national development and Commission For Women. In January 1992, for Women was set up by an Act of Parliament with the specific mandate to study and monitor all matters relating to the constitutional and legal safeguards provided for women, review the existing legislation, to suggest amendments wherever necessary, and safeguard the rights and entitlements of women. The Commission extend financial support to NGOs and educational institutions to conduct legal awareness programme to enable women to become aware of their rights.[11]

Ambedkar is also one of the proponents of social justice in modern India. According to Ambedkar, the term "social justice" is based upon equality, liberty and fraternity of all human beings. The aim of social justice is to remove all kinds of inequalities based upon caste, race, sex, power, position, and wealth. The social justice brings equal distribution of the social, political and economic resources of the community Ambedkar was the chief architect of the Indian Constitution. He was fully aware of the pattern and problems of the Indian society. The aspirations are of the different sections of the society and their conflicting interests. He tried to achieve social justice and social democracy in terms of one man-one value. He treated social justice as a true basis for patriotism and nationalism. Ambedkar did not accept the theories of social justice as propounded by the Varna system, the Aristotelian order, Plato's scheme, Gandhian sarvoday order and not even the proletarian socialism of Marx. The contents of Ambedkar's concept of social justice included unity and equality of all human beings, equal worth of men and women, respect for the weak and the lowly, regard for human rights, benevolence, mutual love, sympathy, tolerance and charity towards fellow being. Humane treatment in all cases dignity of all citizens, abolition of Caste distinctions, education and property for all and good will and gentleness, He emphasised more on fraternity and emotional integration. His view on social justice was to remove man-made inequalities of all shades through law, morality and public conscience, he stood for justice for a sustainable society.[12]

According to Dr. Ambedkar the root cause of social injustice to the Scheduled Castes and Scheduled Tribes is the caste system in Hindu society. He observed, castes are enclosed units and it is their conspiracy with clear conscience that compels the ex-communicated to make themselves into a caste. The logic of their obdurate circumstance in merciless and it is in obedience to its force that some unfortunate groups find themselves closed out with the result that now groups by a mechanical law are constantly being converted into castes in a widening multiplicity. He further maintained that the root of untouchability is the caste system and the root of the caste system is religion, the root of the religion attached to varnashram and the root of the varnashram is the Brahminism, the roof of Brahminism lies with the political power.[13]

Dr. Ambedkar said, we must begin by acknowledging the fact that there is complete absence of two things in Indian society, one of these equality is on the social plane. We have in India a society based on the principle of graded inequality which means elevation for some and degradation for others. On the economic plane, we have a society in which there are some who have immense wealth as against many who lice in abject poverty-How long shall we continue to live this life of contradictions? How long shall we continue to deny it for long, we will do so only by putting our political democracy in peril, we must remove this contradiction at the earliest possible moment or those who suffer from inequality will blow up the structure of political democracy.[14]

His philosophy was occupied with social amelioration, political enlightenment and spiritual awakening. For this it attached due importance to the economic well-being of the masses. To him, Political thought embodied a social dynamism because of man's attitude animal and social being. He had deep faith in fundamental human rights in the equal rights of men and women, in the dignity of the individual in social economic justice in the promotion of social progress and better standards of life with peace and security in all spheres of human life. His study of social facts enriched his political philosophy. Dr. Ambedkar was dead against the Hindu caste structure as he was of the view that this structure has been primarily responsible for committing all sorts of atrocities on the various sections of the society particularly the weaker sections Scheduled Caste and Scheduled Tribes. He was against Manusmriti as it gives a blank cheque to the Brahamins to commit all sorts of atrocities on Scheduled Castes and Scheduled Tribes and justify their evil designs.

Dr. B.R. Ambedkar, being a philanthropic, kind and generous social reformer was much moved with the pitiable and pathetic condition and low status of women in society and he was a torch bearer in the direction of social uplift of women generally and Hindu women specially. Ambedkar chooses his social reform approach only after understanding the reality of the status of women.

Dr. Ambedkar was of the opinion that the Hindu women are tied up with bandage of superstitions which they can till their death. They are also responsible for inculcating these wrong notions learnt by them through baseless traditions and preaching of the shastras in the budding mind of their off spring. Otherwise also the women in India have remained a matter of joy and a source of amusement at such she was used and misused by men guest to serve their evil ends. She has been used just like a machine for procreation. It has also been mentioned in Hindu Shastras that women is the bond slave of her father when she is young to her husband when she is middle aged and to her son when she is mother.[15]

The reforms introduced by Dr. Ambedkar through 'Hindu Code Bill' have been adhered to and have been accepted by and large. He by codifying Hindu law in respect of marriage, divorce and succession, rationalised and restored the dignity to women. It is needless to say, the Bill was a part of social engineering via law, sharp criticism of this Bill in and outside parliament led many to belief that it might inflict heavy damages on the Hindu society[16] Even the president Dr. Rajendra Prasad got scared and issued a threat that he would withhold his assent even it had been passed by the parliament. Justice P.B. Gajendrgadkar while congratulating Dr. Ambedkar for the role he had played in drafting and piloting the Bill said, "If Dr. Ambedkar gives us Hindus our code, his achievement would go down in history as a very eloquent piece of poetic justice indeed". The whole story of Hindu code bill presents the determination of Dr. Ambedkar to bring about the changes in the society. He was the one who just not talked on things; but really worked on them. His concern for women is unquestionable. It is not wrong to say he was a great feminist of his day. Because women's rights form a part of human rights and Babasaheb can rightly be termed as the champion of it.

Dr. Ambedkar says, to the women education was denied by the Manu and he caused both an insult and an injury to the women in India. It was an injury because without any justification she was denied the right to acquire knowledge which is the birth right to every human being. It was an insult because after denying her the opportunity to acquire knowledge she was declared to be allowed to take to 'Sanyas' which was regarded as the path to attain the Brahmin. Not only she was denied the right to realize her spiritual potentiality by the Brahmins but she was also declared to be barren of any spiritual potentialities.[17]

According to Ambedkar, women were treated as mere tools to bear the burdens of the family, restricted to the role of bearing children and fulfilling duties of a wife or mother any. Division of labour is not in their favour, as a result Indian women have lost their identity. They have to face discrimination on gender basis and because of this availability of equal opportunity for remains a dream of them. Poverty, illiteracy lack of health and inequality of class of status and powerlessness, degrades are associated with them. The weight of traditional attitudes that regard them as physically, intellectually and socially, inferior to man subject them to male exploitation and unjustified division of labour. A society where women, i.e., the half of the population, enjoy a low status of women in Indian society is primarily due to the fact that they have no control over material and social resources. This is further compounded by lack of participation opportunities in the decision making process of the family.[18]

Ambedkar impartially concentrates on Muslim women also. He starts with the reference to mother India which created an impression throughout the world that while Hindus were groveling in the mud of social evils and conservative, the Muslims in India were free of them and as compared to the Hindus, were progressive people.[19] Ambedkar takes the help of census report and other data and proves Indian Muslims are equally harsh on their women; of course Muslim law has better provisions for women. But no Muslim girl has the courage to exercise them; there is latitude in their matter of divorce. The wife cannot escape marriage even if it's irksome, the husband can always do it without having to show any course. This destroys the sense of security which is fundamental for a happy life. The right of polygamy and concubine which the Muslim law gives to its men worsens the plight of women. Ambedkar comments are sharp in saying "*Purdah*" deprives Muslim women of mental and moral nourishment. The segregation from the outer world makes them engage their minds in petty family quarrels which develop narrow outlook. These words hold good even today, even after passage of six decades.

At present we find a number of women empowerment programmes, concern for women is show-up by all political parties, even though some time just lip service. Whatever is the issue Babasaheb Ambedkar had totality in his views and sixth sense, perhaps because he did not consider himself belonging to these religions. His arguments were without bias and always probed deep and deep in to the real problem center. His reasoning is fine in all this, whether it is the problems of Hindus or Muslims, women of the religion were just dice in their play. This is clearly presented by Ambedkar.

The fathers of the Indian Constitution had the dream of a new social, economic and political order, the soul of which was social justice. Ambedkar was the chief architect of the Indian Constitution. He was fully aware of the pattern and problems of the society and their conflicting interests. Before the actual work of the constituent Assembly had commenced in full seeing, Dr. Ambedkar proposed a memorandum on 15 March 1947 entitled "States and minorities". What are their rights and how to secure them in the Constitution of free India? This proposed explained the aspect of social justice for minorities in free India. Although no cognizance was taken on this memorandum on the ground of academic interest. However, feeling expressed by Dr. Ambedkar in this memorandum was special to protect the minorities and weaker section.[20] Besides, the proposed memorandum submitted, he was himself presided the meeting of draft for the preamble of the Constitution. After long debate it was passed on 26 November 1947 by the Constituent Assembly. Dr. Ambedkar concluded the debate on the preamble in these words "I say that this preamble embodies what is the desire of every member of the house that this Constitution should have its roots its authority, its sovereignty from the people that it has.[21] His views that "All of us desire that this unfortunate class could be entitled to the same privileges as members of the other Communities without any let or hindrance from anybody. He recreated that if any community or person will violate this provision it will impose duty on the state to stop such violation through the law, because the Constitution contains ample provisions.[22] In this regard Dr. Ambedkar Said:

> It is not the intention to introduce in this part these principles as more pious declarations. It is the intention of the assembly that

in future both the legislature and the executive should not merely pay lip service these principles enacted in this part but that should be made the basis of all executive and legislative action that may be taken hereafter in the matter of the governance of the country.

The ideology of the Dr. Ambedkar influenced the Indian judiciary on the basis of this ideology supreme court of India declared that directive principles of state policy are enforceable with the fundamental rights.[23]

Article 39 of Constitution needs the state to make obtainable to all the countries passable means of livelihood, to issue ownership and switch of material assets. So as to sub serve the common good, to work the economic structure in such a way that. It does not result in attention of wealth and means of manufacture to the common disadvantage, that there is equal pay for equal work, to defend the health and strength of employees, men and women and the caring age of children in contradiction of abuse and that citizen are not compulsory by economic need to enter occupations unfitted to their age and asset, that children are not given chances and services to progress in as healthy manner and in conditions of liberty and self-respect and that childhood and youth are protected against exploitation and against moral and mental abandonment.[24] The state is also obligatory to provide equal justice through the mechanism of free legal aid in order to ensure that opportunities for securing justice are not deprived of to any citizen by aim of economic or other disabilities.[25] To provide right to work, to education and public assistance in cases of joblessness, old age, illness and impairment and other cases of unwarranted want.[26] Article 41 of the Constitution of India. To promote the educational and economic interests of the Scheduled Castes and Scheduled Tribes and other weaker sectors.[27]

VISION OF MARRIAGE RIGHTS

The Cabinet unanimously decided that it should be put through in this Parliament. So the Bill was put on the Agenda and was taken up on the 17th September 1951 for further clauseby-clause consideration. As the discussion was going on the Prime Minister put for a new proposal, namely, that the Bill as a whole may not be gone through within the time available and that it was desirable to get a part of it enacted into law rather than allow the whole of it to go to waste. It was a great wrench to me. But I agreed, for, as the proverb says "it is better to save a part when the whole is likely to be lost." The prime minister suggested that we should select the Marriage and Divorce Part. The Bill in its truncated form went on. After two or three days of discussion of the Bill the Prime Minister came up with another proposal. This time his proposal was to drop the whole Bill even the Marriage and Divorce portion.

Ambedkar cites evidences of higher status of women in the pre-Manu days. She was free and equal partner of man and had the right to education, divorce, remarriage and economic freedom. The story of public disputation between Janaka and Sulabha, Yajnavalkya and Maitrei, Yajnavalkya and Gargi, and Sankaracharya and Vidyadhari show that Indian women in the pre-Manu period could rise to the highest pinnacle of learning and education. It is generally believed that Dr. Ambedkar had completed the books entitled The Riddles of Hinduism, The Buddha and Karl Marx, and Revolution and Counter Revolution. All carry chapters on women entitled Elevation of Women and Degradation of Women which expose how Chaturvarna prioritised "birth" instead of "worth," degraded women and is unable to explain the status and position of women, and endogamy. He found their emancipation in Buddhist values, which promotes equality, self-respect and education.

Ambedkar believes that Buddha treated women with respect. He taught women Buddha Dharma and religious philosophy for women like Vishakha, Amrapali of Visali, Gautami, Rani Mallika, queen of Prasenajith who approached Buddha, as evidences of Buddha's treatment of women as equals. (Paul, 1993:383-84). It was mainly the Hindu culture and social customs, which stood in the headway of women's empowerment.

Ambedkar, The National Policy for the Empowerment of Women 2001, also admits, "the underlying causes of gender inequality are related to social and economic structure…the access of women, particularly those belonging to weaker including Scheduled Castes/Tribes, Other Backward Classes and Minorities…

to education, health, and productive resources, among others is inadequate. Therefore, they remain largely marginalised, poor and socially excluded". (Govt. of India, 2001: 2). Ambedkar philosophical thoughts on women's equal rights and bring women to the mainstream and socio-political awakening from the time of his birth.

Ambedkar created awareness among poor, illiterate women and inspired them to fight against the unjust social practices like child marriages and devdasi system. He was well convinced about the status of women, he tried an adequate inclusion of women's rights in the political vocabulary and constitutional. His key work Human Rights and incorporated the values of liberty, equality and fraternity in the Indian Constitution. He said "political democracy cannot last unless there lies at the base of it social democracy." By social democracy he means a way of life, which recognizes liberty, equality and fraternity as principles of life.

In the Bill, Ambedkar were later passed during 1955-56 in four Bills on Hindu 'marriage', succession', 'minority and guardianship' and 'maintenance,' and later in 1976 some changes were made in Hindu Law, it still remains true that the basic rights of women. His analysis of the Hindu social order and its philosophy that perpetuates inequality, slavery, poverty, ignorance and powerlessness for the oppressed classes and also to women, This was the starting point for women to recognize their position and pursue rights. After women are still fighting issues such as rape, dowry death, communalism, fundamentalism, sexual harassment, violence-domestic and social, poverty and so on. The sexual disparity in marriage problem of caste ultimately marginalised. When woman (widow), and a surplus man (widower) due to spouse's death, their existence was seen as a menace. To regulate them, the methods practiced in the mechanism of caste presents three singular uxorial customs, namely:

1. Sati or the burning of the widow on the funeral pyre of her deceased husband.
2. Enforced widowhood by which a widow is not allowed to remarry.
3. Girl marriage: (Ambedkar, 1987:12-13). Since man has traditional domination over woman. All kinds of iniquitous injunctions,

> religious, social or economic that are made by man. According to Ambedkar, the society must be based on reason, and not on atrocious traditions of caste system. He found education, inter caste marriage and interlined as methods, which may eliminate caste and patriarchy, maintained through endogamy. His dream of society based on gender equality is yet to be realised and therefore his thoughts are important for the social reconstruction that favours women's empowerment.[28]

The Hindu Marriage Act, 1955 was amended in 1976 made the following provisions for women:

1. The legitimization of illegitimate children (Sec.16).
2. Punishment-bigamy (Sec.26).
3. Custody of children (Sec. 26).
4. Marriageable age of females raised to 18 years.
5. Provision for alimony (Sec. 25).

The Act abolishes the difference between a maiden and a widow. The Hindu Succession Act, 1956, this Act contains the following provisions for women:

1. A widow has a right to adopt a son or a daughter which was not there in the Hindu Law.
2. It also provided an opportunity to be independent and dispose of her property by will as she wishes and desires (Sec. 14).
3. A uniform scheme of succession to the property of a Hindu female who dies, intestate after commencement of the Act, was made in Section 15.

Previously under the unmodified law the succession to *stridhan* varied according to the marital status of a woman. While most of the supplies proposed by Ambedkar were later accepted during 1955-56 in four Bills on Hindu 'marriage', succession', 'minority and guardianship' and 'maintenance,' and later in 1976 some changes were made in Hindu Law, it still remains true that the basic rights of women have yet to be reinstated to them even after fifty years of the employed of the Indian Constitution based on the principle of right, equality and justice to all Indian citizens. The nature of controversy on Hindu Code Bill made it clear that the rights for women familiar in the Book of Indian Constitution is very problematic to decode into reality. One can find apassable answer for this in Ambedker's analysis of the Hindu social order and its viewpoint that continues inequality, slavery, poverty, ignorance and powerlessness for the burdened classes and also to women, which has its influence in modern times also. Though, the Hindu Code Bill helped the recovery of feminist movement in India. This battle of Ambedkar to liberate women from injustice inspires the women leaders in Parliament to keep the issue alive until its performing. This was the initial point for women to identify their position and follow rights movement by acquiring strength from 'second wave feminism' started in the early 1960s. Women are still aggressive issues such as rape, dowry death, communalism, and fundamentalism, sexual harassment, violence-domestic and social, poverty and so on.

Ambedkar also talked a meeting of about three thousand women of the Depressed Classes, the first conference of its kind in modern India and advised them to dress well and live a clean life. Do not feed your spouse and sons if they are drunk. Send your children to schools. Education is necessary for females as it is for males.[29]

Ambedkar's approach to women's empowerment is entirely different from other social reformers like Mahatma Jyotiba Phule, Raja Ram Mohan Roy, Ishwar Chandra Vidyasagar and Mahatma Gandhi who tried to reform the Hindu society of certain outdated customs and practices without questioning the hierarchical social order. His approach also differed from Bhakti movement which preached brotherhood without attacking the iniquitous Hindu social order that was based on graded system of caste hierarchy. Dr. B.R. Ambedkar's mission in life was to challenge the ideological foundations of graded system of caste hierarchy that denied equality, freedom and human dignity to women in Hindu society. He believed that society should be based on reason and not on atrocious tradition of caste system. Therefore, in order to reconstruct Hindu society along modern democratic ideas of liberty, equality and fraternity, he suggests in "The Annihilation of Caste System".[30]

The Hindu Minority and Guardianship Act, 1956: Following provisions are come under the purview of this Act:

1. The mother is empowered to change the gurdian, appointed by the father and may appoint a new gurdian by will.
2. The father's right to appoint a guardian for the minor by will during the life time of the minor's mother is prohibited under this Act.

The Adoption and Maintenance Act, 1956: This Act has the following provisions:

1. This Act accepts adoption of a male and a female child without any difference, whereas under the uncodified law a daughter could not be adopted.
2. This Acts permits a wife to adopt a child on her own right even during her husband's life time. She had no such right prior to this enactment.
3. In the uncodified law a spinster or a widow had no right to adopt whereas this Act grants them the right to adopt.
4. Under the old Hindu Law a wife need not be consulted while adopting a child or while giving a child for adoption, whereas this Act made it essential to consult her in both the cases.
5. Section 11 lays down that, a father should adopt a daughter atleast 21 years younger to him.[31]

In 1918, Ambedkar demanded separate electorate and reserved seats for the Depressed Classes in proportion to their population. After fifty years of the working of the Indian Constitution, the Indian women's demand for political reservation and the lower status of other disadvantage sections proves that his theory is correct. Ambedkar started his movement in 1920. He started fierce propaganda against the Hindu social order and lunched a journal Mook Nayak in 1920 and Bahishkrit Bharat in 1927 for this purpose.

His exposure to the west has influenced his perception on feminist issues. it was a time when first wave feminism had been coming to an end with the achievement of franchise rights for women in Britain in 1918, and America in 1920 and Ambedkar's perception of the women question, emphasizing their right to education, equal treatment with men, right to property and involvement in the political process resembled the global feminist demands. It is well known that Ambedkar has the habit to working for more than eighteen hours a day without any difficulty. His reading habit helped him to understand the feminist development in different cultures and countries around the world.

After returning to India he devoted his life fully to work for the depressed classes including women. He was firmly committed to the ideals of equality, liberty and fraternity. In Ambedkar's movement lanched from 1920 onward, women actively participated and acquired the confidence to voice their issues on various platforms. Venbai Bhatkar and Renubai work for the socio- political equality of depressed people and promoting their economic interests.

BROAD VISION OF EQUALITY

According to Dr. B.R. Ambedkar "Dalit women face the paradox of being socially regarded as Untouchable and polluted but still being exploited in the most intimate spheres of their existence." I measure the progress of a community by the degree of progress which women.

He incorporated the values of liberty, equality and fraternity in the Indian Constitution. He said "Political democracy cannot last unless there lies at the base of it social democracy." By social he means a way of life, which recognizes liberty, equality and fraternity as principal of life. He believed primarily in the efficacy of law and legislation, and he struggled to evolve a constitutional mechanism to fashion India of his dreams, where equality, liberty and fraternity would have an unhindered play. So his vision of India, all citizens would be equal before law; they have equal civic rights, equal access to all institutions, conveniences and amenities maintained by or for the public; they possess equal opportunities to settle or reside in any part of India to hold any public office, or exercise any trade or calling, here all key and basic industries would be owned by the state. He pleaded for special privileges and safeguards for the Dalits as scheduled castes. He demanded equality, which would not only lead, to the redresses of the past wrongs but also provide sufficient leverage.

His thought about Harijans women rights. The incidence of poverty, unemployment and underemployment is very large among Harijans and Girijans. Therefore several programmes like the schemes of industrial training, assistance for setting up cottage and small-scale industrial units etc. Dr. Ambedkar militated in favour of the reform of the Hindu personal law. He wanted to implement in a revised manner the Hindu Code Bill that the British had gradually evolved. After more than a century of legislation-ranging from the Abolition of Sati (1829) to the Hindu Women's Right to Property Act (1937).[32] The Hindu Code Bill in 1948 Bill was introduced in parliament and debated on the floor of the house, the opposition was strong against the Bill.

Ambedkar tried his level best to defend the Bill by pointing out the Constitutional principles of equality, liberty and fraternity and that in the Indian society characterised by the caste system and the necessary for a social change in which women have equality in a legal frame. Constitutional provisions emerson has said that consistency is a virtue of an ass. No thinking human and being can be tied down to a view once expressed in the name of consistency. More important than consistency is responsibility. A responsible person must learn to unlearn what he has courage to rethink and change his thoughts. Of course there must be good and sufficient reason for unlearning what he has learned and for recasting his thoughts. There can be no finality in rethinking.[33] Ambedkar the constitution of India provide for equal rights and opportunities for both men and women like:

1. Article 14 guarantees that the State shall not deny equality before the law and equal protection of the laws;
2. Article 15 prohibits discrimination against any citizen on the ground of sex;
3. Article 15 (3) empowers the State to make positive discrimination in favor of women and children;
4. Article 16 provides for Equality of Opportunity in matters of public employment;
5. Article 23 prohibits trafficking in human beings and forced labor;

According to Ambedkar, the most significant feature of the fundamental rights is that these rights are made justice able. The right to move to the Supreme Court for enforcement of fundamental rights under article:

- Article 32 authorizes the Supreme Court to issue directions, orders or writs in the nature of habeas corpus, mandamus, certioraris etc. or any other appropriate remedy, as the case may be, for the enforcement of fundamental rights guaranteed by the constitution.
- Article 39 (a) and (d) enjoins the State to provide equal means of livelihood and equal pay for equal work;
- Article 42 enjoins upon the State to make provisions for securing just and humane conditions of work, and for maternity relief;
- Article 51A(e) imposes a Fundamental Duty on every citizen to renounce the practices derogatory to the dignity of women;
- Article 243D (3) provides that not less than 1/3rd of the total number of seats to be filled by direct election in every Panchayat to be reserved for women, and such seats to be allotted by rotation to different constituencies in a Panchayat;
- Article 243T(3) provides that not less than 1/3rd of the total number of seats to be filled by direct election in every Municipality shall be reserved for women and such seats may be allotted by rotation to different constituencies in a Municipality;
- Article 243T(4) provides reservation of offices of Chairperson in Municipalities for SC, ST, Women in such manner as the legislature of a State, may by law provide.

In pursuance of the above Constitutional provisions, various legislative enactments have been framed to protect, safeguard and promote the interests of women. Many of these legislative enactments have been in the sphere of labour laws to ameliorate the working conditions of women labour.

VISION OF EDUCATIONAL RIGHTS

Education to women is the most powerful instrument of changing their position in the society. Education also brings about reduction in inequalities and also acts as a means to improve their status within the family. In order to encourage education of women at all levels and to dilute gender bias in the provision and acquaintance of education, schools, colleges and even universities were established exclusively for women in the country. To bring more girl children, especially from marginalised BPL families, into the mainstream of education, Government has been providing a package of concessions in the form of free supply of books, uniform, boarding and lodging, clothing for hostilities, mid-day meals, scholarships, free by-cycles and so on. Many universities such as Mother Teresa Women University have been established for the development of Women Studies and to encourage higher education among women and their social mobility. His philosophical thoughts about women's 'you are educate, agitate and organize, have faith in yourself'. With justice on our side I do not see how we can lose our battle to me is a matter of joy. You must abolish your slavery yourselves. Do not depend for its abolition upon god or a superman.

The present paper is an attempt to highlight Dr. Ambedkar's vision of women rights. His ideas of modern India. For this research we have collected secondary data collected from internet, newspapers, published papers and books. The aim of this study is to find how these factors:

1. To view Ambedkar Philosophical vision on women rights.
2. To analyse the Dr. Ambedkar's theory of women equality and empowerment.
3. To evaluate Dalit women rights in the lens of modern India.

CONCLUSION

From the above analysis, it shows that Ambedkar has tried his level best to give dignity to the women's rights and constitution to equality. He framed certain rules and regulations to safeguard the Dalit's. He also opened a new window for the scheduled caste women to equality, and no one is above or below the other. Every human being has self-respect and dignity. There is equality between men and women same. The main objective of this concept is to uplift the women, Scheduled Castes and Scheduled Tribes in the society and pull them to the main stream of the society. This concept also prevents unjust enrichment at the cost of the weaker sections. Dr. Ambedkar gave an inspiring self-confidence to the untouchables who were blind, deaf and dumb. He was a splendid organizer. He began movements to give an identity to the untouchables. Then he built up organizations women rights. His create awareness and democratic through his party practiced equality of human being. Hence, he has been regarded as 'A Ray of Hope" for downtrodden in India. He was a philosopher his thought and idea are women rights. His philosophical approach is to revitalize thoughts and things for the good women rights equal and society is well.[34] So he created human rights for all and tried to bring all men on a par socially. His aim was not communal and related to personal benefit, but it was essentially social and human related to all who suffered from slavery, injustice, tyranny and exploitations. Recognised the social stigma of woman in Hindu society.

B.R. Ambedkar was a path-maker of all the women regardless of religion, caste, creed, gender etc. He brought a new movement for rebellion the women through his vision and beliefs. Not only women all the people of modern India. He spoke about the Muslim women wearing veil, their religious traditions and marriages. On his Jawaharlal Nehru said, "Dr. Babasaheb Ambedkar was a symbol of revolt against all oppressive features of Hindu society". Actual he was a fighter for women liberation. He fought against all kinds of discrimination against women through his whole life. But still taste against women in Indian society is overlooked. We mention here his slogan on Unity, Education and Agitation. "Unity is meaningless without the accompaniment of women. Education is fruit-less without educated women, and Agitation is incomplete without the strength of women".

He felt the need of women human rights. He was realist and had a strong idealism. "The root of his philosophy was not in politics but in religion. His philosophy was such as would facilitate the social revolution in India. The social idealism and political idealism were opposed to each other. The political idealism scarified freedom and equality but social idealism had described them.[35] His strongest ideal society, which consists of social liberty, social equality and social justice rather than political idealism. To Humanism, human beings presence is essential only but not supernatural things. He did not deny the truth of nature, but he believed man is essentially a free human being. He was a liberator. His libertarianism was combined with rationalism and pragmatism. His ethics were utilitarian; his scales of values were determined by the usefulness of an action towards establishment of liberty and equality in the social order.[36]

OBSERVATIONS AND SUGGESTIONS

Ambekdar is a father of social justice. He is a feminist and thinker and practitioner. He is a role model to all in terms of pains and pleasures. His ideology basically equality and equity should provide all people without any discrimination. And new babies should born, live and survive in Indian society without any fear and discrimination. His philosophy should imbibe in all personalities, particularly to women. The results and benefits of humanism, which all reach the door of each and every human being living in human society.

Ambedkar has done for the liberation of women in modern Indian society, we have to highlight his pioneering work to advance the position of women by surrendering the fundamental rights to all regardless of caste, creed, race and sex. Infact during the outline of Hindu Code Bill in the Parliament, he had been strongly opposed by many MPs. Although later on, Ambedkar supported his vision on the earth that woman's right. His liberate women from the cruel knowledge of men, we have to suggestion out the status of women from the Vedic period to British raj. In the first stage of human history, the families were matriarchal. In those days of matriarchal families, it is a well-known fact that women were physically stronger than men. Through menstruation, pregnancy and child birth, she had to depend upon men for food and her defense which then imprisoned her and society took the form of Patriarchal. In this background, we can make some pictures such as according to Swami Vivekananda, "Women will work out their destinies much better than men can do for them". Raja Rammohan Roy worked hard for the closure of sati system. Jyotiba Phule sacrificed his life for the teaching of girls. There were many social workers who had sacrificed and laid down their lives for the rights of women.

Ambedkar's vision to women's right is exclusively different from other social reformers like Jyotiba Phule, Raja Ram Mohan Roy, Ishwar Chandra Vidyasagar and Mahatma Gandhi who tried to reform the Hindu society of certain outdated customs and practices without questioning the hierarchical social order. But Ambedkar made his own view for the women rights and that has been reflected in Indian constitution. His goal was to make a society based on justice. To secure this goal, Ambedkar has given equal status to women on par with men by providing many necessities in the modern Indian law. To him, sexual discrimination should be root out from the society and everyone should get equal chance. The Introduction of Indian constitution assurances socio-economic justice to women and that is because of Ambedkar role.

REFERENCES AND NOTES

1. Md Nisar Uddin (Jan Nisar Moin), Senior Research Scholar, Deptt. of Women's Education, Maulana Azad National Urdu University. Hyderabad. Telangana State.
2. Md Nisaruddin, 'Dr. B.R. Ambedkar's Ideal of Constitution on Women's Rights' *International Journal of Multidisciplinary Educational Research, Volume*, 4, Issue 6(4), June 2015,p.196.197.
3. B. Syam Mohan David Raju, "Life and Philosophy of Dr. B.R. Ambedkar's for Mankind", Volume:3, Issue:5, June-13
4. http://dalitvision.blogspot.in/2013/02/dr-ambedkar-and-women-empowerment. Accessed on 24.05.2016.
5. The philosophy of religion, in Dr. Babasaheb Ambedkar writings and speeches, Vol. 3, p.4.
6. http://gurukuljournal.com. Accessed on 13.05.2016. D. Sai sujata,M.Narmada, 'Ambedkar- A social Activist on Gender equality' Gurukul International Multidisciplinary Research Journal (GIMRJ), Dr. B.R. Ambedkar vision of 'Social Justice' is concerned with the amelioration of the women, Scheduled Castes and Scheduled Tribes in the society. He strongly fought against the prevalent Caste system and Gender discrimination in the society. His struggle for social justice could be visualised in the ideals and philosophy of the Indian Constitution. Thus the Constitutional ethos of the social revolution running through the 'preamble', fundamental Rights and the directive

principles expressly emphasize the establishment of an egalitarian social order and based on human values of justice, Social, economic and political, equality of status and of opportunity and fraternity assuring human dignity. Thus he created a social revolution by awaking. Dr. Babasaheb Ambedkar delivered a speech at Damodar Hall and addressed devadasis, Muralyas and Jogathinis. He gave them a call to come out of their nasty occupation. "Our society has been put to shame because of you, Women are respected in our society, and every society honour's the women of character. Therefore you should forsake this dirty occupation, bring good names to yourself and your society. Many Devadasis, Muralya's and Jogathinis were bewildered by his speech and approached him saying that they wished to come out of their occupations, their marriages were arranged.

7. Meetvili.Com. Accessed on 24.02.2014.
8. S. Radha Krishnan, A. Treu Patriot p.1, B.R. Ambekdar and Human Rights, Vivek Publishing, Delhi.
9. http://samyukta.info/site/node/225. Accessed on 15.06.2016. K.B. Usha, 'Dr.br ambedkar-the champion of womens rights', Mary Wollstonecraft's (1759-97) Vindication of the rights of Women claimed that women also are entitled to enjoy the same rights – right to education, employment, property and protection of civil law- as men do. She also presented th the domestic sphere as a model of community and social order. During the 19th. century women's demand on the right to vote was articulated by feminists such as Elizabeth Candy Stanton (1815-1902), Susan Anthony (1820-1906) in United States, and Harriet Taylor (1807-58) and John Stuart Mill (1806-73) in Britain. Women's rights movements emerged in many countries such as American Women Suffrage Association, Women's Social and Political Union in U.K. and such others. It was when its waves reached India to form a new social awakening, Dr. Bhimrao Ramji Ambedkar was born at Mhow, in the erstwhile Central Province the of British India on 14th April 1891.
10. http://www.legalservicesindia.com. Accessed on 13.05.2016. Society is in a continuous process of evolution. It will take several decades for these imbalances to be rectified. Education of both men and women will lead to change in attitudes and perceptions. It is not easy to eradicate deep-seated cultural value, or alter tradition that perpetuate discrimination. Law can only be an instrument of change that must be effectively used. The absence of effective law

enforcement, results in low rates of conviction, which in turn emboldens the feeling that the accused can get away. It is necessary that deterrent punishments are provided in the statute, and are strictly enforced. A beginning has certainly been made in urban areas. Working women continue to remain primarily responsible for taking care of home and child rearing, in addition to their careers. Increased stress has made them more prone to heart and other stress related diseases. Hence, it is necessary to improve the Support System for working women. The march towards elimination of gender bias has to go on, so as to make it meaningful for the vast majority of women in this country. There is a greater representation now in the legislature, executive and judiciary. India is one of the few countries in the world, which has had a woman Prime Minister. Various States have from time to time, had women Chief Ministers. A woman Judge in the Supreme Court, and in the High Courts, has today become the norm. Women have crossed many barriers, and head various departments in large multinationals today. A beginning has been made in the Army also, when women are being commissioned as SSC Officers. The 73rd and 74th Amendments to the Indian Constitution were brought about in 1993, which served as a break-through towards ensuring equal access and increased participation in the political power structure. The proposed Women's Reservation Bill to provide 33% reservation for women in the Lok Sabha and State Legislature is now under consideration. The empowerment of women in urban areas and the metropolises cannot be the indicator of growth in the country. In a country, where eighty percent of the population is in rural areas, until the lot of women in these areas is also not improved simultaneously, development will remain an illusion to them. The status of women cannot be raised without opening up opportunities of independent in come and employment. In the rural areas, employment of women is concentrated mainly in labor-intensive, unskilled jobs where simple or traditional skills are required. There is lack of access to vocational institutions. Women in the rural areas are wholly oblivious of their rights. It will require a much greater and concerted effort for the various measures to become a living reality for women in the rural areas. This can happen only through the collective effort of the State, NGOs, imparting of formal and informal education, through the media, etc. Empowerment of women so as to enable them to become equal partners with their male counterparts so that they have mutual respect for each other and share the responsibilities of the home and finances should be the ultimate goal that we must aspire to achieve. Enforcement of basic human rights of gender equality must take place, without undermining the institution and sanctity of marriage, and family.

11. Kavitakait "Dr. B.R. Ambedkar's Role in Women Empowerment", http://www.legalservicesindia.com. Access on 11th Jan-15.
12. Purohit B.R., Sandeep Joshi, "*Social justice in India*" Rawat Pub, Jaipur, 2003, p.189.
13. Mohamed Shabbir "*Ambedkar on Law, Constitution and social Justice*" Rawat Pub, Jaipur, 2005, p.309
14. Ibid, p.311
15. D.C. Ahir "*The Legacy of Ambedkar*" B.R. Pub. Delhi, 1990, p.129.
16. J.S. Narayana Rao and A. Somashekar "*B.R. Ambedkar is relevance today*" Shakthi Pub. New Delhi, p.25.
17. Dr. Ambedkar on women's emancipation, Dr. B.R. Ambedkar series Pub of Ambedkar Peeta, KSOU, Mysore, 2005, p.5.
18. Purohit B.R, Sandeep Joshi "*Social justice in India*", Rawat Pub, Jaipur, 2003, p.209.
19. B.R. Ambedkar on "Pakistan or Partition of India" Vol 8, p.225.
20. Many amendments were suggested by the members of Constituent Assembly, viz., L.N. Sahu, Patabi Seeta Ramaiah, G. Durga Bai, Pandith Thakur Das Bhargava, Dr. B.V. Keshkar, T.T. Krishnamchari, M. Ananthasham Iyengar, K. Shantharam, Aututal Chandra, Upendranath Bhraman and Prof. K.T. Shah.
21. CAD Vol. X-XII, p.456.
22. CAD Vol. VII, p.662.
23. Minerva Mills vs Union of India, Air, 1980, S.C 1789.
24. Article 39 of the Constitution of India.
25. Article 38 A of the Constitution of India.
26. Article 41 of the Constitution of India.
27. Article 46 of the Constitution of India.
28. *Samayukta:* A Journal of Women's Studies,"Dr. B.R. Ambedkar-the champion of womens rights", http://samyukta.info/site/node/225, Accessed on 14-02.2015. When he was in Colombia University, he wrote to a friend on the need to educate the depressed classes, especially the womenfolk. To quote him: "We shall see better days soon and our progress will be greatly accelerated if male education is

pursued side by side with female education". (Mathew, 1991:74). Ambedkar perceived education as a catalyst for a movement for self-respect and self-help. The British rule abolished detestable practices like sati but passed several laws to protect customs and traditions of Hindus. Dr. Ambedkar is an architect of Indian Constitution. He provided strong constitutional safeguards to women. The Special Marriage Act sets four essential conditions for a valid marriage i.e, monogamy, sound mind, marriageable age and the parties should not be too closely related. There are some grounds available to the wife only, both in Hindu and the Civil marriages. provided to the women. Violent and forceful abortions and abortions without consent of women are crime under section 313. The Hindu Succession Act gives male and female heirs almost equal rights to inheritance. Section 14 says that any property possessed by a female Hindu shall be held by her as full owner and not a limited owner. Dr. Ambedkar introduced Hindu Code Bill in 1948 which was revolutionary in confinement of proprietary rights to women but when not accepted by the parliament, he resigned from the ministerial post from the cabinet in 1951.

29. Keer, Dhanjay (2009), *Dr. Babasaheb Ambedkar: Life and Mission,* Popular Prakashan, Bombay, p.104.

30. Ambedkar, B.R. (1935), "*The Annihilation of Caste*", text of the Presidential Address to Jat-Pat-Todak Mandal Annual Meeting, Lahore.Hindu minds should be purged from the thralldom of the Shastras. To quote him, "Make every man and woman free from the thralldom of the Shastras, cleanse their minds of the pernicious notions founded on the Shastras and he or she will inter-dine and inter-marry without your telling him or her to do so". He found education, inter-caste marriage and inter-dinning as methods by which caste and patriarchy maintained through endogamy can be eliminated.

31. Volume-I, Issue-I, February 2015, pp.191-195, Accessed on 11.02.2016. Satyajit Das,' Ambedkar and Women Rights: An Analysis', Volume-I, Issue-I, February 2015, pp. 191-195, Volume-I, Issue- February 2015, pp. 191-195.

32. Balakrishna Hedge " Dr. B.R. Ambedkar: A Ray of Hope for Downtrodden in India", *International Journal of Social Science & Interdisciplinary Research,* Vol.2(3), March-13,

33. https://www.google.co.in/search ambedkar+women. Accessed on 14.02.2015.

34. The Philosopher, *D.R. Jatava, B.R. Ambedkar and Human Rights*, Vivek Publishers, p. 132, Delhi.
35. Dr. Ambedkar, India Radio speech, 3 October, 1954.
36. Labour Conference, 7th September, 1943, Speech by Dr. B.R. Ambekdar, Indian Labour Gazette, Vol. 1.

Contributors

Abhishek Mitra, Assistant Professor of Political Science, Bankura Christian College, Bankura, West Bengal.

Aloke Bhowmik, Assistant Professor of History, Khatra Adibashi College, Bankura, West Bengal.

Animesh Raptan, Assistant Professor of History, Bidhan Chandra College, Assansol, Burdwan, West Bengal.

Bedadyuti Barman, Assistant Professor of Economics, Abhedananda Mahavidyalaya, Sainthia, Birbhum, West Bengal.

Bikash Mukherjee, Associate Professor, Department of A.I.H.C & A., Visva-Bharati, West Bengal.

Jitesh Chandra Roy, Assistant Professor of History, Panskura Banamali College, East Medinipur, West Bengal.

K. Mavali Rajan, Assistant Professor, Department of A.I.H.C. & A, Visva-Bharati, West Bengal.

Kartick Chandra Barman, Assistant Professor of History, Hetampur K.C. College, Birbhum, West Bengal.

M. Alankara Masillamani, Associate Professor, Department of Rural Development-Palli Charcha Kendra, Visva-Bharati, Sriniketan, West Bengal.

M.M. Gondi, H.O.D. Department of History, SSMS College, Athani, Belagavi, Karnataka

Madhab Chandra Adhikary, Associate Professor, Department of History, Panchanan Barma University, Coochbehar, West Bengal.

Mala Laha, Assistant Professor of Sanskrit, Saldiha College, Bankura, West Bengal.

Mantu Barai, Assistant Professor of History, J.K. College, Purulia, West Bengal.

Matilal Sen, Assistant Professor of Mathematics, Saldiha College, Bankura, West Bengal.

Md. Nisaruddin, Senior Research Scholar, Department of Education, Maulana Azad National Urdu University, Hyderabad, Telangana.

Md. Salahuddin Munshi, Principal, Azan College of Education, Yadpally, Nizamabad, Telegana.

Mustak Ahmed, Assistant Professor of History, ARS Arts Science and B.Com College, Vijayapur, Karnataka.

N.P. Koti, Assistant Professor of History, Sri Jagadambha First Grade College, Hittinahalli, L.T. Vijayapur, Karnataka.

N.V. Aski, Principal, First Grade Government College, Terdal, Bagalkot, Karnataka.

P. Karuppasamy Pandian, Research Scholar, Department of Sociology, Madurai Kamraj University, Madurai, Tamilnadu.

Sanjay Prasad, Assistant Professor of History, Saltora Netaji Centenary College, Bankura, West Bengal.

Saumyajit Sen, Guest Lecturer, Hetampur K.C. College, Birbhum, West Bengal.

Sreerupa Bhattacharjee, Assistant Professor of History, Khatra Adibashi College, Bankura, West Bengal.

Sudipata Goswami, Assistant Professor, Zakir Hossian B.Ed College & Research Scholar, Department of A.I.H.C& A., Visva-Bharati, West Bengal.

Sujit Kujur, Assistant Librarian, Visva-Bharati Central Library, Visva-Bharati, West Bengal.

T. Chandrasekaran, Guest Lecturer of History, Arigaranna Govt.Arts College, Attur, Salem, Tamilnadu.

Tapan Kumar Das, Assistant Professor of History, Khandra College, Burdwan, West Bengal.

Uday Sankar Sarkar, Assistant Professor of History, B.Z.S.M. Mahavidyalaya, Bankura, West Bengal.